THE

# VESTRY BOOK

OF

## Saint Peter's, New Kent County, Virginia

FROM
1682 - 1758

THE NATIONAL SOCIETY OF THE
COLONIAL DAMES OF AMERICA
IN THE STATE OF VIRGINIA

CLEARFIELD

Originally published
Richmond, Virginia, 1905

Reprinted for Clearfield Company by
Genealogical Publishing Company
Baltimore, Maryland
1995, 1997, 2011

ISBN 978-0-8063-4599-4

*Made in the United States of America*

# INTRODUCTION.

New Kent county was formed from the county of York in 1654, and it seems that the parish of St. Peter's was established about the same time. In 1684-'85 Blissland Parish was cut off from St. Peter's.

The following were the ministers of St. Peter's Parish from 1682. Earlier ones are not known :

Rev. William Sellake, 1682.
Rev. John Carr, 1684-1685.
Rev. John Ball, 1685-1687.
Rev. John Page, 1687.
Rev. John Ball, 1689.
Rev. Mr. Williams, 1689.
Rev. John Gordon, 1690.
Rev. Jacob Ware, 1690-1695.
Rev. Nicholas Moreau, 1696-1698.
Rev. James Bowker, 1698-1703.
Rev. Richard Squire, 1703-1707.
Rev. Daniel Taylor, 1707.
Rev. Samuei Gray, 1707-1710.
Rev. William Brodie, 1710-1721.
Rev. Zacharias Brooke, 1721.
Rev. Mr. Brownscale, 1722,
Rev. Mr. Forbess, 1723.
Rev. Henry Collings, 1723-1725.
Rev. John Lang, 1725-1727.
Rev. David Mossom, 1727-1758.

Of several of these ministers nothing is known.

Rev. John Ball was a signer of a petition to Governor Nicholson in April, 1700.

Mr. Williams was probably William Williams, also signer of the petition just referred to.

Jacob Ware was for many years minister of Henrico Parish.

Nicholas Moreau was doubtless one of the Huguenots who emigrated to Virginia in August, 1696. A letter from him to the Bishop of Lichfield and Coventry, dated April, 1697, is printed in Perry's papers relating to the Church in Virginia.

James Bowker died as minister of St. Peter's, and his will is proved in New Kent, November 17th, 1704. He was brother of Ralph Bowker, minister of St. Stephens', in King and Queen county.

Daniel Taylor had a son of his own name who was educated in an English University, and was for a long time a faithful minister in a Virginia Parish.

The Vestry of St. Peter's Parish must have been in sore need when it employed Rev. Samuel Gray, for shortly before 1699, while minister of a church in Middlesex, he caused the death of a slave by severe whipping.

Rev. Henry Collings, in a letter to the Bishop of London in 1724, reports that this "parish has two hundred and four families in it, forty or fifty communicants, only one church (St Peter's); about one hundred and seventy or one hundred and eighty attendants. His salary eighty pounds, more or less. Glebe and parsonage rented out for six pounds five shillings per annum. Catechising had been much neglected. He intended to introduce it."

"Rev. John Lang came highly recommended from England to Governor Drysdale and Commissary Blair." In a letter to the Bishop of London, February 7th, 1725-26, he says: "I observe the people here (New Kent) are very zealous for our Holy Church as it is established in England, so that (except some few inconsiderable Quakers) there are scarce any dissenters from our communion."

Rev. David Mossom, the last minister who appears in this Vestry Book, was pastor of St Peter's for forty years. He performed the ceremony when George Washington was married to Martha Custis. He himself was married four times. Rev. David Mossom came from Newburyport, Massachusetts, to Virginia. He was born in London, March 25th, 1690, and educated at St. John's College, Cambridge.

St. Peter's Church still stands (the present edifice was built in 1703), and cost one hundred and forty-six thousand weight of tobacco. The steeple was added to the church twelve years after it was erected. As the place where the Widow Custis worshipped, and where, it is supposed, she was sometimes attended by George Washington, it possesses a peculiar interest.

# Vestry Book of Saint Peter's Parish,

## NEW KENT COUNTY, VA.

\* \* \* Jno. Perine & Mary his wife did lately run away &
\* \* \* ye custody of Jno. Barker two children, a boy and order ye s'd Barker shall keep ye s'd children till they come of age and this Vestry do request ye Court that they will be pledged to confirm this their order  \*  \* ye s'd Barker.

This vestry do impower & authorize Mr. Wm. Sellake, Mr. Gideon Macon jointly & severally to go down to Blissland Parish & disburse ye Vestry of ye s'd parish concerning ye Church plan which belongs as well to this parish as to that. And if they refuse to buy either the part belonging to this parish or to sell their part therein. Then this Vestry do impower & authorize Mr. Gideon Macon to continue action against the said Vestry, thereby to recover w't is justly due to the Recordat.

DIOM WRIGHT, Clrk Vest.

Christ's Church in St. Peter's 22nd, 1684, Anno Regis, 37th, Carr, Minister.

REPORT.

Mr. Jno. Carr Minister, Geo. Jones, Jno. Park, Wm. Basset, Mr. Cornl Dabney, Wm. Wyat, Jno. Rever, Mr. Wm. Paisley, Geo. Smith, Vestrymen.

Mr. Cornelius Daboney, Gideon Macon, Church wardens.

St. Peter's Parish is Dr.

To Mr. Jno. Carr minister from ye first of Feb. last & untill ye feast of ye Circumcision of ye lord.

Mr. Gideon Macon by order of Lieut. Coll. Lyddal assigned Diomed Wright for 2 months work Clerk.

Mr. Poindextor as by acct for Surplice & 2000, 6d nails.

Mr. Gideon Mason as by acct.

Mr. Workmour as ye acct for 6000 6d nails.

Mrs. Thos. Mitshel for keeping a bastard child 1000 lb. wher out he allows for him 500 due & to him.
  Mr. Turner for holding tithables last year.
  To ditto for Order Court against Mrs. Littlepage.
  To Mr. John Carr as Assignor of Mr. Ashurst for surplice made.
  To Mr. Carr for fine Diaper Communion Table Cloth.
  To Mr. Macon for Shingling this Church & righting.
  To Thos. Hart Sexton for Church.
  To Rich. Jones Sexton this Church.
  To Wm. Atkinson for Parish Ferry.
  To Mr. Geo. Smith for 5 pts wine from Coll.
  To Cash for 232 lbs. Tob. at ye pecentt.
  Salary for 25,151 Tob. at 5 pts wine from Coll.
  Ordered that Mr. Gideon Macon * * * to Rixoner & received from Mr. Littlepage thousand * *
  Ordered that Mr. Geo. Jones and Mr. Thos. Mitshel Remaine Church wardens in ye place & steadd of Mr. Cornelius Daboney & Mr. Gideon Macon & that they continue in the same office from ye day of the date hereof untill ye expiration of two years & that they collect forty eight pounds Tob' & hold this present year from each tithable in this Parish & therewith discharge the Parish debts et supra.

  Signed        Mr. JNO. CARR, Clerk.
  and this Et Recordat    DIM WRIGHT, Clerk.

A vestry held at St. Peter's Parish this 22nd day of May primo Regno Regis Jacobi Secundi.

### PRESENT:

Mr. Cornelius Dabney, Gideon Macon, Mr. Stephen Carlton, Thomas Mitshell, Mr. Will Peasley, Geo. Joanes, Mr. Jno. Parks.
  It is ordered by this present day vestry that Mr. John Ball shall preach five sermons provided heretofore of & in compensation shall receive twelve hundred and fifty pounds of Tob and Cask.
  It is likewise ordered that Mr. John Ball as minister of parish untill the last of October next for which the vestry agree to

pay * * *thousand Lbs ye worth of Tob' & Cask ye month
* * * promise and aggree to serve as minister of this parish
Sunday * * uper Church and likewise att ye lower Church
as other ministers have done heretofore.

It is ordered that ye order of the last gen'll Cort in this parish
* * Littlepage forthwith comply with all which if the s'd Mr.
Littlepage att twenty days * * itable bills of Exchange for
London payable 20 day of October next that then Gideon Macon
take out Execution Agst the s'd * * for satisfaction of ye
same and that he receive the effects into his hands of ye same
as he hath been formerly ordered.

It is ordered upon ye petition of Mathias Wood being * * *
condition be allowed four hundred pounds of Tob' and Caske
for his maintenance to be levied for him at ye laying of the next
Levy.

Whereas Capt. Mathew Page was by a Vestry held for this
parish elected and of this vestry in the room and stead of Mr.
James Turner Dea'sed and being by Mr. Cornelius Dabney
desired to appear at the nex vestry ensuing then and there to
take the oath accordingly & if he doth refuse to do the same
this vestry hath therefore ordered Charles Turner, Clerk of the
vestry to wait upon the said Capt Mathew Page and request him
to be at ye next ensuing vestry to take ye oath according
to ye law of this country as a vestry man aforesaid & to show
his reasons to ye contrary.

Signed by Jno. Ball, minister, and ye other gentlemen of the
Vestry.

Recordat per me CHARLES TURNER, Clerk of Vestry.

---

Vestry held in St. Peter's Church for St. Peter's parish, New
Kent Co., ye 1686 Ann. Dom. Regis, Jan. 2nd.

Primo, Mr. John Ball, Minister, Mr. Gideon Macon, Mr. Jno.
Rogor, Mr. Stephen Carlton, Mr. Geo. Smith, Mr. Will. Bassett,
Mr. Witt Peasley, Vestrymen.

Mr. Jno. Parks, Mr. Thomas Mitshall, Mr. Henry Wyatt, Mr.
Geo. Joanes, Church wardens.

|  | Tob. & Cask. |
|---|---|
| To Mr. Jno. Ball, Min., to serve untill ye 22 day of this Instant | 7250 |
| To Charles Turner effititing untill 13 day of Dec'er next | 2000 |
| To Richard Joandes Sexton of ye lower Church | 0300 |
| To Thomas Hart Sexton of ye Upper Church | 0300 |
| To Will Atkins to ye 11th Docom'r next | 0300 |
| To Diomi Wright | 035c |
| To Ind. Alford for nursing a bastard child untill ye day of Dec'r next | 1000 |
| To Mr. Geo. Joanes as by acct | 1445 |
| Mr. Gideon Macon as by acct | 1015 |
| Mr. Thomas Mitshall per one gallon of wine | 0120 |
| To Capt. Joseph Forstor Sh'r pr birth arrv'l | 0039 |
| To Mr. James Slattor | 0300 |
| To Cash for 15419 lbs. Tob at 8 pesent | 1232 |
| To Sallory 16651 at 5 pesent | 0832 |
|  | 17483 |
| To Ball. due to ye P'sh lying in ye Church warden's hands. | 0167 |
| to be arrangable at the laying of ye next Levvy | 17650 |

By 542 Tithables at 32 Tob c ½ pr poll.

It is ordered that Mr. Thom. Mitshall, Dim Joandes do collect 32½ lbs. of Tobb pr. poll from each tithable for paying ye above debts.

It is ordered next that Mr. Gideon Macon do at Court in all business relating to this parish as plaintiff or defendant or otherwise.

It is ordered that a thousand pounds of tobacco & cask be paid unto Mary Wilkinson for nursing a bastard child belonging to a servant woman of Capt. Joseph Forster this ensuing year.

It is ordered that Mr. Gideon Macon & Mr. God. Smith & Mr. Jno. Ropor do go down to parish of Blissland & to discover of gentlemen of vestry about dividing line of ye two according a formal agreement, and that they are hereby fully empowered to employ a Surveyor to run a dividing line in full confirmation of ye same.

It is ordered that Mr. Thom. Joanes do aggree & bargain with some one person to keep the Ferry and to pay for the same as formerly.

Signed by Mr. Jno. Ball & other gentlemen of ye Vestry.
Recorded by        MR. CHAS. TURNER, Clk of ye Vestry.

New Kent. At a vestry held at St. Peter's Church for St. Peter's parish, Nov. the 25, 1686, Anno Dom. Regis.

PRESENT.

Mr. Jno. Ball, minister; Mr. Gideon Macon, Mr. Witt Bodlay, Mr. Cornelius Dabney, Mr. Will. Bassett, Mr. Geo. Smith, Mr. Jno. Parke, Vestrymen.

Mr. Geo. Smith, Mr. Jno. Parks, Mr. Steph. Carlton, Mr. Geo, Joanes, Church wardens.

Whereas at this present vestry held for St. Peter's parish at the upper Church Mr. Jno. Ball doth present himself unto ye vestry promising to officiate as minister. Therefore this vestry taking into consideration the present want of ye parish and desirous of the advancement of God's Glory & ye continuance of ye sacred function in this parish do consent & agree with ve said Mr. Jno. Ball Minister to officiate as minister in this s d parish of St. Peter's * * at ye two churches, at ye lower church one Sunday & at ye upper church ye other for this ensuing year from ye date of those presents, at ye rate of one thousand pr month.

It is ordered that Charles Turner do offiate as Clk one complete year beginning from ye thirteenth of Dec'r next ensuing ye date of this order & to be allowed after ye date of two thousand for ye year.

It is ordered that Mr. Geo. Joanes & Mr. Thom. Mitshell Church wardens do prosecute any person or persons whatsoever within this parish of St. Peters that shall be or hath been found guilty of fornication.

It is ordered that Mr. John Lightfoot & family be added to ye Survey or of ye high way of ye lower road between the lower church & Black Creek mill.

It is ordered that Will Atkinson do keep ye Ferry and not to deny Mr. Jno. Ball a passage when occasion shall require and to be allowed as formerly.

Whereas Will Turner hath made complaint to this vestry that his help being too weak in clearing of ye highway, they are not able to perform. It is ordered therefore that the s'd Will. Turner shall have the help of tithables as formerly hath been & followeth viz: Sam'l Wady, Thom. Glass, Will Winston, Robert Anderson, Charles Fleming.

It is likewise ordered that a Register be kept in ye lower church of St. Peter's p'sh & that Charles Turner, Clerk of ye vestry be obligated to keep ye key of ye Chest where ye s'd Register Book is ordered to be kept and to enter all business relating to the parish in ye s'd Register book.

It is ordered that ye widow of Mathias Wood named Mabell Wood be allowed five hundred pounds of Tob & Cask as was formerly appointed for Mathias Wood by this vestry and to be paid at ye laying of the next Levie.

Signed by Mr. Jno. Ball Minister & other gentlemen of ye Vestry.

Recorded by    MR. CHARLES TURNER, Clerk of the Vestry.

At a vestry held at St. Peter's Church for St. Peter's parish ye 23d day of Jan. Anno. Dom. Regis 1687.

Mr. Jno. Ball, Mr. Jno. Page, Minister; Mr. Gideon Macon, Mr. Will Peasley, Mr. Jno. Roper, Mr. Geo. Smith, Mr. Henry Wyatt, Mr. Will. Bassett; Mr. Thomas Mitchell, Church warden.

It is ordered that Mr. David Crafort be elected this day a vestryman in ye room & stead of Mr. Geo. Joanes duly deceased and that he have timely * * * to agree at ye next vestry to take ye oath accordingly.

It is ordered ye Mr. Jno. Ball that he offi'ate as minister of this parish through two ensuing Sundays * * to be requited & to be allowed nine thousand pounds Tob & C.

Mr. Jno. Page minister now presenting himself to ye parish to offiate as Minister thereof, it is therefore ordered that ye time of Mr. Jno. Page, minister, did go in from ye first of July next & ye to be allowed usual allowance as one thousand pounds of Tobb & Csk. pr month, Mr. Jno. Page likewise * * *

Allowed unto Mr. Jno. Ball & C. to be paid at ye laying of ye nex Levie. Likewise ordered that a vestry be held at the Church of St. Peter's parish ye 3rd day of July, 1687.
Recorded by    MR. CHARLES TURNER, Clerk of Vestry.

At a Vestry held at St. Peter's Church for St. Peter's parish this 5th day of October, 1687.
Mr. Jno. Page, minister.
Capt. Mathew Page, Gideon Macon, Mr. Cornelius Dabnee, Steph. Carleton, Henry Wyatt, Mr. Geo. Smith, Jno. Parke Sen, Mr. Thomas Mitchell, David Craford, Will. Peasley.
Jno. Ropor, Sen, Mr. Will. Bassett, Church wardens.

| | |
|---|---|
| To Mr. Jno. Page Minister............................ | 3000 |
| To Mr. Jno. Ball ..................................... | 9000 |
| To Charles Turner ................................... | 2000 |
| To Thomas Hart, Sexton ............................ | 0250 |
| To Mr. Gideon Macon as by assignment of Rich'd Joanes for his Sexton's * * 250, for washing ye Surplice and for cleaning about ye lower church in all......... | 550 |
| To Mr. Jno. Alford for nursing a bastard child ........ | 1000 |
| To Mary Wilkinson for ditto.......................... | 1000 |
| To Mr. * * * on ye acct of ye Es. of Mr. Car....... | 2000 |
| To ye Estate of Mr. * * * * * ...................... | 2000 |
| To Atkinson for roofing Ferry....................... | 0800 |
| To ye Widow Wood ................................. | 0500 |
| To Samuel Waddy for mending ye seats of ye church.... | 0025 |
| To Mr. David Craford for ye Church Lock ............. | 0040 |
| To Cash for 22,165 Lbs. of Tob. at 8 per cent.......... | 1200 |
| In all .................................... | 25210 |

It is ordered that Mr. Jno. Roper Sen and Mr. Will. Bassett be Church wardens for those two next ensuing years, and that they collect forty and two lbs. of Tob. from each tithable in their several precincts, ye payment of ye above debts.

It is ordered that ye forementioned Church wardens do collect from twenty delinquents tithables in ye upper precinct of this parish hereafter mentioned, 32½ Lbs. of Tob. P'r poll, and that they make due payment of same into ye estate of Mr. Geo. Joanes.

It is ordered that Mr. Jno. Page continue as Minister of this parish, and same the vestry hath agreed to pay twelve hundred Lbs. of Tob. per annum. It is ordered that Charles Turner continue as Clerk for the ensuing year, and be allowed two thousand Lbs. of Tob. & C'k.

It is ordered that Will. Atkinson do Levie ye Ferry from ye 11th of December next, for the ensuing year, & to be allowed eight hundred of Tob. & Cs'k.

It is ordered that Mr. Thomas Mitchell do prosecute ye woman servant belonging to Capt. Jo. Forster for having a bastard child, and then to be cleared from ye office of a Church warden, having this day Ball acct. with ye vestry.

It is ordered that Mr. John Alford now having a bastard child in keeping and having two Roads, two thousand Lbs. of Tob. & C'k, doth now discharge ye parish from ye same & is likewise ordered by this vestry to keep the s'd child to serve according to Law & to discharge ye parish from ye same.

It is agreed & understood by this present vestry & is likewise ordered that if any of the s'd vestryment shall at ye appointment of ye vestry be absent from ye same, shall pay fifty Lbs. of Tobb. & Csk. to ye use of ye parish without a lawful excuse showing acct. ye next ensuing vestry.

Recorded by me,      CHARLES TURNER, Clerk of Vestry.

At a Vestry held at St. Peter's Church for St. Peter's parish this 31st day of March, 1688.

### PRESENT:

Mr. Jno. Page, Minister; Captain Mathew Page, Will Peasley, Mr. Gideon Macon, Henry Wyatt, Mr. Geo. Smith, Mr. Jno. Parke, Mr. Thomas Mitchell, Corn. Dabnie.

Mr. Jno. Ropor, Sr., Mr. Will. Bassett, Church wardens.

It is ordered by this present vestry of Mr. Jno. Ropor & Mr. Will. Bassett, Church wardens, of this parish, do employ a Surveyor to run a dividing line line between the parish of St. Peter's & ye parish of Blissland upon ye 30th of May next, according to an agreement of two * * * vestry of Blissland parish in ye year 1678 for ye dividing of ye same & y't ye Church wardens of this parish do give ye Church wardens of Blissland ye twenty days' notice of ye same & ye Mr. Rich'd Littlepage, Capt. Joseph Forster, Mr. Geo. Polegreen, Mr. Henry Benskin, or any two of those be requested to be there on ye same day to take their evidence as shall then be brought before them, ye place of meeting being at the beginning of ye dividing line, called Capt. Bassett's Landing, * * * next by, 10 of ye clock of ye on ye s'd 30th day of May.

It is ordered that Mr. James Moss have notice by ye Clerk to be at the next Vestry, being elected a vestryman in ye stead of Mr. Stephen Carlton, deseased.

It is ordered yt Mr. Will. Bassett do repair ye upper floors according to ye agreement which he has made with ye workman.

It is ordered y't ye Tithables appointed to Mr. Geo. Smith for ye clearing of ye Highway be joined to ye said Tithables belonging to Mr. Gideon Macon & so to keep both roads in repair.

Recorded by me,       CHARLES TURNER, Clerk of Parish.

At a Vestry hold at ye Church of St. Peter's parish for ye s'd parish this 24th day of May, 1688.

### PRESENT:

Gideon Macon, Geo. Smith, David Craford, Thom. Mitsheli, Mr. Cornelius Dabne, Will. Peasley, Jno. Parks, Sr., James Moss. Mr. Will. Bassett, Church warden.

It is ordered by this present vestry y't Mr. James Moss is this day added unto ye vestry of this present parish instead of Mr. Stephen Carlton, deseased.

It is ordered y't Thomas Pontin be allowed 7,000 Lbs. of Tobb. & Cask for building ye Church according to details of agreement, and that all former agreements relating to ye said vestry & Pontin be made void of consent.

It is ordered that Mr. Gideon Macon do agree for shingles, and that * may be thought sufficient to ye finishing ye upper floor, & what he does therein to be allowed by this present vestry.

It is ordered y't ye Church wardens do provide a minister for our Church to officiate once a month untill further order.

Recorded by       MR. CHAS. TURNER, Clk Vestry.

---

At a Vestry hold at St. Peter's parish Church on ye behalf of ye s'd parish this 3rd day of Sept., 1688.

### PRESENT:

Gideon Macon, Corn. Daberni, Geo. Smith, Hen. Wyatt, Mr. Thom. Mitchell, James Moss.

Mr. Jno. Roper, Mr. Will. Bassett, Church wardens.

It is ordered by this present vestry that Mr. Gideon Macon do & is hereby impowered to appear before his Excelansy Francis Lord Howard, Baron of Effingham, his Majes' Left. Gen'l of Virga. & ye Hon'l Counsoll of States upon ye 10th day of ye next Gen'l Court in obedience to an order of his Excell. to y't purpose to answer ye complaint of Mr. Lancelott Bathurst, attorney of ye vestry of Blissland parish, concerning dividing line to be run between ye parish of Blissland & ye parish of St. Peter's, according to an agreement & conclusion of twelve men Elected by an order of vestry of ye whole parish of Blissland before ye same * and this present vestry hath Ratified and Confirmed all whatsoever ye mason shall act or do in & about ye premises above s'd.

It is ordered that Mr. Hen. Wyatt be fined 50 lbs. of Tobb. for not appearing at ye last Vestry and now not give a just Reason at this meeting.

It is ordered that Mr. David Crawford & Mr. Jno. Parks at ye next vestry do show a just reason for their not appearing at this present vestry, and to be fined 50 Lbs. of Tobb., each person according to an agreement formerly made & Recorded.

Jno. Roper, Gideon Macon, Will. Bassett, James Moss, Thomas Mitchell.

Church wardens: Henry Wyatt, Corn'. Dabnei, Geo. Smith. Gideon Macon.

Registered by order of vestry.

MR. CHARLES TURNER, Clerk of Vestry.

At a Vestry held at St. Peter's uper Church on the behalfe of St. Peter's parish, this 3rd day of November, 1688.

PRESENT:

Capt. Mathew Page, Gideon Macon, Mr. Corne' Dabbonie, Thom's Mitchell, Geo. Smith, John Parke, Mr. Henry Wyatt, James Moss, Vestrymen.

Will. Bassett, Mr. John Ropor, Church wardens.

| | |
|---|---|
| To ye Estate of Mr. John Page, deseased | 6150 |
| To Mr. John Ball for foore sermons by agreement | 1200 |
| To Mr. James Slater for 5 sermons by agree't, and 5 sermons before agree't, in all | 2500 |
| To Chas. Turner to ye 13th day December next | 2000 |
| To Rich'd Joanes, Sexton of ye Lower Church (250) for for holding Church plate | 0310 |
| To Thom. Hart, sexton of ye upper Church | 0250 |
| To Rich'd Joanes as Assignee of Will for keeping ferree | 0800 |
| To Mr. Gideon Macon, as assignee of John Edmondson, for work done at ye Lower Church | 0394 |
| To Servt's fees | 0025 |
| To Mr. Will Bassett, Church w'n as by acc't, Charge for work done towards ye uper Church | 6352 |
| To Mr. Macon, Due to Ballance acc't to this day | 0333 |
| To Capt. * * Page for searching ye public record concerning ye division of ye psh. | 0050 |
| To Mr. Ropor as by acct. being Church warden | 1500 |
| To Mr. Macon upon ye delivering 15,000 shingles & two barrels of Tar at 200 Lb. of Tobb | 3400 |
| To Mr. Alford for * ye Glasier foure days | 0030 |
| To Mr. Mitchell for Clk. fees when he was Church warden | 0063 |
| To Mr. Major for posting ye lower Church as by agreement with Mr. Mitchell | 0500 |
| To Stephen Crump for a Stock lock & key for the lower Church | 0050 |
| To Thom. Pontin when it may be adjudged he hath performed half ye work agreed upon with Mr. Bassett to be pay'd | 3500 |

To remain in ye Church warden's hands to give an acc't
at ye laying of ye next levy ........................ 30818
To Cash for 30818 Lbs. of Tobb. at 8 per cent. ........ 2465
To Sallary for 33283 Lbs. of Tobb. at 5 per cent. ....... 1664

Totall ..................................... 3494

Cr't.

By 573 Tithables at 63 per poll ..................... 3494

It is ordered that Church wardens do collect 63 Lbs. of Tobb. from each Tithable for ye payment of ye above charge.

It is ordered y't ye Church wardens doe agree w'th some person to keep ye Ferry, and to give him ye usiall allowance for the same.

It is ordered y't Mr. David Craford & Mr. John Parks doe pay unto Mr. Bassett, Church warden, 5 lb. of Tobb. each of them for not appearing at the last vestry according to a former order mad to y't purpose.

It is ordered y't Charles Turner doe efficiate as Clerke this ensuing yeare & be allowed at ye rate of 2000 lbs. of Tobb & Cask p'r yeare.

Recorded by order, p'r me.

CHARLES TURNER, Clk of the Vestry.

At a vestry heid at St. Peter's parish Church on behalf of ye St. Peter's parish this 4th day of May, 1689.

PRESENT:

Gideon Macon, Thom. Mitchell, Mr. Hen. Wyatt, Corn' Dabnie, James Moss.

John Ropor, Will Bassett, Church wardens.

In pursuance of an Act of Assembly enjoyning ye Remarking of each man's land in each particular parish once in four years.

It is ordered by this present vestry in obedience to an order of New Kent County Court, bearing date ye 28 day of Febroary, 1689, ye date vestry doe putt their parishes into precincts & appoint a time for ye prosessioning and Remarking ye bounds of each man's land.

It is, therefore, ordered by this present vestry y't Charles Turner, Clk. of them, doe forthwith proportion ye persons within ye s'd parish of St. Peter's to go on prosessioning sometime between ye tenth day of this present May and ye tenth day of June next, and y't all of ye s'd orders be forthwith issued out and be delivered to ye s'd persons therein concerned.

It is ordered likewise y't Mr. John Ropor & Mr. Will. Basset, Church wardens, or either of them do agree with Mr. Williams, minister, to officiate once a month at each Church on any day y't ye s'd Mr. Williams & ye Church wardens shall fix.

It is ordered by this vestry y't Mr. David Craford, Mr. John Parke, Mr. Will. Bassett, Mr. George Smith do show a just reason for their appearing at this present vestry, otherwise be fined 50 Lbs. of Tobb. & Cask, each person according to a former agreement made and recorded, & ye reason to be shown at ye next vestry.

Per me, CHARLES TURNER, Clk of Vestry.

GIDEON MACON,
THOM. MITCHELL,
CORN. DABONIE,
HENRY WYATT,

JAMES MOSS,
JOHN ROPOR,
WILL. BASSETT.

The several persons named in Companys y't were ordered to prosession & to Remark ye bounds of each man's land:
Viz.: Capt. Joseph Forster, Mr. Jno. Ropor, Mr. Wm. Bassett, Mrs. Eliz. Littlepage, Wm. Harman & Edmund Bodford, Will. Cox, Jno. Parks, jun.; Mrs. Pierce & Mr. Conding, Mr. Poindexter, sen'r., Mr. Poindexter, jun'r., John Vaughn, Jno. Epecon, Jno. Spurlock, Fr. Day, Will Hodges, Rob't Speare, Rich'd Joanes, Steph. Moon, Wm. Book, Dow Wallton, Rich. Gilliam, Mrs. Botts, Jno. Waddell, Wm. Moss, Mr. Alford, Mr. Geo. Smith, Wm. Major, Hen. Green, Mr. Lightfoot, Mr. Mason, David Clarkston, Mrs. Workman, Mr. Pasley, Wm. Millington, Mr. Clayton, Thom. Jackson, Wm. Stone, Jno. Paine, Thos. Willkins, Thos. Markgold, Steph. Crump, Mr. Field Harte, Pelham Moore, Widow Williams, James Sanders, Steph. Mitchell, Wm. Barne, Will. Cromp, Rob't Chandler, Wm. Moss, Jno. Osling, Mr. Jarrott, Sam'l Weaver, Jno. Dowie, Mr. Mitchell,

Sen'r, Elex. Strange, Mr. Batte, Thos. Paddison, Fran. Hill
Hen. Strange, Ruth Allen, Hen. Martin, Jno. Sands, Wm.
Moss, Wm. Meanly, Mr. Hen. Wyatt, James Sanders, Margaret Prior, Jno. Realy, Rich. Allen, Fran. Warren, Hen.
Turner, Mrs. Isard, Mr. Smithson, Thos. Martin, Mr. Claybourne, Edw. Morgan, Edw'd Ragglin, Chris. Baker, Nic * *
Gilles West, Jno. Joanes, Garrott, Rob't Elleson, Rob't Hughes,
Peter Morse, Jer. Brooke, Jor. Torker, Thom. Moss, Jno. Wakefield, Coll. Pates, Martin Martin, Tho. Meridie, Jno. Alldridge, Wm. Beateson, Edward Haris, Lyon Morriss, Hen.
Turner, Edw. Gross, Wm. Martinn, Mr. Hen. Wyatt, And.
Davis, Wm. Atkinson, Jos. Moon, Edw'd Johnson, Lyon
Moriss, Peter Moss, And. Davis, Wm. Atkinson, Thos. Bird,
Bird Joanes, Dan Britt, Chas. Lovell, Mr. Gentry, Abra.
Venable, Rowland Horsley, Rob't Lansestor, Jno. Medlook,
Renall Allen, Jno. Hight, Chas. Bryan, Chas Bostick, Chris.
Baker, Thos. Moorman, Thos. Snead, James Moor, Edw. Doritt,
Mr. Wm. Bassett, Mr. James Moss, Chas. Fleming, James Austin, Jno. Baughn, James Woody, Thos. Joanes, Nick. Loson,
Tho. Ronalle, Jno. Parks, Sen., Mr. Jno. Lyddon, Thos. Wilkinson, Jno. Lewes, Ronall Allen, Wm. Turner, Geo. Pargeston, Ned Botler, Benj. Balkley, James Blackwell, Young witty,
Rob't King, Jno. Mark, Robt. Harman, Jno. Andrenson, Joanes
Ronalls, Antho. Burrus, Jno. Gontin, Wm. Bassett, jun'r,
Jno. Andrewson, Jonas Ronalls, Jno. Peard, Jno. Engleebricht,
Sam'l Waddy, Mr. Boots, Rob't Thomson, Edw. Bornett, Jno.
Talle, Rich'd Bollork, Sen., Rich'd Bollork, jun'r, James Tate,
Mr. Crawford, Andrew Davis, Edward Broxom, Jno. Wall,
Wm. Winston, Jno. Lewes, Jno. Crawford, David Craford,
jun., Rob't Andrewson, Chas. Fleming, Nic. Mills, Dow. Penix,
Rob't Deprosse, Fran. Eastor, Jno. Mashay, Mr. Polegreen
Jno. Browne, Mr. Dabbony, Geo. Moss, Edw. Howsheus, Capt.
Page, Col'l Page, Rob't Hoghes, Bird Hoghes, Thos. Wattson,
Thos. Clarke, Thos. Tinsly, Sam. Thomas, Widdow Ray, Tho.
Taylor, John Snead, James Hen. Chilloe, James Norkton, Rich'd
Cawdry, Jno. Kinborn & ye rest of his neighbors. The inhabitants belonging to St. Peter's parish in pamanach neck, viz.: Mrs.
Susana Page, Thos. Spenser, Jno. Borross, Mrs. Gooch, James

Henderson, Wm. Turner, Col. Johnson, John Davis, Rob't King, Mr. Gideon Macon, Geo. Cox, Thos. Carr Bird, Chastain James Adams, Thos Nichols, Edm. Smith, Hen. Dillon, Capt. Fran. Page, Mr. Goodin.
By order of ye vestry.
Registered per me, CHARLES TURNER, Clk of ye vestry.

At a Councill held at James City Octo. ye 18th, 1689.
Pres't Nath. Bacon, Esq'r, Pres't Council.
For Determination of ye Difference between Blissland parish & St. Peter's parish in New Kent County, it apearing y't it was agreed as when Blissland parish was to be divided p'r ye dividing line should begin at ye mouth of a Creek called Capt. Bassett's Landing & to run from thence between ye land of Capt, Joseph Forster, Mr. Richmond Terroll, having all ye s'd Forster's tract of Land in ye one parish & ye s'd Terroll in ye other, it is ordered y't a dividing line between ye s'd parish be accordingly Run from ye beginning place to ye s'd Lands & y't ye Lines of Capt. Joseph Forstor lands to ye County bounds be ye division between ye s'd parishes & y't all ye charges which hath arisen about this difference be equally divided on ye poll in both p'shes.
Registered by order of vestry per me
CHARLES TURNER, Clk. of Vestry.

At a Council held at James City, Octo ye 18th, 1689.
Pres't Nath. Bacon, Esq., Pres't Council.
Mr. Will. Phillips & Mr. Jno. Ropor having been summoned Evidences in ye difference between Blissland pa'sh & St. Peter's p'sh in New Kent County & attending in James City each of them three days, it is ordered y't they be paid for ye same by ye s'd Parishes in two days coming to James City, date returning home according to Law with costs.
Registered by order of vestry p'r me,
CHARLES TURNER, Clk of Vestry.

At a Vestry hold at ye Church of St. Peter's parish, in ye behalf of ye s'd parish, this 3rd day of Decem., 1699.

## VESTRY BOOK OF ST. PETER'S PARISH.

### Present:

Capt. Matt. Page, Mr. Gideon Macon, Mr. Henry Wyatt, Mr. Jno. Parks, Mr. George Smith, Mr. Corn. Dabboni, Mr. James Moss.

Mr. Jno. Hopor, Mr. Wm. Bassett, Church wardens.

| St. Peter's Parish. | Dr. |
|---|---|
| To Mr. Williams, Minister, as by agreement | 3600 |
| To Chas. Turner | 2000 |
| To ye 2 Sextons | 500 |
| To Benj. bolskly, for keeping ye Ferry | 800 |
| To Thos. Pontin | 4660 |
| To Wm. Major, as by acc't & ye Church agreement | 2200 |
| To Sam'l Waddy, as by acc't for dietting ye carpen'r, and for getting of 8 lotts of board timber to ye Church | 2470 |
| To Mr. Wm. Bassett, Church warden, as by his acc't | 1052 |
| Mr. Gideon Macon, as by his acc't | 900 |
| To Mr. Ropor & to Dct. Phillips, for attendance at Towne as being Evidences in ye division of ye parishes | 600 |
| To Mr. Ropor, as by acc't | 1150 |
| To Mr. Joanes, mins Surveyor | 400 |
| To Chas Turner, for washing & mending ye surplice & wash ye Communion Cloate & scouring ye plate | 150 |
| To Chas. Turner for effiating on ye work day for what hath been & for part of ye ensuing year | 500 |
| To Cash at 8 pesent | 1678 |
| To Sall. at 5 pesent | 1133 |
| | 23793½ |
| By Peter massy, as by order of Court | 500 |
| By bill ye Sisilly Ellison | 500 |
| By Cash for Ditto | 80 |
| By 603 Tithables at 38 lbs. & ½ ye Polo | 23216 |
| To Remaine in ye Church wardens hands to pay for Glass for ye uper Church, Ball | 503½ |

It is ordered y't Mr. Roper & Mr. Bassett do continue as

Church wardens of this parish untill Easter next ensuing ye date of this vestry & to Collect 38 lbs. & ½ of Tobb. from each Tithable in this parish for ye defraying * * for Charge.

It is ordered y't Jno. Pontin be allowed 330 Lbs. of Tobb. & Cask for six weeks diett for Tho. Pontin beginning from this day to be p'd at ye laying of ye next Levy.

It is ordered y't ye proceedings of ye last vestry be disanold & of no *.

It is ordered y't Rich. Brock for ye future do pay no parish Levy.

It is ordered y't Mr. Williams minister do effiate as Clk for the ensuing year & to be allowed at ye rate of 2000 lbs. of Tobb. & Cask.

It is ordered y't ye Sextons to continue this ensuing year.

It is ordered y't ye Church wardens do agree with some person to keep ye ferry & to be allowed as formerly.

It is ordered y't for ye future ye place of meeting for ye vestry be appointed at ye house of Mr. James Moss.

It is ordered y't sometime between this & Easter Mr. Macon, Mr. * * *, Mr. Roper & Mr. Bassett do appoint a meeting of ye Gentle'n of Blissland parish vestry & to Levvy a Charge according to ye order of ye * * * & Counsel & to run ye dividing line accordingly.

Regis'd by order of vestry pr me,

CHAS. TURNER, Clk of Vestry.

At a Vestry hold on behalf of St. Peter's parish this 17th day of Febr., 1690.

PRESENT:

Capt. Matt. Page, Thos. Mitchell, Gideon Macon, Hen. Wyatt, Mr. Corn'l Dabboni, James Moss, Geo. Smith, Jno. Parks.

Mr. Jno. Roper, Will Bassett, Church wardens.

It is ordered by this present vestry y't Mr. Jno. Gordon be entertained & y't he do offiate as Minister of this parish on ye same terms as other Ministers have done heretofore if ye same Mr. Gordon shall please to arrange ye same.

It is ordered by this vestry y't Mr. Pargesstor do ferry over ye people of ye neck belonging to this parish on Sundays Court days & Mustering days & to be allowed proportionable to wh. he hath been allowed for Sunday.

It is likewise ordered by this vestry y't Capt. Joseph Forster be a vestryman in ye Room & stead of Mr. Wm. Pasly deseased & to have timely noatice of ye meeting of ye next vestry.

It is likewise ordered y't Thom. Pontin do build a platform for ye Communion table, raild & bannistered in according to y't at the Lower Church and to make a new table according to ye s'd platform to lay ye Chancel and Ally wth plank to make two hard blocks & to completely finish all & every of ye aforesaid & ye vestry to find plank sufficient for same & nails. Likewise to be allowed ye sd Pontin Sixteen hundred Lbs. of Tobb. & Cask at ye laying of ye next Levy if ye same work be finished. It is likewise ordered y't Tho. Pontin do saw five hundred foot of pine plank & find himself all necessarrios during ye time of sawing ye same & to be allowed four hundred Lbs. of Tobb. & Cask for ye same.

Registered per me,

CHAS. TURNER, Clk of the Vestry.

At a Vestry held on ye behalf of St. Peter's parish this 12th day of May, 1690, Mr. Jacob Ware Minister.

Capt. Matt. Page, Jno. Parks, Mr. Jos. Forstor, Corn. Dabboni, David Craford, Geo. Smith, Hen. Wyatt, James Moss.

Mr. Jno. Roper, Wm. Bassett, Church wardens.

Whereas Mr. Jacob Ware hath been recommended by ye Hon'l * * unto this parish & having appeared as a minister fully qualified before this vestry, this parish being without a Minister, this vestry being desirous for ye advancement of God's Glory & ye continuance of ye sacred function in this parish do therefore in ye behalf of ye s'd parish consent & agree w'th ye s'd Mr. Jacob Ware to effiate as Minister thereof. It is therefore ordered by this present vestry y't ye afores'd Mr. Ware do effiate as Minister of this parish one Sunday at ye one Church and ye other Sunday at ye other as other ministers have done heretofore and his time to begin from 8 day of this instant May until ye day of June next ensuing ye date of this vestry and to be allowed at ye Rate of twelve thousand pounds of Tobb & Cask pr year.

It is ordered by this vestry y't Capt. Joseph Forster & Capt. Matthew Page or either of them doe by ye first oportunity return ye Hon'l * * * humble thanks for his care and kindness toward this parish in ye sending of Mr. Jacob Ware to this parish.

Whereas this vestry in Octo'r last did order and impower several of ye gentlemen of this vestry to appoint a meeting w'th ye Gentlemen of Blissland, ye vestry to Levy ye Church & Run a dividing line according to ye order of ye P'sh & Council & a time being by them appointed & they failing to appear at ye place & time of their owne appointment this prst vestry doe therefore now order yt ye Capt. Joseph Forster, Mr. Gideon Macon, Mr. Jno. Ropor do appoint a meeting some time between this ye tente day of Octo'r next at ye house of Mrs. Botts giving ye Gents of ye afores'd prst vestry twenty days noatice of ye time & place and the s'd together to Levvy ye Charges * * * a Surveyor to Run a dividing line according to ye order of ye afores'd & Counsoll & in case ye Gen'tle of Blissland p'sh vestry shall refuse or neglect to meet according to this order, then this vestry doe impower & order ye Gen'tle before mentioned to & in behalf of this parish to gether * * * a Surveyor to Run ye dividing line accordingly.

It is ordered yt Eliz. Faulkner be allowed five hundred Lbs. of Tobb. & Cask towards her maintenance accordingly to be Levied for her at ye Laying of ye next Levy ys year beginning as from ye date of this vestry for one whole year.

Mr. Geo. Poindexter Sen'r is this day Chosen & Ellected as a vestryman in ye Room & stead of Mr. Thom. Mitchell disseased & it is likewise ordered yt he have timely noatice of ye meeting of ye next vestry.

It is ordered by this present vestry yt Capt. Matthew Page & Mr. Henry Wyatt do effiate as Church wardens of this parish for two years ensuing as from Easter last past.

Registered per me,
      CHARLES TURNER, Clk of Vestry.

The line dividing ye parish of St. Peter's & Blissland as follows viz: Beginning at Pamonky River side at a small * mouth known by ye name of Bassett's landing where there is a small oake markt poynt and bottoms untill ye come to ye maine Roade to a markt Corner Red oak of ye lands of Richmond Powoll throwe by ye lines of ye s'd Powoll's land having all ye s'd Powoll's land in Blissland parish throwe by ye s'd Powelles land, & by Capt. Joseph Forster including all ye land of ye s'd Capt. Joseph Forster in St. Peter's parish, this done by order of the Governour and Counsoll dated at James City ye 18th day Oct., 1689, Pr James Minge.

At a Counsoll held at James City ye 18th, 1689.

PRESENT:

Nath. Bacon, Esq., Presd't Councoll.

For determination of ye Difference Between Blissland parish & St. Peter's parish in New Kent County, it appearing yt it was agreed on when Blissland parish was to be divided ye dividing line should begin at ye mouth of a Creek call'd Capt. Bassett's Landing & to Run from thence between ye lands of Capt. Joseph Forster & Mr. Richmond Powoll's leaving all ye s'd Forster's dividend of land in ye one parish & ye s'd Powoll's land in ye other, it is ordered yt a dividing line between ye s'd parishes be accordingly from ye beginning to ye s'd lands & y't ye lines of Capt. Joseph Forster's land to ye County Court so yt division between ye s'd pshs & yt all ye Charge w'ch hath arisen about this difference be equally Levied on ye poll in both psh's.

Veria copia, test,

W. EDWARDS, Clk Court.
NATH. BACON.

At a Vestry hold in ye behalf of St. Peter's parish this 20th novem., 1690.

Mr. Jacob Ware minister, Capt. Joseph Forster, James Moss, Capt. ——— Macon, Wm. Bassett, Corn'l Dabboni, Jno. Parks.

Capt. Matt. Page, Mr. Hen. Wyatt, Church wardens.

## VESTRY BOOK OF ST. PETER'S PARISH. 25

| | |
|---|---|
| Mr. Jacob Ware minister to ye 8 of this instant.......... | 6000 |
| To Mr. Ware from this 20th day of nov. to ye 8th of Jan. | 2000 |
| Mr. Williams for preaching ten sermons 300 lbs. of Tobb. as by agreement between ye s'd Desem'r to ye 8 of May pr. sermon ..................................... | 3000 |
| To Charles Turner for effiating as the Sexton of ye Lower Church ........................................ | 2250 |
| To Thos. Hart Sexton of ye uper Church.............. | 0250 |
| To Thos. Pontin for finishing ye uper Church........... | 2000 |
| To Mr. Macon 509. 10 5\|\| 10 1 300:6................. | 0100 |
| To Mr. Botte as by acct............................ | 0165 |
| To Mr. John Lyddall, for Iron work for uper Church ... | 0070 |
| To Capt. Matt Page as by acct...................... | 0300 |
| To Jno. Gontin as by an order of vestry.............. | 0355 |
| To Mr. Bassett as by acct........................... | 0371 |
| To Mr. Macon as by acct........................... | 0110 |
| To Mr. Wyatt as by acct........................... | 0218 |
| To Jno. King * * for two delinquents.............. | 0077 |
| To Mr. Pargistor for keeping ye ferry on Sundays, Coort days & more days................................ | 0960 |
| To Mr. Thos. Wilkins for boarding ye widow faulkner one year ....................................... | 0500 |
| To Mr. Thos. Wilkinson for dyett whilst sawing at ye uper Church ................................... | 0030 |
| | 18576 |
| To Cash for 18576 Lbs. of Tobb. at 8 pesent is.......... | 1500 |
| To Cash for 20256 Lbs. of Tobb. at 5 pesent is......... | 1018 |
| | 21274 |

Cr.

| | |
|---|---|
| By 609 Tith'bls at 34½ of Tobb. pr polo............. | 21010½ |
| By Thos. Spenser by order of Coort ................ | 0500 |
| | 21510½ |
| To Remaine in ye Church warden's hands to give an acct at next vestry ................................. | 0236½ |

It is ordered by this vestry upon petition of several inhabitors collect 34½ Lbs. from date Tithables to defray ye parish of ye above debts.

It is ordered that Charles Turner do effiate as Clk & Sexton this ensuing year & to be allowed 2250 Lbs. of Tobb. & Cask.

Lyonell Morriss hath agreed w'th this present vestry to keep ye widow faulkner & to find her sufficient accommodations it is therefore ordered yt he be allowed one thousand Lbs. Tobb. ye whole year.

Chas. Baker hath agreed w'th this present vestry to keep Jno. Hanowell to find him sufficient accommodations & is to be allowed one thousand Lbs. of Tobb. & Csk at ye laying of ye next Levy.

It is ordered by this vestry upon petition of several inhabitors of ye neck belonging to this parish yt so soon as ye time of Mr. Pargestor's keeping of ye ferry be expired by then Robt. King do provide a sufficient ferry boat & to be allowed at same rate as Mr. Pargestor was for ye year being so ofered by s'd King. Whereas Mr. Ware hath been allowed 2000 Lbs. of Tobb. & Cask to offiate as minister of this parish from ye 8 of this instant untill 8th of Jan. next as was by our first agreement it is therefore ordered yt he do offiate from ye s'd of ye afores'd Jan. untill ye 8th of Nov'r next and be allowed 10000 Lbs. of Tobb. & Cask.

This vestry being informed by Mr. Ware minister yt Mr. Geo. Poindexter Sen'r doth refuse to offiate as a vestryman ye Clarke of this vestry declaring to this vestry yt he did give ye s'd Mr. Poindexter timely noatice of their meeting and Mr. Tho. Smith is elected as a vestryman in his stead & that ye Clark do send ye s'd Mr. Smith timely noatice of ye next meeting of this vestry.

Registered pr me,         CHAS. TURNER, Clk of Vestry.

---

At a Vestry held at the Lower Church of St. Peter's parish this second day of Novemb'r, 1691.

PRESENT:

Mr. Jacob Ware, minister.

Capt. Jos. Forster, Mr. David Craford, Mr. Jas. Moss, Mr. Thos. Smith, Mr. Jno. Roper, Mr. Corn'l Dabonni, Vestrymen.

## VESTRY BOOK OF ST. PETER'S PARISH. 27

Capt. Matt. Page, Mr. Hen. Wyatt, Church wardens.

Capt. John Lyddall being present at ye meeting of this vestrie & this vestrie being vacant of a vestrieman it is therefore ordered by this present vestrie that Capt. John Lyddall be now henceforward a vestryman in ye Room & stead of Mr. George Smith deseased.

| | |
|---|---:|
| To Mr. Jacob Ware minister with Convenience at 6 pesent | 10000 |
| To Charles Turner for effiating as Clk & Sexton of ye Lower Church | 02250 |
| To Thomas Hart Sexton of the Uper Church | 00250 |
| To Lyonell Morriss for keeping Eliz. Faulkner one whole year | 01000 |
| To Mr. Xtoph'e Baker for keeping John Hannewell one mon. & buriing him | 00150 |
| To Mr. Littlepage for the keeping & burying Mary Wattenedgo | 00350 |
| To Capt. Jno. Lyddall for one Delinq't & 8 Feridges after ye levy laid & ye prsh ferrie ceased | 00074 |
| To Capt. Matt. Page pr acct as being Church warden | 00470 |
| To Idem for Tobb. overpaid the last year | 00147 |
| To Thomas Pontin as pr Acct | 00150 |
| To Mr. James Moss for a pr of Duff * for the Communo | 00020 |
| To Mr. Hen. Wyatt as pr Acct being Church warden | 01084 |
| To Robt. King for keeping parish ferry untill ye Divid. of ye Co'ut | 00480 |
| To Mr. Jno. Roper as ye Acct | 00100 |
| To Cash for 16526 Lbs. of Tobb. ½ at 8 pecent | 01322 |
| To Ball for 17848 Lbs. ½ of Tobb. at 5 pr cent | 00892 |
| To the convenience of the minister & Tob. being 12250 at 6 pr cent. | 00735 |
| | 19475 |
| By 531 Tithables at 37 lb. of Tob. pr poll | 19647 |
| To remain in the Church warden's hands to give an acct of at ye laying of ye next Levy | 172 |

It is ordered that Capt. Matt Page, Mr. Hen. Wyatt do collect 372½ pr polo to defer the above charge as being Church wardens.

Reg'd pr me, CHARLES TURNER, Clk of ye vestrie.

At a Vestry hold at the uper Church of St. Peter's parish this 28 day of April, 1692.

PRESENT:

Mr. Jacob Ware minister.

Mr. James Moss, Mr. Wm. Bassett, Mr. Tho. Smith, Mr. John Parks, Mr. Corn'l Dabboni, Mr. Jno. Roper.

Capt. Matt Page, Mr. Hen. Wyatt, Church wardens.

It is ordered by this present vestry yt Capt. Joseph Forster & Mr. James Moss do offiate as Church wardens of this parish two whole years from this present time according to a former Costom of this vestrie upon the petti. of Thomas Kerby to be Levy free & ye s'd Kerby having appeared to this vestrie that his is free from publique & County Levy. It is therefore ordered by this present vestry yt henseforward yt s'd Thomas Kerby pay no parish Levy.

Reg'd pr me CHARLES TURNER, Clk of Vestrie.

At a Vestry hold at the house of Capt. John Lyddall on ye behalf of ye St. Peter's Parish on this 20th day of December, 1692.

Mr. Jacob Ware, Minister.

Capt. Jno. Lyddall, Mr. David Craford, Mr. Thos. Smith, Mr. John Roper, Mr. Corn. Daboni, Mr. Hen. Wyatt, Mr. Gideon Macon, Mr. John Parker, Mr. Wm. Bassett.

Capt. Jos. Forster, Mr. James Moss, Church wardens.

St. Peter's parish Debtor to this following Charge, viz:

Tobb,

To Mr. Jacob Ware minister w'th Casque & Convense. 12000
To Chas. Turner Clk of ye parish & Sexton of ye lower
    Church with Casque & Conveniense.................. 2250
To Edward Clark Sexton of ye uper Church........... 0250
To Charles Turner for ye washing ye Communion Cloath
    & Surplice & scousing ye plate..................... 0150

| | |
|---|---|
| To Capt. Joseph Forster for * * & Commu. wine..... | 0385 |
| To Capt. Batthorst Acct of Mr. Winn Edwards for * * upon ye dividing of the two parishes................ | 0250 |
| To Mr. James Moss pr Acct being Church warden....... | 0140 |
| To Capt. Matt Page as by Acct for Comu. wine......... | 0150 |
| To Mr. Jno. Lightfoot ye keeping & bording a lame woman as by agreement with Mr. Wyatt Church warden ........................................... | 0550 |
| To Mr. Wm. Bassett w'ch should have been raised in ye year 1689 ........................................ | 0091 |
| To Rich. Cox for making a window frame for ye lower Church behind ye pupitt & finding nails & for ye glass.. | 0050 |
| To Richard Scrugg for keeping Mary Fisher being a poor child & for finding it Cloathes as per notiace........ | 1200 |
| To Mr. Gideon Macon for Charges about a Deed of Sale concerning ye land belonging to the uper Church...... | 0055 |
| To Mr. Wyatt as by Acct 900 Lbs. of Tobb. he having allowed his deed and being 406 remain Due.......... | 0507 |
| To Rowland Forster for keeping Susana Barnes one whole year & finding Cloathes..................... | 1200 |
| To Geo. Bradby for keeping John Bhadshow four months & one day & burying him......................... | 0433 |
| To Lyonell Morriss for keeping ye widow foulkner one year ............................................. | 1000 |
| To Wm. Millington for keeping Eliz. Green about five months & boarding her........................... | 0500 |
| To Robt. Sporlock for keeping Thos. Rodge & burying him .............................................. | 0300 |
| To Mabell Wood Widow towards her maintanace...... | 0500 |
| To Chas. Turner for ye clearing wood round ye lower Church this present year .......................... | 0050 |
| To Steph. Crump for a pair of Doftailes............... | 0049 |

| | | |
|---|---|---|
| | | 22051 |
| To Cask for 22051 lbs. Tobb. at 8 pesent........ | 1764 | 1764 |
| To Cask for 500 lbs. of Tobb. to be paid by Mr. * * | 40 | 40 |
| To Conven'e for ye Minister & * *.............. | 855 | 855 |

To Soll for * * *.............................. 1235  1235
                                              _____  _____
                                                      25945

To remain in the Church wardens hands to give an Acct at the laying of ye next Levy 0031¾ lbs. Tob.

It is ordered by this psent vestry yt Capt. Joseph Forster & Mr. Jas. Moss Church wardens do collect 50 Lbs. & ¼ of Tob. from Each Tithable to defray ye above Charge.

It is ordered yt Charles Turner doe offiate as Clk of this parish sexton of the lower Church this ensuing year & to be allowed at ye rate of 2250 Lbs. of tobacco and Cask convenient pr annum.

It is ordered yt Mabell Wood widow be allowed after ye rate of two hundred pounds of Tob. & Cask yearly doeing ye vestry pleasure.

It is ordered yt Mr. Warkman be allowed after ye rate of one thousand pounds of Tob. & Cask pr year for keeping yr widow faulkner this ensuing year & to be paid at ye laying of ye next Levy.

Whereas it appeared to this vestry yt Thomas Jackson did take his sister Mrs. Green into his Care and first brought her into this parish. It is ordered by this vestry yt ye s'd Jackson do keep this parish harmless of all trouble & Charge yt may Arise by this said Eliz. Green & to reimburse this parish five hundred pounds of Tob. & Cask paid to William Millington for his Care in looking after & bording her ye s'd Eliz. Green & yt ye Church wardens are ordered to take care yt ye same be effectually done.

It is ordered yt ye Church wardens do take Care to secure ye tobacco to this parish by bill from Sam'l Bogg being by a fine according to law. In obedience to a late act of Assembly made at James City 1691 yt each vestry divided their parish into & certain precincts to so mark ye bounds of last man's land some time between ye month of September & ye last of March. It is therefore ordered yt ye do give out orders to ye severall precincts as has been formerly divided by this vestry.

Benjamin Bolsly being appointed Surveyor of the high way do in ye place & stead of Mr. Geo. Pargitor & making his Survey to this vestry for help. It is therefore ordered yt he have all the Tithables on ye south side of the road from Mattodequin Creek up to Capt. Page's mill to board & make good ye s'd Roade according.

Registered p me,         CHARLES TURNER, Clk Vest'y.

At a Vestry hold at ye house of Mr. James Moss on ye behalf of St. Peter's parish this 8th day of Mars 1692-3.

PRESENT:

Capt. Matt Page, Mr. David Craford, Mr. Thom. Smith, Mr. Jno. Roper, Mr. Gideon Macon, Mr. Hen. Wyatt, Mr. Corn'l Dabboni, Mr. John Parks, vestrymen.

Capt. Jos. Forster, Mr. James Moss, Church wardens.

Whereas Mr. Jacob Ware late minister of this parish did at ye Vestry hold ye 20th day of December, 1692, desire a presentation to his Excell. to be minister of this parish w'ch proposition did likewise ye vestry and ye vestry now having made and confirmed ye same do therefore order Capt. Jos. Forster & Mr. James Moss Church wardens doe request Mr. Jacob Ware to accompany them to his Ex & to whose ye Church wardens are ordered and desired in the behalf of this vestry to go to his Excell. yt ye said Mr. Jacob Ware may be restored to this parish w'th an induction to be our minister.

At a vestry held at the house of Mr. James Moss on ye behalf of St. Peter's parish this 25th day October, 1693.

Mr. Jacob Ware minister.

Capt. Jno. Lyddall, Mr. Henry Wyatt, Mr. Geo. Smith, Mr. Wm. Bassett, Mr. Con'l Dabboni, Mr. Jno. Parks, Vestrymen.

Capt. Jo Forster, Mr. James Moss, Church wardens.

St. Peter's parish Dr. to this following Charge

To Mr. Jacob Ware w'th Casq't, Considering two months wanting in paying & s'd Mr. Ward acc't one agt ye other   12720

To Chas Turner as Clk of this parish & Sexton of ye Lower Church ....................................   2385

To Edward Clark, Sexton of ye uper Church........   250

To Mrs. Butts for keeping Margaret Swanson & her Bastard child sixty-eight days ........................   680

To Jon. Giles for keeping Margaret Swanson & Child 11
  days & other attendance ........................... 175
To Rich'd Scruggs for keeping Mary Fisher after ye
  rate of one thousand pounds of Tob. p'r year & p Acct. 1034
To Wm. Booth for keeping ye Widdow Davis two months
  after ye rate of one thousand pounds of Tob. p'r year.. 167
To Mr. Rob't Napier for keeping ye widdow faulkner and
  for some things she hath had as p Acc't after ye rate of
  1000 Lbs. of Tob. p'r year, according to a former order
  of this to Mr. Warsman .......................... 1160
To Benj. Bulkly as by agreement & Acc't for paling in ye
  Uper Church .................................... 2700
To Capt. Matt. Page as p Acc't .................... 1896
To Mr. Jas. Moss as Church Warden p'r Acct......... 940
To Wm. Daniell for falling & removing two trees from ye
  uper Church .................................... 0025
To Chas. Turner for laying of Lower Church Alley ..... 0060
To Capt. Forster for two bottles of wine for A Commun-
  ion at ye rate of a penny p pound for Tob. ......... 0060
To Mabel Wood, widdow, towards her maintanance .... 0500
To Capt. Forster & Mr. Moss for their expense James
  Towne concerning ye presenting of Mr. Ware in order
  to his induction according to a former order, they giv-
  ing an Acc't next Levy .......................... 01000
To Jo'n Webb for Clearing round ye uper Church yar'd
  burning ye leaves to secure ye same this present year.. 0050
To Chas. Turner for clearing room ye lower Church to se-
  cure ye same ................................... 0050
To Capt. Lyddall for a Case to secure ye Register Book.. 0060
To Thomas Miller p agreement w'th ye Church warden
  for carrying Margaret Swanson's child from Mrs. Butts
  to Mr. Moss's house ............................. 0030
To Casks for 25944 lb. of Tob. at 8 p'ct is ............. 2075
To Ditt. for 28019 of tob. at 5 p'ct is ................. 1400
                                                    ─────
                                                    29419
  CR.
By 539 Tithables at 55 lbs of Tob. p polo is ........... 29645

VESTRY BOOK OF ST. PETER'S PARISH. 33

To remain in ye Church wardens' hands to give an acc't . . 00226
At ye laying of ye next Levy ....................... 00183
By Samuel Waddy
By what remains in ye Church warden's hands last year 0313/4

00440

It is ordered y't Capt. John Lyddall, high Sheriff of New Kent. Co. do collect 55 lbs. of Tob. from each Tithable in this parish for defraying the above charges, making payments to ye severall creditors & give an acc't of ye same at ye next vestry.

It is ordered y't Capt. John Lyddall do collect from four Tithables belonging to Geo. Pargitor according to w'ch is raised p'r polo they not being in the list of Tithables.

It is ordered that Capt. Joseph Forster ye Bill of ye Sam'l' Bugg into the hands of Capt. Jno. Lyddall & y't he take care to review ye same & render an Acc't thereof at ye laying the next Levy.

Registered. CHARLES TURNER, Clk of Vestry.

At a Vestry hold at ye house of Mr. James Moss on ye behalf of St. Peter's parish this 1st day of May, 1694.

PRESENT:

Mr. Jacob Ware Minister.

M- ... Smith, Capt. Matt. Page, Mr. Gideon Macon, Capt. Jo'n Lyddall, Mr. David Craford, Mr. Jno. Roper, Mr. Jo'n Parks, Mr. Hen. Wyatt, Vestrymen.

Mr. James Moss, Church warden.

It is ordered by this present vestry y't Capt. John Lyddall & Mr. John Parks do offiate as Church wardens of this parish two years ensuing ye date of this present vestry according to a former order & * * *

Mary Fisher, an orphant child, having been a Charge to this parish for some time past, & Mr. Jacob Ware offering to this vestry to have ye s'd orphant bound to him thro' vestry considering ye same, do, therefore, order y't ye Church wardens doe bind ye same orphant to Mr. Ware according to law.

It is ordered y't Mr. William Clopton do have lawfull noatisa of ye next vestry meeting, he being chosen & elected as vestryman in ye Room & stead of Mr. Cornelius Dabboni, Deas'd.

This vestry understanding y't Mr. John Bouston, late of this parish, in his last will & Testament did bequeath some part of his estate to ye use of this parish. It is, therefore, ordered y't James Austin doe bring ye s'd will to ye next vestry whereby ye s'd vestry may be sattisfied y't ye Case may be take on thereof.

Registered. CHARLES TURNER, Clk of vestry.

At a vestry hold at ye house of Mr. James Moss on the behalf of St. Peter's Parish this 2nd day of Octob'r, 1694.

PRESENT:

Mr. Jacob Ware, Capt. Joseph Forster, Capt. Matt. Page, Mr. James Moss, Mr. Da. Craford, Mr. Jo'n Roper, Mr. Wm. Bassett.

Capt. Jo'n Lyddall, Mr. Jo'n Parks, Church wardens.

ST. PETER'S PARISH, Dr., to ye following Charge:

| | |
|---|---|
| To Mr. Jacob Ware, minister | 12720 |
| To Charles Turner as Clk of this Parish | 2120 |
| To Jo'n Webb as sexton of ye uper Church | 0250 |
| To Jo'n Webb for clearing about ye Church, to secure ye same | 0050 |
| To Jo'n Hillton as Sexton of ye Lower Church | 0250 |
| To Jo'n Hillton for clearing about ye Church, to secure ye same | 0050 |
| To Mr. Rob't Napier for keeping ye widdow Faulkner one whole year | 01000 |
| To Mabell Wood, widdow, for her year's maintanance | 00500 |
| To Mr. Curteen for keeping William Wittin 8 days & burying him | 00400 |
| To Capt. Page for Communion Wine | 00060 |
| To Mr. James Moss as Church warden as p acc't | 00160 |
| To Mr. Wyatt for Communion Wine | 00060 |
| To Capt. Forster for Delinq't Tithables in ye year 1691 | 00?? |
| To Charles Turner for ye washing ye Surplice & Commu: Cloathe, Scouring ye plate being usually allowed | 00150 |

VESTRY BOOK OF ST. PETER'S PARISH.     35

To Mr. Jacob Ware for Cloathes for Mary Fisher, an
orph't ........................................... 00153
                                                    —————
                                                    17960
Cr. pd fine laid on Mary Turber .................. 01332
By w'h laying in Church wardens hands............. 00440
                                                    —————
                                                    16187¼
To Casq's for 16187¼ of Tob at 8 p cent, is ...... 01294
To Ball. for 17589¼ of Tob. at 5 p cent, is ...... 00874
                                                    —————
                                                    18355¼
By 534 Tithables at 35 lbs. of Tob. p'r polo ..... 18690
To remaine in ye Church wardens' hands to give an acc't
at ye laying of ye next levy ..................... 335

It is ordered y't ye Church wardens do Collect 35 Lbs. of Tob. from each Tithable in this parish to defray ye above Charge making payment to ye severalle Credit's and render an acc't of ye same at ye next vestry.

It is ordered y't Tho. Mimb be allowed for keeping ye widdow Faulkner this ensuing year after ye rate of 1000 lbs. of Tob. & Cask.

It is ordered that ye Church wardens take Care in receiving ye fine due from Mr. Macon Concerning Rich'd Rhodes & his servant woman and render an acc't thereof at ye next vestry.

It is ordered that ye Church wardens take Care to take out A Copy of Bouster's Will & present ye same soe far as ye parish * * lye therein.

Whereas divers of ye parishoners have so petitioned to this vestry y't course may be taken with some persons for their mis-

It is, therefore, ordered y't ye Church Wardens doe take care demeanors at ye Church in ye time of Divine service.

to give in their presentments agt all such persons for ye future yt they may be proceeded against according to law.

Registered pr me. ...  CHARLES TURNER, Clk of ye vestry.
                       —————

At a vestry hold at ye house of Mr. James Moss in ye behalf of St. Peter's parish octob'r ye 10, 1695.

36        VESTRY BOOK OF ST. PETER'S PARISH.

PRESENT:

Mr. Jacob Ware, Mr. James Moss, Mr. Thomas Smith, Mr. David Craford, Mr. Hen. Wyatt, Mr. Jo'n Roper, Mr. Wm. Clopton, vestrymen.

Mr. John Parks, Church warden.

ST. PETER'S PARISH, Dr., to ye following Charge:

| | |
|---|---:|
| To Mr. Jacob Ward, Minister | 12720 |
| To Chas. Turner as Clk of ye parish | 02120 |
| To Jo'n Webb as Sexton of ye uper Church | 00250 |
| To Jo'n Hillton for clearing about ye Church to secure the same | 00050 |
| To Mr. Job Howes p acc't of Ch. fees for persons summoned to ye Court p ye Church wardens | 00040 |
| To Jno. Webb, Sexton of ye uper Church for clearing abot ye same | 00050 |
| To Mr. William Clopton for 4 summons pr ye Church wardens' order | 0040 |
| To Thomas Wingfield for keeping Hanah Ross' child one year | 01000 |
| To Mr. Parks as Church warden for Acc't for W. Pedley for haveing a bastard child | 00150 |
| To Thos. Wingfield p acc't of charge for Hanah Ross' child | 00071 |
| To William Walker for acc't paid to ye widdow Faulkner & to Mary Gibson upon an acc't drawn by ye Church wardens. | 00208 |
| To Jos. Gibbs pr acc't for ye care of Boe wounded by ye Indians | 02000 |
| To Edward Burnett for keeping Gulshell 8 weeks & burying him | 00350 |
| To Mr. David Craford as by acc't for Cloathing of Rich.: Boe & some lining to Edward Burnet for Thos. Gulshell | 00558 |
| To Mabel Wood, widow, for her maintanence | 00500 |
| To Thomas Gibson for keeping a bastard child a year and a half | 01500 |

To Thomas Minne for keeping ye widow Faulkner one

whole year ..................................... 01000
To Thomas Minne for one pair of shoes for ye widow
Faulkner ....... ............................. 00040
                                                    ──────
                                                     22897
To Casq's for 22897 Lbs Tob. a 8 p cent., is............  1831
To Sall for 24728 Lbs Tcb. a 5 p cent., is.............  1236
                                                    ──────
                                                     25964
CRE'T.

By Tobacco in Capt. Lyddall's hands ye half year......0335¼

By 538 Tithables at 48 Lbs of Tob. pr polo..........25824
By 538 Tithables at 48 Lbs of Tob. pr polo............25824
                                                    ──────
To lie in ye Church wardens' hands to give an acc't at ye
laying of ye next levy ........................... 00186

It is ordered that ye Church wardens doe collect 48 Lbs. of Tob. from each Tithable in the parish to defray ye above Charge, making payments to the severall Creditors & render an acc't of ye same at ye next vestry.

Registered est CHARLES TURNER, Clk of ye vestry.

At a Vestry hold at ye Lower Church of St. Peter's Parish, on the behalf of ye s'd parish this 5 day of Jan'y, 1695.

PRESENT:

Mr. Jacob Ware, minister.
Mr. James Moss, Mr. Thos. Smith, Mr. Gideon Macon, Mr. Hen. Wyatt, Mr. Jo'n Roper, Mr. Wm. Clopton.
Mr. John Parks, Church warden.

Whereas, Mr. Jacob Ware was inducted as minister of this parish, and for some time ye Induction did soe remain, and now publishing & declaring his intention of leaving this parish, & upon a motion of this vestry toward considering ye s'd Induction, he doth utterly renounce & lay downe ye same as never hereafter to take any advantage ov any person by from or under him any ways relating to ye same, and yt this parish have full and free liberty to provide a minister to serve ye sd parish as fully & freely as though no such thing as an induction had ever been and doth likewise now surrender up to ye Church wardens in ye behalf of this parish ye Church belongings thereto, and this vestry doth descard Mr. Jacob Ware hath fully effiated for in Tob. hath been raised for him by the parish.

Registered per CHARLES TURNER, Clk of ye vestry.

At a vestry hold at ye Lower Church of S'n't Peter's parish on ye behalf of ye s'd parish this 10th day of Aprill, 1696.

Capt. Jo. Forster, Capt. Matt. Page, Mr. Jas. Moss, Mr. Thos. Smith, Mr. Hen. Wyatt, Mr. Will. Bassett, Mr. John Roper, Mr. Tho. Smith, Mr. Gideon Macon, Church wardens.

It is ordered yt Mr. Gideon Macon & Mr. William Clopton doe officate as Church wardens of this parish two years ensuing ye date hereof in ye Room & Stead of Capt. John Lyddall & Mr. John Parks, who have officiated ye time aforesaid.

Capt. Matt. Page acquainting this vestry of ill rec * * * * of ye being removed out of this parish and County. It is therefore, ordered yt Mr. John Lewis be appointed as a vestryman in ye Room & Stead of ye s'd Capt. Page, ye s'd Mr. Lewis being present at this vestry.

It is ordered yt ye Church wardens doe make application to his Excellency concerning a minister for this parish being now vacant. This Parish being vacant of a minister & ye vestry considering ye necessity and want thereof did request Mr. Monrowe yt he would offiate some certain Sundays to ye w'ch ye s'd Mr. Monrowe hath agreed & doth promise to offisiate at ye uper Church ye first Sunday after Easter next, & yt day three weeks at this Lower Church in ye afternoon & so to continue untill this parish be provided with a minister; it is, therefore, ordered yt ye Church wardens take Care to provide yt ye S'd Mr. Monrowe may have a passage over ye River on those particular days aforementioned.

Registered pr CHARLES TURNER, Clk vestry.

At a Vestry hold at ye uper Church of St. Peter's Parish in ye behalf of this s'd parish this 16 day of November, 1696.

Capt. Joseph Forster, Capt. Jo'n Lyddall, Mr. James Moss, Mr.

Thos. Smith, Mr. David Craford, Mr. Jo'n Lewis, Mr. Hen. Wyatt, Mr. Jo'n Parks, Mr. Wm. Bassett.

Mr. Wm. Clopton, Church Warden.

Whereas, Mr. Nicholas Moreau hath been recommended by his Excell. and Mr. Camesery unto this parish and appearing to this vestry as a minister fully qualified this parish being vacant of a minister and ye vestry being desirous of ye advancement of God's Glory & ye continuance of ye Sacred function in this parish do therefore in ye behalfe of ye s'd Parish Covenant & agree w'th ye s'd Mr. Moreau to offiate as minister thereof for this ensuing year from ye day and date of this present vestry & he ye s'd Mr. Moreau do offiate one Sunday at ye one Church and ye other Sunday at ye other as other ministers have done heretofore, and to be allowed for ye same according to law, but if not well understood by this parish then by agreement this parish to be at their liberty at ye expiration of ye afores'd year.

Read and approved of p ye vestry & is Registered p

CHARLES TURNER, Clk of Vestry.

---

At a vestry held at ye uper Church of Snt. Peters Parish in ye behalf of ye s'd parish this 16th day of November, 1696.

PRESENT:

Mr. Nicholas Moreau, minister.

Capt. Joseph Forster, Mr. Jno. Lewis, Capt. Jo'n Lyddall, Mr. Hen. Wyatt, Mr. James Moss, Mr. Jo'n Parke, Mr. Thos. Smith, Mr. Wm. Bassett, Mr. Daniel Craford.

Mr. Wm. Clopton, Church warden.

St. Peter's Parish, Dr. to ye following Charge:

| | |
|---|---|
| To Mr. Monroe, minister for nine sermons at 250 Lbs of Tob pr serm.................................... | 2250 |
| To Charles Turner as Clerk of this parish............. | 2120 |
| To Idem for serving extraordinary when no minister.. | 0500 |
| To Jo'n Webb as sexton of ye uper Church............ | 0250 |
| To Idem for clearing around ye s'd Church to secure ye same ......... ..................................... | 0050 |
| To Jo'n Hilton, Sexton of ye lower Church............ | 0250 |

| | |
|---|---|
| To Thos. Wingfield for keeping Hanah Ross' child 1 year & for finding same necessarys .............. | 1075 |
| To John Giles for keeping Rich' Bowe who was wounded p ye Indians ................................. | 2750 |
| To Mabell Wood Widdow for her maintanence ......... | 0500 |
| To Mr. Job Howes for lb feed concerning Eliza Pedly's having a bastard child .......................... | 0110 |
| To Jo'n Gunton for three bush'll Indian Corn delivered to Anthony Burruss ........................... | 0060 |
| To Thom. Minns for keeping ye widdow faulkner 1 year & providing her a pr of Shoes as pr acct........... | 1040 |
| To Tho. Gibson for keeping a Bastard Child 10 months & a half ............................................. | 0850 |
| To Mr. Jo'n Lightfoot for keeping Anna Chapman 14 mon's & for * * trouble with her .................. | 1450 |
| To Jon. Hilton for mending some pews & pales abo't ye lower Church & fetching Mr. Monrowe once over ye River with Mr. Littlepage's overseer ............... | 0110 |
| To Capt. Lyddall pr acct for delinq't Tithables & goods for cloathing Rich'd Bowe wounded by Indians...... | 0855 |
| To James Nees for himself & two horses going w'th Mr. Moreau minister ................................ | 0150 |
| | 14370 |
| To Casq's for 14370 lbs. Tob'o at 8 p Ct. is............ | 1149 |
| To Sall'r for 15519 lbs. tob. at 5 p Ct. is ............. | 775 |
| | 16294 |
| By 541 Tithables at 30 lbs. tob'r p polo is.............. | 16230 |
| To be repaid ye Church wardens at ye laying of ye next levy being now wanting .......................... | 64 |
| Totall ......... ........................... | 16294 |

It is ordered yt ye Church wardens do take Care to collect from each date Tithable person in this parish, 30 lbs. of Tob. for ye defraying of ye above Charge & to make payment to ye severall persons unto whom it is proportioned.

It is ordered yt ye Church wardens take Care to receive ye

## VESTRY BOOK OF ST. PETER'S PARISH. 41

moyete of ye fine due from Mr. Gideon Macon concerning Rich. Rhodes & his servant woman & render an acct. thereof at ye next vestry.

Whereas Anthony Burrass of this parish is stricken blind & his wife is very ancient by what means they are incapable of getting their living & that ye s'd Anthony addressing himself to this vestry for a maintanence.

It is therefore ordered yt ye Church wardens forthwith cause ye s'd Anthony Burros to convey over unto them for ye use of this parish forever his plantation, Cattle, horses & hoggs & yt there be allowed to each of them five hundred pounds of Tob. & Casq's for their maintanence during their or either of their natural lives or till he may be recovered of his eye sight. It is ordered yt ye Church wardens take care as soon as may be binde out Hanah Ross's child now at Thomas Wingfield's to any person that shall be willing to take ye same according to law.

It is ordered yt ye Church wardens forthwith endeavour to find out some person yt may take & keep Anna Chapman now at Mr. Lightfoot's house at as little Charge to ye parish as they can.

It is ordered yt the Church wardens doe by the first opportunity Return his Excell. humble thanks for his Care & kindness in Recommending to this parish a minister.

Mary ye wife of William Leah declaring to this vestry yt her husband aforesaid is willing to keep Richard Bowe this ensuing year and Mr. Tho. Smith assume yt what shee did declare her s'd husband would performe. It is therefore ordered yt Wm. Leah do keep ye s'd Richard Bowe this ensuing year ye vestry finding him Cloathes during ye s'd time & ye s'd Leah to be allowed after ye rate of foure hundred pounds of Tob. & Casq p year.

Jeffery Daniel making appear to this vestry yt he is discharged for paying any Publique or County levy p order of Coort. It is likewise ordered by this present vestry yt ye s'd Jeffery Daniel pay noe parish levy for ye future.

Sam'll Buggs Bill was this day delivered to Mr. Wm. Clopton.

Church warden, to receive and give acct. of at ye laying ye next levy.

Registered p order of vestry.

p CHARLES TURNER, Cl. of ye vestry.

At a Vestry held at ye house of Mr. Wm. Bassett on ye behalf of S'nt Peter's parish this 19 day of Jan'y, 169

Mr. Nicholas Moreau, minister.

Capt. Joseph Forster, Mr. Hen. Wyatt, Capt. Jo'n Lyddall, Mr. Wm. Bassett, Mr. James Moss, Mr. Jo'n Roper, Mr. John Parke, vestrymen.

Mr. Wm. Clopton, Church warden.

Whereas this vestry did upon ye presentation of Mr. Nicholas Moreau, minister on ye 16th day of November last past agree with ye s'd Mr. Moreau as minister of this parish and to offiate ye ensuing year from ye date aforesaid and yt s'd Mr. Moreau having considered ye afores'd agreem't and finding many disadvantages yt may attend to him in ye performing ye same did appoint a vestry, ye which vestry have accordingly met & ye s'd Moreau acquainting this vestry his desire to returne for England & therefore to be acquitted from ye afores'd agreement. This vestry doe consent to ye same if it be Mr. Moreau's pleasure so to doe or other way or to continue minister as afores'd Mr. Henry Wyatt assuming to this vestry yt he will pay unto Mr. Moreau wt. Tob. is due to him from this parish for ye time of his offiating in this parish, And this vestry hath promise to repay to s'd Mr. Wyatt at ye laying of ye next levy ye w'ch paying Mr. Moreau doth like and request.

Registered p CHARLES TURNER, Clk. Vestry.

St. Peter's Parish at a Vestry held at the house of Mr. Gideon Macon this 18th day of Dec'r, 1697.

PRESENT:

Capt. Joseph Forster, Mr. Thomas Smith.

Capt. John Lyddall, Mr. John Lewis, Mr. James Moss, Mr. Will Bassett.

Mr. Gideon Macon, Church warden.

VESTRY BOOK OF ST. PETER'S PARISH. 43

Charles Turner, late Clerk of this Vestry, being dead William Clopton in his stead to offiate in his place and to have the same allowance the late Clerk had.

Capt. Thomas Bray is elected to be one of the vestry of this parish in place and stead of Will Clopton who was this day chosen Clark of the vestry & requested to be at the next vestry to take the oath according to Law & that the Clark give him notice thereofe.

St. Peter's Parish, Dr.

| | |
|---|---:|
| To Mr. Nicholas Moreau, minister, 16000 Comm't 800.. | 168000 |
| To Charles Turner, Late Clerk | 2289 |
| To John Hilton, Sexton of the Lower Church | 0270 |
| To Idem for Clearing about the Church | 0054 |
| To John Webb, Sexton of the uper Church | 0270 |
| To Id for Clearing ab't y'd Church & wash ye Surplis.. | 0108 |
| To Robert Walker p acct. of Smith's work | 0150 |
| To Anto. Burrows for himselfe and wife's maintainance but to Lye in the Church warden's hands for his use. Severall payments taken out | 0540 |
| To Edm. Bedford for keep Eliz. wimsherfers Child Six wekes | 0270 |
| To Idem for fees ab't Pedley | 0015 |
| To Capt. Lancelott Bathurst for the fees | 0030 |
| To Mr. Job Howes for Clark's fees | 0173 |
| To John Lightfoot, Esq., p acct. regulated | 0847 |
| To Mr. Hen'e Wyatt for Cloathes for ye wid. Faulkner. | 0292 |
| To Thom. mims for keeping ye wid. Faulkner one year.. | 1080 |
| To Idem for one pr Shooes for her | 0030 |
| To Capt. John Lyddall for Releefe of Anth. Burrows.... | 0540 |
| To Mr. Macon & Clopton, Church wardens, p acct. for Antho. Burrows | 1188 |
| To Mr. Macon ballance of an acct. | 0015 |
| To Will' Clopton p acct. as Church warden | 0065 |
| To Mabell wood, widow | 0540 |
| To will'e Leake for keeping Hen'e Bow one year | 0432 |
| To Sallery for 25662 at 5 p Cent | 1283 |
| | 27491 |

| | |
|---|---|
| P. Centra, P. Cap' John Lyddall paid Edmond Badford for six weeks nursing two children .............. | 0270 |
| p Mr. Nicho. Morean for his servant woman's find .... | 0540 |
| P Capt. Lyddall for ½ of Perdy's find ................ | 0270 |
| P Wm. Clopton upon the moyetee of a find Rec'd of Mr. Macon, p Serv't and overseer ..................... | 1512 |
| p 575 Tithables at 42 Lbs. Tobacco p polo............ | 24150 |
| p Capt' Lancelot Bathurst for Deposits to b'd showed him in the next Levy ................................ | 00749 |
| | 27491 |

Registered p. WM. CLOPTON, Clk Vestry.

St. Peter's Parish At a Vestry held at the uper Church the 14th June, 1698.

PRESENT:

Capt. Joseph Forster, Mr. Hen' Wyatt, Mr. Jno. Roper, Mr. Wm. Bassett, Mr. James Moss, Mr. Dan Crawford, Mr. Jno. Parke, Capt' Tho. Bray, vestrymen.

Mr. Gideon Macon, Church warden.

Mr. Gideon Macon, Mr. Thomas Bray and Mr. John Roper the oaths enjoyned by act of Parliament in Stead of the oaths of Alegence and Supremacy Duly Administered to them by Capt' Joseph Forster and also doe subscribe to be Conformable in all things relating to the Church of England as it is now Established. Gideon Macon.

Signed THOMAS BRAY,
JOHN ROPER.

Mr. David Craford and Mr. Thomas Smith were this day elected and Chosen Church wardens of this parish for this present year.

The Church wardens of this parish are ordered forthwith to Caus the Lower Church yard to bee fenced in with a Good Ditch and that there bee a Good gate with Seader posts on that side next to the Road.

It is ordered that the Church wardens forthwith Caus the uper Church to be put in Good repair.

Stephen Crump applying himself to this vestry for help to Cleer the Roads in his presints is ordered the s'd tithables following, viz.: Capt' Thomas Bray, Step. Mitchell, Step. Mitchell fun, Will Fergisson, Will Bournd, Will' Crump, Pelham moore, and his own family and that the aforementioned help to Cleer to the new mill Damm upon the Black Creeke.

Registered p WM. CLOPTON, Clk. to Vest.

Alexander Mackeney, producing an order of Court to this vestry for help to Cleer the roads in his presints is ordered those familye following, viz.: Christopher Clarke, Thomas Stanley, Edw'd Clarke, Thomas wharton, Nicholas Purde, Will Martin, Jno. Martin, Edmond Harris, Will Reese, Thos. Harris, Barnell Chappell, martin martin, Thomas Delahay, John Aldridge, michael Johnson, John Jones, Thomas moss, Sam'l moss, John Willmore Garrat, Robert Ellison, Francis Amos.

Mr. Hen. Wyatt producing an order of Court for help to Cleer the Roads in his presints is ordered the s'd following Tithables, viz.: will mackgeehe, Edw. Tony, Will Walker, Robert Allin, will Daniell, John Yeomans, Richard Scruggs, James Neenes, Thomas Ashcraft, Edw'd Flinch, Thomas Wilkinson, John Rayle, Evan Raglan, Mr. Thomas Smith's quarter, Edw'd Morgan, Will Dollard, Thomas martin, Thomas Gibson, Will Gardner, Christopher Baker, William Johnson, Peter Moss, Robert Hughes, Thomas Howard, Geo. Bradbury, Hen'e Turner, Thomas minns.

Registered WM. CLOPTON, Clk of Vestry.

---

St. Peter's Parish, July the 10th, 1698.

PRESENT:

Capt. Joseph Forster, Capt. Jno. Lyddall, Mr. Jam's Moss, Capt. Thomas Bray, Mr. John Lewis, Mr. Jno. Parke, Mr. Wm. Bassett, Mr. Hen'e Wyatt, Vestrymen.

Mr. David Craford, Church warden.

Whereas Mr. James Bawker having appeared as a minister

fully qualified before this vestry, this parish being vacant of a minister, this vestry being desirous of the advancement of God's glory and the continuance of the Sacred function in this parish doe therefore in the behalf of the s'd parish Covenant and agree with the said Mr. James Bowker toe offiate as minister thereoffe; it is therefore ordered by this present vestry that the aforesaid Mr. James Bowker doe offiate as minister of this parish one Sunday at the one Church and the other Sunday at the other, as other ministers have done heretofore and his time to begin from the 26th day of June last past and to continue till the 2nd day of December next & to be paid * *

WM. CLOPTON, Clk. to ye vestry.

St. Peter's Parish, July the 10th, 1698. At a Vestry held at the uper Church.

PRESENT:

Mr. James Bowker, minister.

Capt. Jos'ph Forster, Mr. John Lewis, Capt. Jno. Lyddall, Mr. John Park, Mr. James Moss, Mr. Will Bassett, Capt. Tho. Bray, Mr. Hen. Wyatt, vestrymen.

Mr. David Craford, Church warden.

Whereas Capt. Thos. Bray by the Information Will'm Hughes hath informed this vestry that there is a man child Lately brought to the house of Richard Gillam in this parish and noe parents Can be found for the same: the Church wardens are therefore ordered forthwith to take Care that the said Child be returned to the place from whence it Came or to Caus the said Gillam to give good Securities to save the       parish harmles.

It is ordered that the Church wardens forthwith take out a Copie of Bruster's will and prosecute the same soe far as the parish Interest Lyes.

Registered. WM. CLOPTON, Clk. to vestry.

St. Peter's at a Vestry held at the House of Mr. Gideon Macon this 18 day of December, 1697.

PRESENT:

Capt. Jose. Forster, Mr. Thos. Smith, Capt. John Lyddall,

Mr. John Lewis, Mr. James Moss, Mr. Will'm Bassett, vestrymen.
Mr. Gideon Macon, Church warden.

Capt. Lancelott Bathurst, high Sheriffe of New Kent County, is ordered to Collect from each tithable person in this parish forty-two pounds of Tobacco: to defray the parish Charge and make payment to the severall persons to whom it is proportioned: and in cas of non payment to make Destres according to Law, and that the Clark deliver a copy of Charge to Capt. Bathurst and take his Receit for the same.

Registered. WM. CLOPTON, Clk. of the vestry.

St. Peter's Parish, New Kent Co. At a Vestry held at the uper Church Octo. the 3rd, 1698.

PRESENT:

Mr. James Bowker, minister.
Capt. John Lyddall, Mr. James Moss, Mr. John Roper, Capt. Jos. Forster, Mr. Will Bassett, Mr. Hen. Wyatt, Mr. John Lewis, Mr. John Park, vestrymen.
Mr. David Craford, Mr. Thos. Smith, Church Wardens.

St. Peter's Parish, Dr.

| | |
|---|---|
| To Mr. James Bowker, minister for ½ the year........ | 8000 |
| To Idem for Cash & Convenience of ditto ........... | 1120 |
| To Will Clopton, Clk............................. | 2289 |
| To Idem for reeding Homiles there bein' noe minister.. | 0250 |
| To Will Major p acct............................ | 0148 |
| To Mr. Thom. Smith, p acct...................... | 1670 |
| To Idem p acct................................. | 1140 |
| To Mabell Wood, widdow ......................... | 0540 |
| To Mr. John Roper ............................. | 0010 |
| To Wm. Sanders for his bro'l goeing to James * * *.... | 0150 |
| To Will Leake for keeping Hen'e Bow & burial of him.. | 0700 |
| To Mr. Gideon Macon, p acct..................... | 0280 |
| To John Gonton for Corne for Antho. Burrows........ | 0065 |
| To Mr. James Moss ............................. | 0030 |
| To John Hilton Sexton, of the Lower Church......... | 0300 |

48    VESTRY BOOK OF ST. PETER'S PARISH.

| | |
|---|---|
| To John Webb, Sexton of the uper Church ........... | 0300 |
| To Will Clopton p acct............................ | 0456 |
| To Thom. Mims for maintaining ye wid. Faulkner one year | 1080 |
| To Capt. Lancelott Bathurst for Deposito. last year..... | 0854 |
| To Idem p acct. for The fees ....................... | 0100 |
| To John Gonton for goeing to Court to prove Anthony Burrows deed of sale to the parish ................ | 0040 |
| To Mr. David Craford & Mr. Thom. Smith, Church wardens for ye maintanance of Antho. Burrows and wife.. | 1728 |
| To Capt. Matthew Page for 6 Bush'l of Corne for Antho. Burrows in 1696....... ........................ | 0129 |
| To Mr. Craford & Mr. Smith, Church wardens, towards the getting of Blocks ............................ | 0648 |
| To Idem for getting timber and bringing it in place..... | 0648 |
| To Thom's Ponton for Covering the uper Church but to Lye in the Church wardens' hands till the work be dun | 1693 |
| To Idem for blocking the uper Church making 2 hors blocks and Steps to both doors, but to Lye in the Church wardens' hands till the work be dun................ | 1728 |
| To Sallery of 26096 Lbs. Tob. at 5 p cent. is.......... | 1305 |
| Lbs Tob. ............................................ | 27401 |

P. Conte, Cr.

| | |
|---|---|
| By 618 Tithables at 44 Lbs. p polo.................. | 27192 |
| By Capt. Lancelott Bathurst for deposito to be alowed the next year .................................... | 00209 |
| | 27401 |

Capt. Lancelott Bathurst, high Sheriffe of this County, is ordered to collect from each tithable inhabitant in this parish fortyfoure pounds of Tobacco to defray the parish charge and that he make payment to the several persons for whom it is Levy'd: and in case of non payment to make destress according to Law, and that the Clerk give a Copy of this Charge to the said Capt. Bathurst and take his receipt for the same. Will. Clopton was this day sworn Clark of this vestry.

VESTRY BOOK OF ST. PETER'S PARISH.     49

Anthony Burrows being sent for to this vestry doth accept and is contented with one thousand six hundred pounds of Tobacco and Cask yearly for himself wife's maintainance during their Lives.

Whereas at a vestry held for this parish on the 27th Sept'r, 1697, it was ordered that Mr. Gideon Macon, Mr. John Roper and Will Clopton should meet sutch Gen'l as the vestry of Blissland parish should apoynt & reamark the line between the two parishes, which order hath not yet been executed; it is therefore ordered that Mr. Thomas Smith, Mr. Hen. Wyatt and Mr. John Roper or any two of them doe meet sutch Gen'lmen as the vestry of Blissland parish shall apoynt: and at sutch time as they shall apoynt and reamark the said Line.

Whereas Mr. James Bowker, at a vestry on the 10 July, 1698, did agree with this vestry to preach in this parish till the 26 day of December next following, and this vestry Considering the uncertinty of another meeting doe therefore Covenant and agree to and with the said Mr. Bowker for the next ensuing year and the time to begin from the 26th day of December next following: to offiate as formerly and to be paid Sixteen thousand pounds of Tobacco and Cask Convenient for the year.

Mr. John Alford aplying him self to this vestry for help to Cleer the Roads in his presints, it ordered all the tithable which formerly belonged to David Clarkson and within his presints.

Registered.  WM. CLOPTON, Clk. of ye vestry.

St. Peter's Parish, at a vestry held at the uper Church the 19th March, 1698-9.

PRESENT:

Mr. James Bowker, minister.
Capt. Joseph Forster, Capt. Jno. Lyddall, Mr. James Moss, Mr. John Lewis, Mr. Hen. Wyatt, Mr. Will Bassett, Mr. John Parke, vestrymen.
Mr. David Craford, Mr. Thos. Smith, Church wardens.
Mr. Nicholas Meriwether was this day chosen vestryman in the place & stead of Mr. John Roper, late dec't and the oathes injoyed by act of Parlament duly administered onto him by Mr. James Moss and did likewise sincerely promise and sware as a vestryman of this parish that he would be Conformable in all

things Relating to the Church of England as it is now Established.

Upon the petition of Thos. Wilkins it is ordered that the Church wardens provide such things as are necessary for him.

Upon the motion of Mr. David Craford, Church warden, Jeffrey Davis is ordered the same.

It is ordered by this present vestry that Capt. John Lyddall Carry Anthony Burrows in his Sloop to the Springs in Maryland and provide such necessarys for him as he shall think fitt; and to be paid for his Charge and trouble at the laying the next Levy.

Mr. David Craford and Mr. Thom. Smith are Chosen and Elected Church wardens of this Parish for this Insuing year.

WM. CLOPTON, Clk. of Vestry.

St. Peter's Parish. At a Vestry held at the uper Church the 20th Sept., 1699.

PRESENT:

Mr. James Bowker, minister.

Capt. Joseph Forster, Mr. Nicho. Meriwether, Capt. John Lyddall, Mr. Will Bassett, Mr. John Lewis, Mr. Hene. Wyatt, Vestrymen.

Mr. David Craford, Mr. Thomas Smith, Church wardens.

Whereas Mr. Charles Turner, late Clark of this vestry, hath omtted the Registring Severall orders of vestry and Baptizmes therefore ordered that Will. Clopton the present Clark, Comit all such orders of vestry and Baptizmes as he thinks verily to be of the hand writing of the late Clark or signed by the Gentle'n of the vestry in the Register book of this parish.

Capt. Lancelott Bathurst, Late high Sheriff of this County, having undertaken the last year's Collection of the parish Dues, and having fully satisfied the same is Discharged.

This vestry doe agree with Mr. James Bowker, minister for this next ensuing year, and to be paid Sixteen thousand pounds of tobacco and Cask Convenient as formerly.

Whereas Thomas Ponton, at a vestry held at the uper Church of this parish the 3rd October, 1698, did agree with the said parish to Double Cover the said uper Church as pr his Bond of the above date may more Large appear and the s'd Ponton failing to Come to work accordingly and the timber Lyeing upon Soyle this vestry Doth therefore agree with John King Carpenter, of this parish, to performe Thomas Ponton's bargin evere Respect and the said King doth promise to begin upon the said work upon the second day of October next. * * *

St. Peter's Parish, Dr., 1699.

| | |
|---|---|
| To Mr. James Bowker minisster for one year......... | 16000 |
| To Idem for Cask & Conve. of Ditto ................. | 2240 |
| To Wm. Clopton, Clark of the parish for one year...... | 2280 |
| To Idem for a Register Book ....................... | 0114 |
| To Mabell Wood, widdow ......................... | 0540 |
| To Jno. Hilton, Sexton of ye Lower Church, 300 Ca' 24. | 0324 |
| To Id. for Cask of 300 omited Last year............. | 0024 |
| To Jno. Webb, Sexton of ye Uper Church 300 Ca'—24.. | 0324 |
| To Idem for Cask of 300 omited last year ............. | 0024 |
| To Capt. Lanc'lt Bathurst for Deposito. Last year ...... | 0238 |
| To Idem for Sheriff's fees ......................... | 0040 |
| To Mr. Job Howes for Cla'k fees .................. | 0219 |
| To Thomas mims for maintaining ye wid. faulkner 1 yr. | 1080 |
| To Jno. Hillon for grubing round ye Church, &c......... | 0050 |
| To Tho. mims for 1 pr Shoes for wid. faulkner 30 lb., &c. | 0034 |
| To Jno. King for work done ab't ye Lower Church.... | 0100 |
| To Tho. Smith, Chu'h warden, p acct................ | 0168 |
| To Mr. David Craford, Chu'h warden, p acct. 445 lb. 62.. | 0507 |
| To Capt. Jno. Lyddall p acct....................... | 1275 |
| To John Webb for washing ye Surplis ............... | 0050 |
| To Wm. Sanders by Mr. Smithes, note as Church warden for maintaining Tho's Wilkinson, 500 l a 40 ......... | 0540 |
| To Capt. Lanc't Bathurst, Late she. for Delinq't tithables | 0176 |
| To Thos. moss for keeping Lettice Bayle the time of her Lying in ...................................... | 0300 |
| To Alex'r mackeney for keeping Anne Peggs the time of her Lying in ...................................... | 0300 |
| To Mr. David Craford, Chu'h warden p ball. of his acct. | 1512 |
| To Wm. Clopton, Clk for Registering Severall orders and Baptizmes omited by the Late Clk................. | 0500 |
| To James Blackwell for 20 Cutte timb'l at 30 p cut 600 Ca, 48 ......................................... | 0648 |

| | |
|---|---|
| To Mr. David Craford and Mr. Thos. Smith, Church wardens for ye maintainance of Ant. Burrows.......... | 1728 |
| To Sall'e of 31344 at 5 p Cent. ...................... | 1567 |
| To Lye in the Collector's hands to reimburse the parish next year ..................................... | 0213 |
| | 33124 |

P. Coute                              Cr. Lb. Tobacco
P. 676 tithables at 49 lb. tobacco p polo.............. 33124

Capt. John Ldyall is ordered to Collect for each tithable inhabitant in this parish forty nine pounds of Tobacco to Defray the parish Charge and mak payment to the severall p'sons for whom it is Levyed and in Case of non payment to make Destress according to Law and that the Clark give a Copy of this Charge to the s'd Capt. Lyddall and take his receipt for the same.

Ordered that William Sanders take care and provide sufficient meate, Drink, washing and Lodging for Thomas Wilkins and to be alowed one thousand pounds of Tobacco and Cask for the year.

This vestry doe give Anthony Burrows the mare which he formerly acknowledged to the parish.

Whereas by order of vestry the Church wardens of this parish were ordered to presente James Austin conserning Brustor's Estate and the vestry now considering the Same the Church wardens are ordered to desist from any further prosecution.

Whereas Lettice Bayle was delivered of a bastard Child at the house of Thomas moss sum time the last winter, and being summoned to Court upon her oath doth lay the same to Thomas Harris. Therefore ordered that the Church wardens prosicute the said Harris according to Law.

Registered p WM. CLOPTON, Clark. Registe.

St. Peter's Parish, at a Vestry held at the Lower Church the 29 march, 1700.

Mr. James Bowker, minister.

PRESENT:

Gideon Macon, Hene. Wyatt, James Moss, Wm. Bassett, John Lewis, John Park, Gent Vestrymen.

David Craford, Tho. Smith, Gent Church wardens.
It is ordered that Mr. Hen. Wyatt & Mr. William Bassett do offiate as Church wardens for this insuing year in the place & stead of Mr. David Craford and Mr. Thomas Smith.

Reg'd. WM. CLOPTON, Clk. Reg't.

For St. Peter's parish, Nek Kent County. At a vestry held at the house of Mr. James Moss 13th August, 1700.

PRESENT:

Mr. James Bowker, minister.
Capt. Joseph Forster, Mr. Thomas Smith, Mr. Gideon Macon, Capt. John Lyddall, Mr. John Lewis, Mr. David Craford, Mr. James Moss, Capt. Nicho. Merewether, Mr. John Park, Vestrymen.
Mr. Hene. Wyatt, Mr. Wm. Bassett, Church wardens.

Whereas the Lower Church of this parish is very much out of Repair and Standeth very inconvenient for most of the inhabitants of the said parish. Therefore ordered that as soon as conveniently may be a new Church of Brick Sixty feet long and twenty fower feet wide in the Cleer and fourteen feet pitch with a Gallery Sixteen feet Long be built and Erected upon the maine Roade by the School House near Thomas Jackson's; and the Clark is ordered to give a Copy of of This order to Capt. Nicho Merewether who is Requested to show the same to Will Hughes and desire him to draw a Draft of the said Church and to bee at the next vestry and Mr. Gideon Macon and Mr. Thomas Smith are Requested to treat with and buy an acre of Land of Thomas Jackson whereon to build the said Church and for a Church yard.

New Kent County. At a vestry held for St. Peter's parish at the house of Mr. James Moss the 26 September, 1700.

PRESENT:

Mr. James Bowker, minister.
Capt. Joseph Forster, Capt. Jno. Lyddall, Mr. Thomas Smith. Mr. Jno. Lewis, Capt. Nicho. Merewether, Mr. James Moss, Mr. Gideon Macon, Mr. Jno. Parke, Vestrymen.
Mr. Wm. Bassett, Mr. Hene. Wyatt, Church wardens.
The upper Inhabitants of this parish by their Pettiteon Set-

ting forth that they Live very Remote from the Church, therefore pray that they may have a place apointed and preaching amongst them which is Refered to the Consideration of the next vestry.

Whereas there is Layed before this present vestry an order of Court held for New Kent County dated the 28th day of August last past wherein is Resighted an order of his Excellence and Councill dated at James City the 10 day of July, 1700, wherein the first part thereof signified that severall frauds and Abuces have been commited heretofore in Concealing County and parish tithes and Converting severall Gifts and Donations made to School and other Pious uses to other uses then were by the Donors Intended, and whereas the Said order Doeth direct that this vestry doe Returne to the next Court held for this County aforesaid an exact List of all and Every Indeveduall Tythable in this parish this present yeare 1700 and a true and p'fect acct. Debtor and Creditor of the Parish Levy the last yeare 1699 and allso the Exact bounds and Limetts of this Parish, together with an acct. of what Gleabes or Gleabe Lands thereunto belonging of what value and Estimation what gifts and Donations for the Advancement of scools and other pious uses when and by whom Given, &c. In answer to all which this present vestry doeth Returne as followeth, first an exact List of all and Every Indevidual! Tythables in this parish which doeth amount to 738 tythables and allso an acct. Debtor and Creditor of this parish Levy the last year 1699 and alsoe that the Bounds of this Parish doeth begin at a Certain place on Pamaunkey River commonly known by the name of Capt. Bassett's ould Landing from thence Runing up the Said River to the Extent of this County and soe over to Chickcohominy Swamp which Devides this from Henerico County and Soe Down the Said Swamp to the upper Eand of James City County and from thence by a line of marked trees to the place it first began and for the Gleabe Lands there is where the two Severall Churches Belonging to this Parish doeth Stand about 100 acres of Land at Each place of Little value and Estimation there being noe Improvement on either, and the Lower Church Speedely to be removed and as to Gifts and Donations for the advancement of schools and other pious uses there is not any in this Parish and the Clark is ordered to make Returne hereof to the next County Court.

Whereas Robert Magrime, who for some years past hath lived with the Hon'ble Jno. Lightfoot, Esq., and hath not been Listed this two years past and Mr. Gideon Macon offering to this vestry to take the said Magrime and keep him as long as he Can work and pay his Levys and keep him from being a Parish Charge During his natural life, therefore ordered that the Sheriff sumon the said Magrime to appear at the next Court to answer what the Court shall therein order.

This present vestry having taken into their Consideration the order of his Excellence and Councill baring date at James City the 10th July, 1700, together with an order of this County Court baring date the 28th August, 1700, this day Layd before them Conserning the Returning an acct. of the number of Tythables in this parish, together with the bounds and Limits of the Same in order to be Layd before the next Generall Assembly and the same being just at hand, and whereas this present vestry having Designed to build a Brick Church out of hand they have therefore thought good to Refer the laying of the Parish Levy for this present year and all other proceedings about the building the aforesaid Church till after the Eanding the Sessions of the next Gen'l Assembly, and all Persons that are Desirous to undertake any part of the said work Relating to the Building of the said Church shall have notice given of the time and place where the next vestry shall be held when they will then and there be Recorded.

Cop'a Test: WM. CLOPTON, Clk. Vestry.

New Kent County Sct. At a vestry held for St. Peter's Parish at the uper Church the 25 November, 1700.

PRESENT:

Mr. James Bowker, minister.
Capt. Joseph Forster, Mr. Thos. Smith, Capt. Nicho. Meriwether, Mr. John Lewis, Mr. David Craford, vestrymen.
Mr. Hene. Wyatt, Mr. Wm. Bassett, Church wardens.

St. Peter's Parish. Lbs. Tobacco.

To Mr. James Bowker, minister for one year ........ 16000
To Cask and Convenience for Ditto ................. 02240
To Wm. Clopton, Cla'k of the parish for one year ...... 02289
To John Hilton, Sexton of the Lower Chu'r, 300 Cas 24. 00324

56   VESTRY BOOK OF ST. PETER'S PARISH.

To John Webb, Sexton of the uper Church, 300 Cas 24.. 00324
To Capt. Nicho. Merewether, acct. of Sheriff's fees .... 00040
To Mr. Geo'e Clough his acct. of Clark's fees......... 00138
To Mr. David Craford, late Chu'r warden, the ball. of
 his acct. ....................................... 01240
To Mr. Thomas Smith, late Chu'r warden, his 397 lb.,
 44 .... ....................................... 0045
To Mr. Gideon Macon for 1 pr Large hooks and hinges.. 00060
To James Teate for worke done for Antho. Burross... * * *
To Mabell Wood, widdow, 500 Cask, 40.............. 00540
To Thomas Mins for maintaining ye wid. Faulkner and ye
 1000 Ca. ...................................... 01080
To Jno. Webb for washing ye Surplis & 2 days' work at ye
 Chu'h, 70 Ca. ................................;..... 0075
To John Hilton's acct. ............................. 0190
To Capt. John Lyddall the ball. of his acct............ 0083
To Mr. Hene Wyatt, Chu Warden, his acct........... 0686
To Wm. Sanders for keeping Thos. Wilkinson one yea:
 1000 Ca., 80 .................................... 1080
To Clopton, his acct. for Recording proclamations and
 Drawing over the Lists of tithables ................ 0220
To James Sanders, his acct. ......................... 0460
To Sallery of 27571 at 5 lbs. tobacco p Cent........... 1378
To lie in the Collectors hands to reimburst the parish next
 year ......... .................................. 0379
                                                    ─────
P. Conte, Wm. Timson ..,......................... 29328

                            Cr.
P. 752 tithables at 39 lb. tobacco p polo............... 29328
                                                    ─────

It is ordered that the parish Levy for this present year be thirty nine pounds of Tobacco p polo to be paid for Every tithable inhabitant in this parish to Defray the parish Charge, and that Capt. Nicholas merewether Receive and Collect the same and make payment to the severall persons for whom it is Levyed and in Case of non payment to make Destress acording to Law and that the Clark * him a Copy of this Charge and take his Receipt for the same.

This present vestry doe hereby agree with Mr. James Bowker,

minister for this ensuing year and to be paid sixteen thousand pounds of Tobacco and Cask Convenient as formerly.

Copa Test, WM. CLOPTON, Clk. vestry.

Ordered that William Clopton be Continued Clerk of that parish and vestry for this insuing year, and to be paid as formerly. William Clopton being apointed Surveior of the highwayes in the place and stead of Stephen Crump and aploying himself to this defráy for help to doe the work is ordered those tithables following, viz.: Capt. Thomas Bray, Stephen Michell, Stephen Nicholl, Jun., Will Forgison, William Crump, William Bourne, Stephen Crump, Richard Crump, the widdow Crump's tithables, Pelham more and John Crumps Jun: all which did formerly belong to Stephen Crump's presincts.

Registered p WM. CLOPTON, Clk. Vest.

New Kent County. At a vestry held for St. Peter's parish at the house of Mr. John Lewis, 14 Febe., 1700-1.

PRESENT:

Mr. James Bowker, minister; Capt. Joseph Forster, Mr. James moss, Capt. John Lyddall, Mr. Gideon Macon, Mr. Thomas Smith, Mr. David Craford, Mr. John Lewis, Mr. John Park, Capt. Nicho. merewether, vestrymen.

Mr. Hene Wyatt, Mr. Wm. Bassett, Chu'h wardens.

Where as at a vestry held for this parish the 13 Janue last the Clark was ordered to sum Mr. John Park Jne to be one of the vestry for this parish in the place and stead of Capt. Thomas Bray, Late dec't, who haveing appeared according sumon and taken the oathe enjoyned by act of Parlament to be taken in stead of the oathes of alegence and Supremacy together with the oath of a vestryman: and subsented the test and associacion it admited into the vestry.

Mr. John Park, Jne aded.

Thomas Jackson having appeared at this present vestry hath agreed toe and with the said vestry to make one hundred thousand good and well burnt brick fit for building each and Every brick to be moulded in a Shod mould of 9 inches ¾ in length and 4¾ in width and 4 inches ½ thick in the Cleer all the afore said bricks to be layd down or delivered upon the Ground where the Church is to be built and in consideration of the said work this vestry doe promise and agree to pay the said Jackson ten thousand pounds of Legall sweet-sented tobacco and Cask Conv't in this parish this present year, 1701, and teen thousand pounds of Like qualified tobacco as afores'd and Cask Convt. in this parish in the year 1702.

Vincent Vaughn hath this day agreed too and with this present vestry to doe all the sawyers work belonging to the Church Compleated and workman Like be the same Either Plank or Skantling for one pound of Tobacco and Cask, to be paid Conv't in this parish p feet, and to Lay all the said plank and timber down upon the Ground where the said Church is to be built as fast as the Carpenter shall require the same.

Recorded p WM. CLOPTON, Cl.

David Craford, Nicholas Merewether and Wm. Bassett absent whereas at a vestry held for this parish at the House of Mr. James Moss the 13th Aug't, 1700, it was ordered and agreed that as soon as Conveniently could be made a new Church of Brick 60 feet Long 24 feet wide and 14 feet pitch in the Cleer with a Gallerey 16 feet long Should be built and Erected upon the main Roade by the School house neer Thomas Jackson's and for the performance and forwarding the said work according to the aforesaid order this vestry do Request and apoint Jo'n Lewis and Gideon Macon, Gent'n Supervisers and Directors of the said work to agree with and toe any workmen that shall offer themselves to undertake any part of the S'd work that hath not been allwady agreed with and for what ever the Superavisers doe agree for in Tobacco and Cask Conv't this vestry doe promise to performe and abide by and make punctuall payment of the Same and that the Collector make noe payment to any workman but upon a note sign'd by the S'd Superviasers and the Superviasers are Requested to take bond with Good Securities of all workmen that have or shall undertake any part of the S'd work for due performance of the same, and that all bonds be taken paiable to the Superavisers and Directors for the use of the parish and that the Superavisers give bond in behalfe of the parish to all workmen for due payment of their tobacco according to agreement.

William Hughes, Carpenter, hath this day agreed toe and with this vestry to doe and performe all the Carpenters, Joyners and hewers work of a Church to be built neer the house of Thomas Jackson and acording to the Severall Drafts this day Subscribed by the said Hughes and to performe all the said work Compleated and workman Like of Length, breadth and pitch acording to an order of vestry dated the 13th Aug't, 1700, and in Consideration of the s'd work this vestry are to pay the S'd Hughes twenty-five thousand pounds of sweet sented tobacco and Cash Convenient in this parish that is to say one halfe at the * all after the Raising and Covering the said Church and the other halfe at the Compleate finishing the said work and when the whole work is finished if it be done to the Liking of the major part of the said vestry then this vestry doe promise to pay him, the Said Hughes, one thousand pounds of Sweet sented Tobacco and Cask Conv't over and above the aforesaid mencioned * * * and further the said Hughes doeth promise to Enter into bond with Good Securities when Required.

Recorded p W<small>M</small>. C<small>LOPTON</small>, Clk. Vestr.

N<small>EW</small> K<small>ENT</small> C<small>OUNTY</small>.

At a vestry held for St. Peter's parrish at the House of Capt. nicho merewether the 4 June, 1701.

P<small>RESENT</small>:

Mr. James Bowker, minister.

Joseph Forster, Nico. Merewether, John Park, Thos. Smith, Gideon Macon, John Park, Jr., John Lewis, David Craford, Gent., Vestrymen.

Hene. Wyatt, Wm. Bassett, Gent., Church wardens.

It is ordered that Mr. Hen'e Wyatt and Mr. Wm. Bassett are Continued Church wardens for this ensuing year.

It is ordered by this present vestry that the Church wardens from time to time provide all such nailes and other necessarys as are necessary and Conven't for Carrying on the building of a brick Church in this parish and that they hire some man to see the oyster Shoals measured and give a Receipt to the Sloopman for the same.

Upon the mocion of Mr. James Bowker, minister of this parish, whose sermons for thanksgiveing or upon Holydays should be preached it is the opinion of this vestry that the Sermons are successively preached one at the one and the other Church having noe Regard to Sabbath days.

Recorded p   WM. CLOPTON, Clk vest.

At a vestry held for St. Peter's Parish at the house of Mr. John Park the 22 October, 1701.

PRESENT:

Mr. James Bowker, minister.

Joseph Forster, John Park, Thomas Smith, John Park, jun'r, Gentlemen vest.

Wm. Bassett, Hen.e Wyatt, Gent'n, Church wardens.

| ST. PETER'S PARISH. | Dr. Lbs. Tobacco. |
|---|---|
| To Mr. James Bowker, mini'r, for one year, 16,000 Lbs. C. C., 2240 | 18240 |
| To William Clopton, Cla'k, for one year | 2289 |
| To John Hilton, Sexton of the Lower Chu'h, 300 Ca., 24.. | 324 |
| To John Webb, Sexton of the uper Chu'h, 300 Ca., 24.... | 324 |
| To Wm. Bassett, Chu. ward., for Comu. wine, 180 C. C., 25 | 205 |
| To Mr. Tho. Poindexter, p acc't, 80 Ca., 6 | 120 |
| To Mr. Henr. Wyatt, Chu. warden, p his acc't | 1341 |
| To Thomas Wingfield, to keep a bastard child 8 months.. | 700 |
| To Idem p acc't | 106 |
| To Cha'r Bryan, for keeping Eliz. Brown 9 weeks, 190 Ca., 15 | 205 |
| To John Hilton, p acc't, 110 Ca., 9 | 119 |
| To Nicho Gentry for Clothes for Mabell Wood, 899 Ca., 72 and Sunderall Charges for Idem | 971 |
| To Tho. Mims for keep ye widd. Faulkner 1 year, 1000 Ca., 80 | 1080 |
| To Wm. Sanders for keep Tho. Wilkinson 1 year, 1000 Ca 80 | 1080 |
| To Idem p acc't | 060 |
| To James Blackwell the ball of his acc't | 272 |
| To Mr. Geo. Clough, Cla'r, his acc't of fees | 060 |

To Tho. Jackson, for one acre of land to build a Chu'h

upon acording to agreement, but to Lye in the Superaiviser's hands till it be acknowledged, 200 C C 28.... 228
To Tho. Jackson his 1st payment for bricks for ye Chu'h 10000 C. C., 1400 .............................. 11400
To the Superaivisers for vincent vaughn, Sawyer for plank and timber for the S'd Chu'h, 12000 C. C., 1680. 13680
To Idem for 120 hhds. Oyster Shoals at 45 Tobo. per hhd 5400 C C 756 ............................... 6156
To Idem for Carting 120 hhds. Shoals at 25 p hhd., 3000 C. C., 420 ....................................... 3420
To Idem to Lye in Ch'r wardens' hands to be desposed of for nailes for ye S'd Chu'r, 2000 C. C5., 280........ 2280
To William Clopton for Record, procla................ 110
To Saller of 63856 lbs. of Tobacco at 5 p cent.......... 3192

The Parish Levy being proportioned amountts to Eighty-fouer pounds of tobacco p polo, which same of Eighty-fouer pounds of Tobacco William Clopton is hereby ordered and impowered to Collect and Receive from Each and Every tythable person in this parish, and in Case of non-payment to Levy the same by Destress, and that the same Clopton give bond to the Church wardens for the said Collection.

It is ordered by this present vestry that the Church wardens provide Three sufficient Laborers to atend the bricklayer or bricklayers in building a brick Church upon a acre of Land bought of Thomas Jackson upon Stone Swamp neer the said Jackson's house, and that they be ready some time in the month of March, and that they take Care the said Laborers have Sufficient Dyet, washing and Lodging for 6 months, and soe proportionable for a Longer or a Shorter time bein' for the Said wages and Dyet.

Whereas, this vestry taking into their serious Consideration the remotenes of the upper inhabitants of this parish from the upper Church, and not to hinder the propagation of Christianity, have Requested and accordingly ordered Mr. James Bowker, minister of the said parish, to preach a Sermon one Sabbath day in Every month at Such Convenient place as the aforesaid inhabitants shall pleas to apoint and the said Mr. Bowker is Likewise desired to give notice in the Churches what Sundays he will be absent upon the said ocation, and William Clopton, the Cla'k, is Likewise ordered to give his attendance with the minister.

It is ordered that Thomas Sneade's bill of 500 lbs. of tobacco and Cask Lye in the hands of Mr. William Bassett, Church warden, and by him to be desposed of for nails for and towards the building the Church and to returne an acc't to the next vestry.

Mr. Hen'r wyatt hath this day agreed toe and with this present vestry to get 20000 Good Sound Sipres Shingles for Covering for the brick Church Each and every Shingle to be 18 inches in Length, and none to be more than 5 inches in breadth, or none over than 3 inches, and not to be Less than ½ an inch or more than ¾ of an inch thick, and all to be well rounded and bundled up fit to be Layed into a Cart by the 10th Septemb'r next, and Delivered on this Side Chickahomana Swamp, where a Cart may Conveniently Come to take them up in the neck below and adjacent to the Land where Richard Scrugs now Lives with in the County of New Kent, and that he be payed for the same two thousand pounds of tobacco and Cask Conven't.

Convenient at the Laying the next Levy. Likewise the said Mr. Henry Wyatt doth further agree with this vestry to send for England in this present Shipping for Ironwork, Glass for Sash windows, and paint for the aforesaid Church acording as the Carpenter shall Give Directions, and to be alowed 45 lbs p Cent. from the Superaviser's notes * in tobacco and Cask. Convenient at the middle markuit price, and that Mr. Wyatt take his Directions for Sending for the aforesaid Goods from Mr. William Hughes, the Carpenter, who is to build the said Church.

Thomas Jackson hath this day agreed with this vestry to Cart all Shingles for Covering the Brick Church to be built in this parish from Chickahomany Swamp to the place where the said Church is to be built at 25 Lbs. of Tobacco and Cask, Convenient p thousand, and to begin the said Carting by the 10th day of September next, and Soe to be Continued the same till they are all brout in place.

Whereas, Elizabeth Brown is in a very Deplorable Condition, and noe way able to help herself it is therefore ordered that Mr. Charles Bryan take the Said Eliz. and provide nessecarys for her, and to be alowed at the rate of 1200 Lbs. Tobacco p annum Soe long as She shall remaine in that Condition.

Ordered that John More forthwith Cleer and make good the Roads and Sutable briges from Coll. Lyddall's ould field to the mill upon black Creeke and thence to the Lower mill on the Same Creeke, and Soe back by Geo. Yorke into the main Roade by Coll. Lyddall's.

This present vestry do hereby agree with Mr. James Bowker, minister, for this ensuing year, and to be payed sixteen thousand pounds of Tobacco and Cask Convenient as formerly.

Ordered that Will. Clopton be continued Cla'k of this parish and vestry for this insuing year, and to be paid as formerly.

Rege'r p             WM. CLOPTON, Clk of Vest.

At a Vestry held for St. Peter's parish at the House of Capt. Joseph Forster.

PRESENT:

Capt. Joseph Forster, Mr. Thomas Smith, Maj'r Nicho meriwether, Mr. James Moss, Mr. David Craford, Capt. John Lyddall, Mr. John Parks, Mr. John Parks, Ju'r, Vestrymen.

Mr. Wm. Bassett, Mr. Henry Wyatt, Chu'r wardens.

In Compliance with an order of Court dated the 28 Januery last, it is ordered that the Clerke forthwith send out orders to the Severall Inhabitants of this parish to prosession their Lands.

Whereas, Mr. John Alford and Mr. Will. major made Complaint to this vestry that they have never had their Lands prossessioned acording to Law, the orders being Lodged in the hands of Coll. John Lightfott, who never put the Same in Execution; Therefore, ordered that John wilson, John Lightfoot, Esq'r, Mr. Will. major, Mr. John Alford, Dan'll Parks, Esq., and William Millington forthwith goe on prosessioning and reamark Each others' bounds, and make returns of this order to the next vestry.

In Compliance with an order of the vestry of Blissland parish for prosessioning the bounds between this parish and the parish of Blissland, Capt. Joseph Forster, Mr. Thomas Smith, Mr. Hen'r Wyatt and Mr. John Park, Ju'r, or any two of them are requested to meet the Gen't of Blissland parish at the House of Mrs Butts on the 16th of this instant, and prosession and reamark the bounds between the two parishes, and the Clerke is ordered to give a Copy of an order of vestry dated the 4 May, 1689, relating to the bounds between the S'd parishes to the Gen't apoynted.

Whereas, at a meeting of Certaine Gen't of the vestry of this parish at the House of Mr. Gideon Macon the 8th December, 1701, the power of Superavisers invested in the Church wardens for the time being it is, therefore, ordered that the power of Superavisers be still continued in the Said Church wardens.

Whereas, Mr. Gideon Macon, one of the vestry of this parish, is lately de cest, and Mr. John Lewis lately Departed this County, it is ordered that Mr. Henry Childs be a vestryman in the place and stead of Mr. Gideon Macon, and Mr. Richard Littlepage be a vestryman in the place & stead of Mr. John Lewis, and the Clerke is ordered to Request them to meet at the next vestry.

Ordered that the Church wardens forthwith Send to Thomas Becket and Zackery Ellis or any other Bricklayers to Come and view the Bricks made by Thomas Jackson for the building a brick Church in this parish whither they are good and well burnt, fitt for building and that the viewers make Report thereof, and that the Church wardens pay them for their Trouble.

Rege'r p                 W. CLOPTON, Clk vest'r.

---

At a vestry held for St. Peter's parish at the House of Mr. Hene. Wyatt, the 6 Aprill, 1702.

PRESENT:

Mr. James Bowker, minister.

Capt. Joseph Forster, Capt. John Lyddall, Maj. Nicho Meriwether, Mr. John Park, Mr. John Park, Ju'r.

Mr. Hen'r Wyatt, Mr. Wm. Bassett, Church wardens.

Whereas, at a vestry held for this parish the 4 March last, the Clerke was ordered to Request Mr. Hen'r Childs and Mr. Rich'd Littlepage to be Vestrymen in the places of Mr. Gideon Macon, accordingly, and Mr. John Lewis and Mr. Hen'r Childs haveing this day appeared and taken the oathes injoyned by act of Parlament to be taken in Stead of the oathes of allegiance and Supremesy together with the oath of a vestryman and Subscribed the test and assosiacion is admited into this vestry.

Mr. Henry Childs aded.

It is ordered that Mr. James Moss and Maj. Nicholas Meriwether doe offiate as Church wardens for this Insuing year in the place and Stead of Mr. Wm. Bassett and Mr. Hene. Wyatt.

Whereas, there is a great Church of Brick a building in this parish, and the Churchwardens Liveing somewhat remote from the said building, therefore, Capt. John Forster and Capt. John Lyddall with the Churchwardens as Superavisers from time to time to give their direction and assistance for Carrying on the Said work.

Stephen Moon aploying himself to this vestry of help to Cleer the Roades in his precincts is ordered beside what he had formerly all the tithables at the quarters of Mr. John Page and Mr. Geo. Poindexter.

Whereas, Mr. Hene. Wyatt and Mr. Wm. Bassett, Late Church wardens, have bought of and Supose to have paid Excep about 6 mos., Maj'r Nicolas meriwether one of the present Church wardens, 30m. 6 25m 10'h 15m 20'h and 10m 4'd nails, the Said maj'r meriwether doeth promise to send (by the first oppertunity) the Said nailes to Robert Pasley's Landing, and Thomas Jackson is ordered to bring them up to his House and deliver them to the workmen from time to time as they shall have need of them for and towards the Carrying on the Said building.

Reger'd p　　　　　　　　　Wm. Clopton, Clk vest'r.

New Kent County, Sct. At a vestry held for St. Peter's parish at the house of Mr. John Park, Ju'r, the 23rd Sept, 1702.

Present:

Mr. James Bowker, minister.

Joseph Forster, John Lyddall, Nicho. Meriwether, James Moss, Hene. Childs, David Craford, Wm. Bassett, Hene. Wyatt, John Park, John Park, Jun'r, Gen. Vestrymen.

St. Peter's Parish.　　　　　　　Dr. Lbs. Tobacco.
To Mr. James Bowker, minister, for 1 ye'r, 16000 C. C. 2240 ............................................. 18240
To Wm. Clopton, Cle'k, for 1 year ................. 2289
To John Hilton, Sexton of ye Lower Church, 300 Cs., 24　324
To John Webb, Sexton of ye uper Church, 300 Ca., 24..　324
To Wm. Clopton, misscast Last year, 128 C. C., 101......　829
To John Webb for wash ye Surplis ..................　50
To John Hilton for the Same ......................　50
To Jno. Gonton for Anth, Burrows p Mr. Bassett's obligation, 900 C. C., 126 ............................ 1026

To Cha's Bryan for maint. Eliz. Browning 4 mo., 335 C.
C., 46 .......................................... 381
To Mr. David Craford for 1 pr Stockins for Id., 25 C. C.. 328
To Maj'r Nicho. Meriwether p acc't, 676 C. C., 94 ...... 770
To James Sanders for keep'g Thos. Wilkins 1 yr, 1000
Ca., 80 ......................................... 1080
To Idem for Cask of 700 Lbs. Toba., omitted Last year.. 56
To Idem p acc't, 125 C. C., 17 ...................... 142
To James Sanders p acc't .......................... 15
To Mrs. Alice Butts p acc't ........................ 60
To Nicho. Amoss for keep 1 of Bur'll Chapell's Child'r.. 100
To Rob't Pasly p acc't, 235 Ca., 18 .................. 253
To Tho. Mims for keep wid. faulkner 1 y'r, 1000 l., 80... 1080
To Mr. James Moss p acc't ......................... 36
To Mr. Tho. Poindexter, an error in a Levy and 1700 .. 39
To Mr. Hen'r Wyatt p acc't, 1165 C. C., for 978, 136.... 1301
To the Supervisers for vin. vaughn, 6000 C. C., 840.... 6840
To * * * * * * * * * *
To the Superviser for Mr. Wyatt for paint, Glass, Lead,
&c., for ye Brick Church ........................ 4500
To Idem towards building a Church upon Mechams'
Creeke, 7000 C C, 98 ........................... 7980
To Robert Pasley for Conv. for his acc't .............. 16

                      98193
To Sallery of 98193 Lbs. Tobacco at 5 lbs tobacco p * * 4909
                      103102

  C'R.

p 895 tithables at 115 Lbs. tobacco p polo ............ 102925
p Ball to reaimburse ye Collec'r nex year .............. 177
                      103102

The parish Levy being proportioned amounts toe one hundred and fifteen pounds of Tobacco p polo which same of one hundred and fifteen pounds of Tobacco Maj'r Nicholas Meriwether is hereby impowered to Receive and Collect of and from Each and Every tithable p'son within this parish, and in Case of non payment to make destress for the Same and to make payment accordingly as the same is proportioned, and enter into bond with Security for the said Collection.

It is ordered by this vestry that the Churchwardens forthwith bind out Sam'll Chapell, Burnell Chapell and William Mallitt, three poore Children of this parish.

Upon the petition of the upper inhabitants of this parish presented by John Kimburrow, James nuckols and Richard Corley Laying down that they are very remote from the Church, it is ordered that a new Church or Chapell be built upon the upper Side of mechamps Creeke adjoining to the Kings Roade forty feet Long and twenty weet wyde, framed and planked in Every respect like to the upper Church: Mr. John Kimburrow assuming to this vestry that he will Give two acres of Land Convenient to the Saide roade and a Spring and Likewise all maner of Timbers for building the Said Chuchr, and maj'r Nicholas Meriwether and Mr. Henrey Childs are requested and impowered to agree with any workman or workmen that shall offer themselves to undertake all or any part of the said worke.

Upon the petition of Elizabeth Johnson, a poore woman, in this parish, it is ordered that Mr. John * * * keep the said Elizabeth Johnson and toe find her sufficient Clothing, meete, drink, washing and Lodging, and all other nessicaries whatever, and to be paid for the Same Six hundred pounds of Tobacco and Cask p annum, and soe proportion * for a longer or shorter time.

Upon the petition of James Turner Setting forth that he has been visited with Lameness and sickness severall years in Somuch that he hath spent all his substance upon Phesitians and nessicaries, therefore, ordered that Samuell Waddy keep the same James Turner during Life and to find him sufficient Clothing, meate, drink, washing and Lodging, and all nessicaries, and to be paid twelve hundred pounds of Tobacco and Cask p annum, and soe proportionable for a longer or a shorter time the said Wadde assuring to this vestry to keep the said Turner for the Sume of 1200 lbs. of Tobacco, and bring noe Claime against the parish for the same.

This vestry do hereby agree toe and with Mr. James Bowker, minister, for the ensuing year and to be paid Sixteen thousand pounds of Tobacco and Cask Convenient as usuall.

Ordered that Wm. Clopton bee Continued Clerke for the ensuing year, and to be paid as usual.

Recorded p  WM. CLOPTON, Clk of Vest.

At a vestry held for St. Peter's Parish at the house of Mr. James Moss the 27th day of febe', 1702-3.

PRESENT:

Mr. James Bowker, minister.

Capt. Jas. Forster, Mr. Hen'r Childs, Mr. David Craford, Mr. Will Bassett, Mr. Jno. Park, Jun'r, Vestrymen.

Mr. James Moss, Mr. Nicho. meriwether, Chu'h wardens.

Whereas, his Excellence by his Proclamation dated the 16 January, 1702, Requiring the County Courts within this Colony to Give Strict Charge to the vestrys of their Respective Parishes to send by the Burgesses for next assembly a True account of their Respective parish Levys together with an account of any Gleabe belonging to the Said parishes, and of what value what Lands, Houses, Donations or Legases have ben given for the promoting of Scholes or for other pious uses when and by whom given and how Employed to the Eand the said accounts may be Layd before the Gen'ell Assembly which order being now Layd before this vestry to Consider doe Returne as followeth, viz.: a true Copy of the parish Levy for the last year, 1702, and that there is two parcells of Gleabe Lands Each Containing about 100 acres and noe improvement upon Either, and for Lands, Houses, Donations or Legases there is none Given.

James Knott, plasterer, doeth and hath this day agreed with this vestry to drive and naile on the Lathes and doe all the Lathing plastering and painting work that is to be done in, on or about a Brick Church now built in this parish, and to doe and performe all the said worke Compleated and workmanlike and to Enter upon the work with in a forth night and not to doe any other worke till it be Compleated and finished, and in Consideration of the Said worke this vestry doe promise to pay the Said James Knott foure thousand five hundred pounds of Tobacco and Cask Convenient at the Laying of the nevt Levy, and the Said Knott to find him help to send him and Enter into bond to the Churchwardens for the performance of the same.

Mr. Richard Littlepage haveing met at this vestry acording

to Sumons and taken the oathes of alegence and Supremecy together with the oath of a vestryman and Subscribed to the test is admited to the vestry.

Mr. Richard Littlepage, Mr. Hen'r Wyatt, present.

Richard Hood upon his petition to this vestry is declared free from paying any parish Levy.

William Moore, a sick and Lame man, belonging to this parish, brought to this vestry by Wm. Martin, is promised to be alowed for his meate, drink, washing and Lodging Six hundred pounds of Tobacco p annum and so proportionable for a longer or a shorter time.

George Alais aplying himself to this for hedpe to Cleer the roades in his precincts is ordered John Tyler, Richard maidlin, Nicholas Gentry, Thomas Tinsley, John Burley and all the tithables from thence up the North side of Totopatomoys Creeke.

Mr. Robert Anderson, Jun'r, aploying himselfe to this vestry for help to Cleere the roades in his precincts is ordered those tithables following all the tithables on the South side the Queene's high roade that goeth by afasven and so up the South Side of Totopotomoys Creeke to Chickhaminy Swamp and down the said Swamp to the north side of Beverdam Swamp and up the said Swamp to the head of Mattadecon Creeke and thence down the said Creeke to Mr. Lewis's mill.

Peter mafe upon his motion to this vestry is ordered to his tithables the tithables on Mr. Edloes' plantation John Jones and Michael Johnson.

Cornelius Hall doeth this day agree to and with this vestry to doe and performe all the underpinning brick worke acording to the direction of Wm. Hughes, Carpenter, that is to be done in the Brick Church now built in this parish, and to be paid fouer hundred pounds of Tobacco and Cask Convenient for the same at Laying of the next Levy.

John Lyddall present.

Thomas Jackson hath this day agreed with this vestry to find lumber sufficient for Lathes, Sand and wood to burn the Lime and bring the Same in place and to find sufficient helpe, to send the plasterer during the plastering the Brick Church and to give his assistance to Cornelius Hall while he is underpining the place for the pews and Communion table, and to be paid for the same five thousand pounds of Tobacco and Cask Convenient at Laying the next Levy, and the Clerke is ordered to take his bond paiable to the Church wardens for the performance of the same.

James Moss and Nocholas Meriwether, Gentlemen, are chosen and elected Churchwardens for the Insuing year, and to begin their time from Easter next.

Reger.                Wm. Clopton, Clk Vest.

---

At a Vestry held for St. Peter's Parish at the house of Mr. James Moss, 23 Apr., 1703.

PRESENT:

Capt. Joseph Forster, Mr. Hen'r Wyatt, Mr. Wm. Bassett, Capt. John Lyddall, Mr. John Parks, Jun'r, Mr. Rich'd Littlepage, Vestrymen.

Maj'r Nicho. Meriwether, Mr. James Moss, Churchwardens.

Upon the petition of Mary Pyrant setting forth that she is very ancient, Lame and altogether unable to get her own Liveing, it is, therefore, ordered that she be alowed five hundred pounds of Tobacco and Cask p annum, and so proportionable for a Longer or shorter time.

Richard Harvy upon his petition to this vestry is Declared free from paying any Parish Levy.

Ordered that the Clerk Request Capt Nathaniel West to be at the next vestry to be sworne a vestryman in the place of Mr. Thomas Smith, Late Dec't.

Whereas, the Reverend Mr. Richard Squire is Recommended by his Excellence to this parish as a minister fully quallified, and the parish being vaquent of a minister by the death of the Reverend Mr. James Bowker, this vestry doe, therefore, in the Behalf of this parish agree with the said Mr. Richard Squire to offiate as minister in the said Parish, as Mr. Bowker used to doe, that is to say, one Sunday in Every month. * *

---

At a vestry held for St. Peter's parish at the Brick Church the 13 July, 1703.

PRESENT:

Mr. Richard Squire, minister.

Capt. Jos. Forster, Mr. Hen'r Wyatt, Mr. Wm. Bassett, Mr. Rich'd Littlepage, Mr. John Parks, Mr. John Parks, Ju'r, Vestrymen.

VESTRY BOOK OF ST. PETER'S PARISH. 71

Mr. James Moss, Maj'r Nicho. Meriwether, Churchwardens.
It is ordered that the pulpet in the said Brick Church be Sett upon the north Side thereof.
Mr. Richard Littlepage is Requested and acordingly joyned with Capt. Joseph Forster to be Superaviser of the worke to be done about the Brick Church in the place of Capt. John Lyddall, Late dec't.
Mr. John Scott haveing mett att this vestry and taken the oathes of alegence and Supremacie together with the oath of a vestryman and Subscribed the Test, is admited to the vestry in the place of Capt. John Lyddall, Late Dc't.
Cornelius Hall, Bricklayer, hath this day agreed with this vestry to brick the Ile of the Brick Church from dore to dore Compleated and workman like and to be paid for the same Seven hundred pounds of Tobacco and Cask Conv't at Laying the next Levy, and that he find all Laborers to doe the said worke and doe the said worke when Ever the Supervisors shall call for the same.

Reg'd p          WM. CLOPTON, Clk Vest'r.

New Kent County. At a vestry held for St. Peter's Parish at the Brick Church ye 27th Octo'r, 1703.

PRESENT:

Mr. Richard Squire, minister.
Capt. Joseph Forster, Mr. Wm. Bassett, Mr. Jno. Parks, Capt. Richard Littlepage, Mr. John Parks, Jun'r, Mr. Jno. Scott, Mr. Hen'r Childs, Vestrymen.
Capt. James Moss, Maj'r Nicho. Meriwether, Churchwardens.

ST. PETER'S PARISH.          Dr. Lbs. Tob'o.

| | |
|---|---|
| To Mr. Ralp Bowker, Exec for Mr. James Bowker, for 5 month and | 7693 |
| ½ To C. C. for ditto at 14 p Cent. | 1077 |
| To Mr. Wm. Williams for 3 sermons | 1200 |
| To C. C. for Ditto | 0168 |
| To Mr. Rich'd Squire from the 11 April to 11 January, 9 months | 12000 |
| To C. C. for Ditto | 1680 |
| To Will. Clopton Clarke for 1 year | 2289 |

72     VESTRY BOOK OF ST. PETER'S PARISH.

To Jno. Hilton, Sexton of ye Lower Church, 300 Ca., 24    0324
To Idem for wash'g ye Suplis and nailes for ye window..   0060
To Jno. Webb, Sexton of ye upper Church, 300 Ca., 24..    0324
To Idem for washing ye Surplis .....................      0050
To Mr. Geo. Clough, his acc't of fees ................    0450
To Mr. John Stamp Sherr acc't of fees ................    0045
To Will'm Clopton, his acc't ........................     0174
To Mr. John Scott his acc't 215 C. C., 30 ..............  0245
To Mr. Tho. Mins for ye wid. faulkner, 1 y'r, 1000 Ca., 80 1080
To Wm. Martin for Wm. Moore, 600 Ca., 48 ...........      0648
To the wid. Per'ant, 500 Ca., 40 .....................    0540
To John Gonton for keep Antho. Burrows 1 y'r, 1000 Ca.
   80 ............................................       1080
To Sam. Wadde for keep Jam. Turner 1 y'r, 1200 Ca., 96    1296
To John Kimburrow for 1 y'r rent for the use of his house
   to preach in, 600 Ca., 48 ........................     0648
To Tho. More for trouble a Ct. Indian Ross ..........     0220
To Will. Atkinson, 600 Ca., 48 .....................      0648
                                                         ———
                                                         33939

To Maj'r Nicho. Meriwether ye ball. of his acc't .......  1387
To C. C. for Ditto .................................      0193
To Mr. Jam's Moss his acc't, 345 C. C., 46 ...........    0361
To Cha's Bryan for Trouble ab't Eliz. Browne .........    0100
To Madam Sarah Bray her acc't, 540 C. C., 73 ........     0613
To David Clarkson his acct, 57 C. C., 8...............    0065
To Mr. Geo. Poindexter's acc't, 200 C. C., 28 ..........  0228
To Mr. Rich'd Littlepage's acc't, 1518 C. C., 212 .......  1730
To the widd. King for keep a bastard Child born at Mrs.
   Butt's, 6 months, 500 Ca., 40 .....................     540
To James Sanders for keep Tho. Wilkins,3 months, 8 days
   at 1000 p annum ................................       0282
To Idem p acc't .................................         0195
                                                         ———
                                                         6329½

To ye Supervisers for Tho. Jackson p agre'm 5000 Ca., 400  5400
To Mr. Wm. Major p acc't .........................        0050
To Tho. Jackson his acc't regulated, 1840 Ca., 143......  1983

## VESTRY BOOK OF ST. PETER'S PARISH. 73

| | |
|---|---|
| To the Supervisers for Corn'l Hall, 700 C. C., 98...... | 0798 |
| To Idem for Wm. Hughes 2 paym't, 1250 C. C., 1750 .. | 14250 |
| To Idem for Jam. Knott, 4500 C. C., 630 ............. | 5130 |
| To James Knott p acct ............................. | 0075 |
| To the Supervisers for Jno. Uppehew p ord'r of Vincent Vaughn, 3223 C. C., 423 ........................ | 3446 |
| To Idem for Vinc't Vaughn ye ball. of his acc't 601 C. C., 84 .......................................... | 0684 |
| | 31916 |
| To Jno. Kimburrow, Ju'r, and Jam. Babbitt, Lawyers, but to Lye in Maj'r Merriwether and Capt. Childs' hands as Supervisors of the Chapell till the work be done, 2659 C. C., 272 ..................................... | 2931 |
| To Idem p acc't, 200 C. C., 28 ...................... | 0228 |
| To Mr. Hen'r Childs p acc't, 185 C. C., 25 ............ | 0210 |
| To John Dod p acc't, 65 C. C., 08 ................... | 0073 |
| To the Supervisers of the Chapell for Jno. Dod, 6000 C. C., 840 .......................................... | 6840 |
| | 10282 |
| Sum Totall ........ ............................. | 82466½ |
| So Salle'r of 82466½ at 5 p cent. ................... | 4128 |
| | 86589½ |
| Cr. p 936 Tithables at 91 lbs. Tobacco p polo.......... | 86376 |
| To the Collect'r for deposits to be p'd next year........ | 213 |
| | 86589 |

P. Conte,          Cr.

| | |
|---|---|
| P Coll'e Joseph Forster .......................... | 0070 |
| P Maj'r Merriwether for 1 Lock mischa'e ............ | 0050 |
| P Mrs Butts, 500 Ca 40 ........................... | 0540 |
| P Capt. Lyddall for Eliz. Portlock's bastard, 500 Ca 40. | 0540 |
| The Parish Levys being proportioned amounts to...... | 1200 |

Ninety one pounds of Tobacco p polo which Sum of ninety one pounds of Tobacco William Clopton is hereby impowered and ordered to receive from Each tithable person in this parish, and in case of non payment to make destress, and that he make payment of the same to the Severall persons to whom it is Levyed an that he enter into bond with Sufficient Securitie to the Church wardens for the use of the parish for the due payment of the Same.

Whereas this parish have been at greate Charge in building a Brick Church and Chappell and at present can not find a suitable place for a Gleabe doe therefore agree with Mr. Philip Levermore for the house and plantation where Capt. John Lyddall lived at the yearly rent of one thousand pounds of tobacco and Cask Conv't so long as the parish shall think fit to hire the same for the minister to Live upon, but if Mr. Levermore or his Lady should happen to Come into Virginia that then the said Plantation be immediately surrendered to them if Required.

Whereas Mr. Philip Levermore hath appeared at this vestry and agreed with the said vestry in behalfe of the parish that he doeth Lett them the Plantation whereon he now Lives Lately belonging to John Lyddall, Gen. dec't from year to year and Longer if the parish shall think fit, the parish paying him the Said Levermore the annual Rent of one thousand lbs. sweet sented tobacco and Cask Conv't for the same, and that the Church wardens take a Lene for the same.

Whereas upon the mocion of Mr. Richard Squire, this Parish doe Levy his Saller to the 11 day of Januery next.

Peter Maye did this day produce an order of Court wherein he is Sett Levy free.

Upon the mocion of Mr. John Kimburrow, it is ordered that he be paid proportionable at the rate of 600 lbs. Tobacco p annum.

Maj'r Nicho. Merriwether, upon his mocion to this vestry, is discharged from the last year's Collection, and Every part thereof noe Claimers appearing against him.

This vestry doe hereby in the behalfe of the Parish agree with Mr. Rich'd Squire for the insuing year.

Will Clopton is Continued Clarke of parish and vestry for the insuing year.

It is ordered that Coll'r Joseph Forster and Capt Richard Littlepage be Supervisers of the Brick Church and maj'r nicholas merriwether and Mr. Hene. Childs be superavisers of the Chappell upon mechumps Creeke, and that the Collector make noe payment of any Tobacco Levyd to them p their order.

Rege'r p WM. CLOPTON, Clk. vest.

The vestry held for St. Peter's parish the 27 march, 1704.

PRESENT:

Mr. Richard Squire, minister; Joseph Forster, Wm. Bassett, John Parke, Jun'r, Delaid Craford, John Parke, John Scott, Hene. Childs, Gen't'men vestrymen.

James Moss, Nicho. Meriwether Gent: Church wardens.

It is ordered that maj'r nicholas merriwether send for Glass, Lead Sodder and Casments for the Chappell and to be paid for the same in sweet sented Tobacco and Cask Conv't at the middle marquit price with fifty p Cent. upon his Goods.

Rege'r p WILL CLOPTON, Clk. rege.

At a vestry held for St. Peter's Parish in New Kent County the 3 Aprill, 1704.

PRESENT:

Mr. Richard Squire, minister; Joseph Forster, Rich'd Littlepage, David Craford, John Parke, Hene. Childs, John Parke, Jun'r, Jno. Scott, Gent Vestrymen.

James Moss, Nicho. Meriwether, Gent'n Church wardens.

This vestry taking into their serious Consideration the Largeness of this parish there being two Churches and one Chappell in the same, and the major part of the parish being desirous of a devision becase they Cannot have the word of God duly preached to them, doe accordingly agree upon a devision and that it begineth at the mouth of maddadecan Creeke so up the Said Creeke to Mr. Lewis mill, thence down the Queens high Roade to the rowling Roade that goeth from Edward mores to Geo'e Turners so along the Said Roade including the Said more in the upper parish, thence along the Said Roade to the Plantation of John Baughn Senr who is to be in the upper parish, thence upon a Line between the plantation of Nicholas Lawson and John Sandige the said Lawson to be in the Lower parish and Sandige in the upper and soe upon a Straite Line to Chickahominy Swamp including Edw'e Clark in the uper parish and Capt. James Moss and Maj'r Nicholas Merriwether Church wardens are Requested by this vestry to Suplicate his Excellence by way of Petition for his Concurrence with this order which if he be pleased to grant that the Lower parish may Continue the name of St. Peter and that his Excellence would be pleased to give a name to the upper parish as to his wisdom may seem meete and the Gleabe Lands w'ch are about 200 acres remaine as they were that is 100 acres in the Lower parish to remaine to the Brick Church and 100 acres to remaine to the upper Church and what plate or ornaments in the parish to be Equally divided between both parishes and that which is Called by the name of the upper Church to be left in Good Repair and that the Chapell to be finished all at the Cost of both parishes and Mr. Richard Squire was Requested by this vestry to declare what parish he would make Choice of if his Excellence were pleased to admit of a Division who accordingly accepts of the Lower parish.

Regeristered p. WM. CLER: Rege.

St. Peter's Parish, June the 1st, 1704.

Pursuant to an act of Assembly made at a Generall Assembly begun the 20th Aprill, 1704, for the division of this Parish the free houlders and hous keepers of this parish have this day meet and Chosen and Ellected a vestry for the said parish who are Capt. Richard Littlepage, Mr. Geo. Poindexter, Mr. Will Bassett, Mr. Rich'd Allen, Mr. Thomas Butts, Ju'r, William Clopton, Collo. John Lightfoot, Mr. John Forster, Mr. John Parke, Jun'r, Mr. John Scott, Mr. Thomas massie, Mr. William Waddell, who have accordingly taken the oathes pointed by Law subscribed to the Test and to be Conformable to the Doctrin and Dissipline of the Church of England, all the above gentlemen Except Mr. William Bassett and Mr. John Parke Ju'r, Sworn before Coll'e Joseph Forster.

At a vestry held for St. Peter's parish the 1st June, 1704.

PRESENT:

Mr. Rich'd Littlepage, Col. Jno. Lightfoot, Mr. Geo'e Poindexter, Mr. Jno. Forster, Mr. Rich'd Allen, Mr. Jno. Scott, Mr. Tho. Butts, Ju'r, Mr. Thos. Massie, Will Clopton, Mr. Wm. Waddell, vestrymen.

This vestry do agree with Mr. Richard Squire, minister of this parish to be paid according to Law and to Eand the year upon the first day of Jan'e next. Present: Mr. Rich'd Squire, minister.

Capt. Richard Littlepage and Capt. John Scott are Chosen and Elected Church wardens of this parish for the insuing year.

The Church wardens are requested and impowered to forewarne Robert Hughes from building or Cleering upon the Gleab Land and in Case he will persist in building or Cleering upon the Said Land then to Commence Sute against him and imploy an atturney or atturneys against him and Likewise to get the Churchyard very well paled in and Cleered as they shall think fitt.

WM. CLOPTON, Cler. Rege.

---

At a vestry held for St. Peter's parish the 14th June, 1704.

PRESENT:

Mr. Richard Squire, minister; Col. Jno. Lightfoot, Wm. Clopton, Mr. Geo. Poindexter, Mr. Jno. Forster, Mr. Rich'd Allen, Mr. Tho. Massie, Mr. Tho. Butts, Ju'r, Mr. Wm. Waddell, Vestrymen.

Capt. Rich'd Littlepage, Capt. Jno. Scott, Church wardens.

Mr. Will Bassett and Mr. John Parkes, Ju'r, being Elected two of the vestry for this parish and haveing appeared according to notice given them have had the oathes apointed by Law duely administered to them by John Lightfoot, Esq'r and Likewise subscribed the Test and to be Conformable to the Church of England as by Law Established are admitted to the vestry.

Present: Mr. William Bassett and Mr. John Parkes, Ju'r.

William Clopton not any way Relinquishing or foregoing the place and office of a vestryman, but that he is Continued in the full power and office of a vestryman is Continued Clerke of this vestry and parish till the 1st day of Januery next, and to be paid as formerly.

John Hilton is Continued Sexton of this Parish till the first day of Januery next, and to be paid at the rate of five hundred and forty pounds of Tobacco p annum.

Upon Reeding of his Excellence in Council his order Concerning S'r Edw'd northe Knight her maj'ter att'r Gen'ell his opinion on the acts of Assembly of this Collony relating to the

Church and perticularly Concerning Inductions the Clarke is ordered to Commit the same regester.

Rege p. W<small>M</small>. C<small>LOPTON</small>, Cle'k reg'e.

On Consideration of the Laws of Virginia provision being made by the act Entitulated Churches to be built or Chappell of Ease for the building a Church in Each parish and by ye act intitaled ministers to be Inducted that ministers of each parish Shall be Inducted on the presentation of ye paritioners and ye Church wardens being by the Act Entitled Church wardens to keep the Church in repaire and provide * aments to Collect the minister's dues & by ye Act for the better support and maintainance of the Clergy provision being made for ye ministers of the parishes by the Said Act for Inducting ministers ye Governer being to Induct ye ministers to be presented & thereby he being Constituted ordinary & as Bishop of the Plantation and with a power to punish ministers preaching Contrary to ye Law: I am of opinion the Advowson & right of presentation to the Churches is subject to ye Laws of England, there being no Express Law of ye Plantation made further Concerning the same; therefore, when ye Parishioners present their Clark & he is Inducted by the Governer (who is to and must Induct on the presentation of ye parishioners) ye Incumbant is for his Life and Can not be displaced by the parishioners; if ye parishioners do not present a minister to the Governor w'thin six months after any Church shall become voyde ye Governer as ordinary Shall and may Collate a Clerk to Such Church by Laps & his Collate shall hould ye Church for his life if the Parishioners have never presented they have a reasonable time to present a minister, but if they will not present, being required so to doe ye Governer may allso in their default Collate a minister in Inducting ministers by the Governer on the presentation of the parish or his own Collation he is to see ye ministers be quallified according as ye act for Inducting ministers requires. In Case of ye avoydance of any Church the Governer as ordinary of ye Plantation is according to ye Statue of 28 |-| 8 Chap. 11th ecl. 5th to appoint a minister to officiate till the parish shall present one or ye six months be Lapsed and such person appointed to officiate in ye vacancy is to be paid for his service out of the profits thereof from the time ye Church shall become voide. By a Law a bond stated no minister is to officiate as such till he hath showed to ye Governer he is quallified according as ye Said Act for Induction directs, if ye vestry do not levy ye Tobacco ye Court then must decree ye same to be Levyed.

EDW'D NORTHE, July 29th, 1703.

At a Council held at Williamsburg ye 3d day of March, 1703. Present: His Excellency in Councill.

Upon reading at this board S'r Edwarde Northe Knight her ma'te Attorney Generall his opinion upon ye acts of Assembly of this Collony relating to ye Church & particularly concerning Induction of ministers & His Excellency is pleased to order yt a Copy of the S'd S'r Edw'd Northe his opinion be sent to ye Church wardens of Each parish within this Colony Requiring them upon receit thereof forthwith to Call a vestry and there to Cause the Same to be read and Entered in the vestry booke to the Eand the Said vestrye may offer to his Excellence what they think proper thereupon.

WILL ROBERTSON, Cl. Cou.

At a Vestry held for St. Peter's parish in New Kent County the 7th July, 1704.

PRESENT:

Mr. Richard Squire, minister; John Lightfoot, Esq'e Mr. Rich'd Allen, Mr. Geo. Poindexter, Mr. Wm. Waddell, Mr. Jno. Forster, Mr. Tho. Massie, Mr. Wm. Bassett, Wm. Clopton, vestrymen.

Mr. John Scott, Church warden.

Capt. John Scott, Capt. Rich'd Littlepage, Mr. William Bassett, Mr. Rich'd Allen and Mr. Thomas Massie or any fouer of them are Requested to meet such gentlemen of the vestry of St. Pall's parish to run the Dividing Line between this parish and the parish of St. Pall and that it be done by the County Suvaeior at the Charge of both parishes and the Clerke is ordered to waite on the Church wardens of St. Pall's parish with a Copy of this order that it may be done forthwith.

John Lightfoot, Esq'r, Capt. Richard Littlepage, Capt. John Scott, Mr. George Poindexter and Mr. Thomas Butts or any fouer of them are Requested to meet such Gentlemen as shall be apointed by the Gentlemen of the vestry of St. Pall's parish to

Devide what orniments were belonging to this Parish when it was all in one and Likewise to adjust and Settle all maner of accts. belonging to the Said parish when it was all in one intire parish according to the order for the Devision of the Said parish and the Gentlemen of St. Pall's parish are Requested to meet at the Brick Church and to give the Gen'ts of this parish a forthnight's notice for the time of meeting.

Capt. John Scott and Capt. Richard Littlepage, Church wardens, are Requested and acordingly ordered to Imploy a Carpenter to build one Dwelling House 20 feet Long and 16 feet wide, with an Inside Chimney, posts in the Ground 8 feet pitch't double joiest and Lofted upo the Gleabe Land belonging to this parish formerly Given by Reece Hughes. Whereas Edw'd Morgan Complaines to this vestry that he hath in his house a very poore, Lame and impotent woman named Jane Clarke, ordered that he keep the Said Jane Clarke and to be alowed as others are in the same Case.

Rege. p WM. CLOPTON, Cle'k Veste.

At a Vestry held for St. Peter's parish ye 18th day August, 1704.

PRESENT:

Mr. Richard Squire, minister; Mr. Thos. Butts, Mr. Wm. Waddill, Mr. Geo. Poindexter, Mr. Thos. Massey, Mr. Rich'd Allin, Wm. Clopton, vestrymen.

Capt. John Scott, Capt. Rich'd Littlepage, Church wardens.

Whereas the Church wardens have laid before this vestry Sr Edw'd Northe her Maj'hgt Att'r Gen'lle opinion Concerning Inductions & his Ex'cye ord'r in Council on the Same together w'th his Ex'cye Proclamation Requiring ye Vestrye to give him an act w't Gleabe lands in ye Respective parishes in Virga & wt building thereon & likewise whether they have Rec'd any of ye Great Bibles Sent in by S'r Geofrey Geofrye to be this vestry answer that they are not for Inducting the Minister nor for any dislike they have to him, but that the whole p'sh in Gen'll is agt. Gleabe Lands no building upon it at present there being some dispute in law about it & for ye Great Bibles sent in by S'r Geof'r Geofreys do not know of any that hath been brought heither, orderd ye Clerk Send a Copy of this ord'r to ye Sec'rs office.

Ordered by the Church wardens forthwith a good pr of Stocks

to be Built & Set up just w'th out ye Church yard & to be Paid at ye laying ye next levie.

Ordered yt Pelham Moore Scoure up ye dich about ye old Church to ye full Depth & width it was at first, & cut Quite through ye place where people went in & doe it between this & ye last of October & to be pd three hundred pounds of Tob'o & Cask Conv't at Laying ye next Levy.

Mr. Richard Squire is Requested to preach two Sermons in every year at the old Church, commonly known by ye name of ye Broken back'd Church.

Recorded p WM. CLOPTON, Clk veste.

New Kent County.

At a meeting Capt. Rich'd Littlepage, Capt. Jno. Scott, Jno. Lightfoot, Esq'r, Mr. Tho. Butts, Gen't in trust for St. Peter's Parish & Mr. David Craford, Maj'r Nicho. Merriwether, Mr. Henry Childs, Capt. Rob't Anderson & Mr. Jno. Moss, Gen't in truste for Saint paul's pr'sh at ye Brick Church in St. Peter's pr'sh ye 29th Aug't, 1704.

| St. Peter's pr'sh. | Dr. |
|---|---|
| To Mr. Rich'd Squire for 5 months, CC............... | 6665 |
| To CC for Do........................................ | 933 |
| To Wm. Clopton, Clerk for 5 months ................ | 895 |
| To Jno. Hilton, Sexton for 5 months, 125 CC 10........ | 135 |
| To Idem for washing Surples ...................... | 025 |
| To Jno. Webb for 5 mo'th, 125 CC 10................ | 135 |
| To Idem for washing ye Surples .................... | 025 |
| To Tho. Mins for widdow faulkner, 5 mo'ths, CC...... | 450 |
| To Wm. Martin for Wm. Moore .................... | 270 |
| To ye widdow Pyrant for five mo's ................. | 225 |
| To Peter Plantine for Antho. Burrows, 5 mo's.......... | 450 |
| To Sam'l Waddy for James Turner, 540.............. | 540 |
| To Jno. Kimbrow for 5 mo'hs ..................... | 270 |
| To Wm. Atkinson for 5 mo'hs ..................... | 270 |
| To Mrs. Roper for a bastard child .................. | 450 |
| To Nicho. Mills for keeping a bastard child........... | 403 |
| To Maj'r Nicho. Merriwether ye ball. his acct........ | 1447½ |
| To Sam'l Waddie his acct. ......................... | 700 |
| To Joseph Baughn, Chain Carrier .................. | 030 |

| | |
|---|---|
| To Jno. Landige ye Same | 030 |
| To Thos. Snead ye Same | 030 |
| To Rich'd Clark, Ju'r, for pelating ye Surveyor | 100 |
| To Jno. White's acct Regulated | 180 |
| To ye Church wardens of both pr'she for ye Trouble about ye division of ye parish | 400 |
| To Capt. Scott for Trouble about ye Survey'r | 100 |
| To Capt. Littlepage for paid Care foot ye Glazer Ll-18st-6d at 1d p pound | 949 |
| * * * | 056 |
| * * * | 1190 |
| * * * | 166 |
| * * * | ** |
| To Capt. Rob't Anderson | 045 |
| To Thos. Jackson, his acct. | 1179 |
| To Coll. Joseph Forster, 500 6d nailes | 020 |
| To Idem p acct. more | 140 |
| To Mr. Geo. Poindexter's acct. Regulated L1 13s 9d, at 10 p C | 338 |
| To Mr. David Clarkson p acct. | 140 |
| To Mrs. Alice wiat ye Ball. her acct. p 20 lb 10s at 10qd p Cent. | 108 |
| To Capt. James Moss his acct. | 170 |
| To Capt. Geo. Clough's acct. | 163 |
| To Vincent Vaughn's acc't 808 C. C. 113 | 921 |
| To Wm. Clopton's acct. | 2330 |
| To Jno. Hilton's acct. keeping goody Al | 380 |
| To ye Collector for ye minister's Rent, 3 mos. 250 C C 35 | 285 |
| To Wm. Clopton for Extreordinary Trouble about 3 De Devision, &c., 600, 100 | 27396 700 |
| To Jno. Hilton's atendance here to Sall at 5 p Cent | 1404 |
| In all | 29503 |
| Cr—By 947 Tithables at 31 p polo is | 29357 |
| By ball. due to ye Colect'r | 146 |
| | 29503 |

St. Paul's pr'sh,            Dr.

| | L | z | d |
|---|---|---|---|
| To ye half of ye Church plate & Table Cloath | 2 " | 5 | 0 |

To Ball. due St. Paul's parish ..................... 0 " 5 " 0

2 " 10 " 0

By halfe of Mr. Henry Wyatt Legacy ............... 2 " 10 " 0

Whereas we, the Subscribers, were apointed by both parishes to adjust & Settle all accts. between ye S'd parishes & having this day mett p'suant to ye Same, doe find ye pr'sh debt to amount to Twenty Nine Thou'd five hund'r & three pounds of Tobo. w'ch being divided by 947 ye Number of Tithables for this pr sent year amounts to 35 lbs. Tobo. p polo, Saving 146 lbs. Tobo. to be paid by both p'rish's to ye Colect'r next year, each Tithable in both ye S'd pr'shs for Defraying ye afores'd Charge upon ye division of ye plate & all other ornaments there is due to St. Paul's p'rishes five Shill's, & if there should happen to be any mistake or Error of either Side to be Equally Rectified.

John Lightfoot, Thos. Butts, Nicho. Meriwether, David Craford, Reich'd Littlepage, Jno. Scott, Henry Childs, Robt. Anderson, Jun'r, John Mask.

At a vestry held for St. Peter's p'sh in New Kent County ye 1st Nov'r, 1704.

PRESENT:

Mr. Richard Squire, Minister.

Coll. John Lightfoot, Mr. Wm. Waddill, Mr. Wm. Bassett, Mr. Rich'd Allen, Mr. Jno. Park, Jun'r, Mr. Tho. Massey, Mr. Jno. Forster, Wm. Clopton, vestrymen.

Capt. Rich'd Littlepage, Capt. John Scott, Church wardens.

| St. Peter's Parish, | Dr. |
|---|---|
| To Mr. Rich'd Squire for 7 months ................. | 9335 |
| To C C for Ditto at 14 p cent........................ | 1306 |
| To Wm. Clopton, Clerk, for 7 months ............... | 1394 |
| To Jno. Hilton, Sexton, for 7 months ............... | 315 |
| To Tho. Mins for widow faulkner 7 months........... | 630 |
| To Wm. Martin for Wm. More, 10 * ................ | 125 |
| To Mrs. Roper for a bastard child 7 mon............. | 630 |
| To James Stringer, p acct........................... | 350 |
| To Capt. John Scott, p acct......................... | 490 |
| To Wm. Martin p his acct. Regulated ................ | 310 |

| | |
|---|---:|
| To James Sanders p acct............................... | 400 |
| To Tho. Jackson p acct 1200 C C 168................. | 1368 |
| To Jno. Hilton p acct. .............................. | 050 |
| To Jno. Hilton for keeping Widd. Astill 7 mon.......... | 630 |
| To Capt. Rich'd Littlepage p acct. 3550 ................ | 4047 |
| To Tho. Mins for a pr Shoes for wid. * * .............. | 040 |
| To Wm. Clopton p acct. ............................ | 100 |
| To Rich'd Harvey for his Troub. * * * ................ | 100 |
| To Mr. Levermore for 9 mos. rent.................... | 855 |
| To Ex. pd. toward a Bell, but to Lye in ye Collector's hands till it be ordered p ye Church wardens 1500 C C 210 .......... ..................................... | 1750 |
| To Sall'r of 24639 at 5 p Cent....................... | 1232 |
| To Ball. due to ye p Ch. ............................ | 233 |
| | 26104 |

Cr. By 502 Tithables at * * 2610.

The Parish Levey being proportioned to fifty two pounds of Tobo. pr polo w'ch with thirty one upon ye Settlement before ye Division of ye parish amounts to Eighty three pounds of Tobo. p polo, w'ch Sume of Eighty three pounds of Tobo. p polo Capt. James Moss, Sherife of this County, is hereby impowered & ordered to Receive & Collect of & from Each & Every Tythable p'son w'thin this p'sh, & in Case of non payment to Levy ye Same by Distress.

Coll. Jno. Lightfoot, Capt. Rich'd Littlepage, Capt. Jno. Scott, Mr. Tho. Butts, & Mr. Jno. Park, Ju'r, or any 4 or 3 of them are Requested to meet Such Gent as ye Gent of St. Paul's p'sh Shall apoint at ye Lower Church of their p'sh one Wensday ye 8th of this Enstant by tenn of ye Clock in ye forenoon in ord'r to ye Settle of Severall accts. belonging to both p'shes.

Rich'd Squire, Clerk; Jno. Park, Jun'r, J. Lightfoot, Wm. Waddill, Wm. Bassett, Rich'd Allin, Jno. Forster, Wm. Clopton. Rich'd Littlepage, Jno. Scott, Church wardens.

At a Vestry held for St. Peter's ye 6th Jan'e, 1704.

PRESENT:

Mr. Rich'd Squire, min'r; Jno. Lightfoot, Esq'r, Mr. Jno. Forster, Mr. Wm. Waddill, Mr. Tho. Butts, Mr. Rich'd Allin,

Wm. Clopton, Mr. Wm. Bassett, Mr. Tho. Massey, Mr. Jno. Park, Jun'r, Mr. Geo. Poindexter.

Capt. John Scott, Church warden.

The order of Vestry made w'th Mr. Rich'd Squire, min'r, bearing date of ye first day of June, 1704, is Received for ye insuing year.

Ordered that Wm. Clopton be Clerk of this Vestry & to be paid five hundred pounds of Tobacco p annum.

Ordered that Mr. Norris is chosen Reader of this p'sh & to be allowed eight hundred pounds of Tobacco p annum.

Ordered that John Hilton be Sexton of this Church & to be paid five hundred & fifty pounds of tobo. p annum.

RICH'D SQUIRE, Clarke.

Jno. Forster, Jno. Lightfoot, Rich'd Allin, Jno. Parke, Ju'r, Tho. Butts, Tho. Massey, Jno. Scott, Wm. Waddill, Wm. Bassett.

Chu'r wardens, Wm. Clopton, Geo'e Poindexter.

---

At a vestry held for St. Peter's p'sh in New Kent County ye 14th of May, 1705.

PRESENT:

Mr. Wm. Bassett, Mr. John Parke, Jun'r, Wm. Clopton, Mr. Geo. Poindexter, Mr. Tho. Massey, Mr. Rich'd Allin, Mr. Wm. Waddill, vestrymen.

Capt. John Scott, Church warden.

Mr. Wm. Bassett & Mr. Geo. Poindexter are Chosen & Elected Church Wardens & to act & doe therein accordingly from this time till Easter next.

Wm. Clopton, one of the Surveyors of this County, applying himselfe to this vestry for help to clear ye Road in his presinct is ordered all ye tythables belonging to those persons following, viz.: Madd. Sarah Bray, Dan'l Park, Esq'r, Ju'r Ashew, Steph. Mitchell, James Crump, Wm. Burrow, Steph. Mitchell, Ju'r, Wm. Forgasen, Robt. Crump, Wm. Crump, Jno. Waddill, Jun'r Rich'd Crump, Steph. Crump, Chas. Barker, Tho. Shroasby, Eliza Crump, widdow & Tho. Brigman.

Jno. Scott, Tho. Massey, Jno. Park, Jun'r, Wm. Clopton, Wm. Waddill, Geo. Poindexter, Rich'd Alin, Wm. Bassett, Chu'r wardens.

86        VESTRY BOOK OF ST. PETER'S PARISH.

At a Vestry held for St. Peter's p'sh in New Kent County 7 10th. 1705.

PRESENT:

Mr. Rich'd Squire, min'r; Capt. John Scott, Mr. Rich'd Allen, Mr. Tho. Butts, Mr. Wm. Waddill, Mr. Jno. Park, Jr., Wm. Clopton, Mr. Jno. Forster, Mr. Tho. Massie.

Mr. Wm. Bassett, Mr. Geo'e Poindexter, Ch. Wardens.

Mr. Tho. Butts, Mr. Geo. Poindexter & Mr. Jno. Park, Jun'r, or any two of them, are apointed to meet Such Gent'm as Shall be apointed by ye Vestry of St. Paul's parish at Such times & place as ye Gen'n of St. Paul's parish Shall apoint.

Ordered yt ye Church wardens forthwith bring Suit agt. ye Extr'e of Jno. Lyddall, Gent. late of this County, dec'd for a Legacy Left to this p'sh by ye S'd Lyddall.

Whereas there was a Leese taken by this p'sh Philip Levermore, as marrying ye Ex'trx of Mr. Lyddall, Gent Dec'd for ye house & Plantation where (ye S'd) Jno. Lyddall Lately lived upon at ye annual Rent of 1000 lbs. Tobo. & Cask Conv't p annum & ye Parish being desirous to acquit them Selves of yt Leese or agreement Mr. Richard Squire doth hereby agree to & w'th this p'sh & hereby acquit ye S'd p'sh of & from ye Sd Leese at ye end of this yeare ye Parish paying him ye S'd Mr. Squire ye Same Sume of tobo. they were to have paid Mr. Levermore till such time yt ye Parish can provide a Suficient Gleabe for ye min'r to live upon.

Ordered yt Mr. Geo. Poindexter & Mr. Wm. Bassett, Ch'r wardens, to be a Saile from Rob't Hughes to this ps'h for all that Land Given to this p'sh by his father, Rees Hughes.

Rich'd Squire, Wm. Bassett, Geo. Poindexter, Church wardens.

Jno. Scott, Thos. Butts, Jno. Forster, Jno. Park, J'r, Thos. Massie, Rich'd Allin, Wm. Waddill, Wm. Clopton.

---

At a vestry held for St. Peter's p'sh in New Kent County ye 15 octob'r, 1705.

PRESENT:

Capt. Rich'd Littlepage, Capt. Jno. Soctt, Mr. Tho. Butts, Mr. Rich'd Allin, Mr. Wm. Waddill, Mr. Tho. Massie, Mr. Wm. Clopton.

Mr. Wm. Bassett, Mr. Geo. Poindexter, Chu. Wardens.

St. Peter's Parish.

| | |
|---|---:|
| To Mr. Rich'd Squire, C. C., for 1 year | 16000 |
| To Cask & Conv't to Do. | 2440 |
| To Mr. Wm. Norris, Cl. of ye Ch'r, for 1 year | 800 |
| To C. C. to Do. | 112 |
| To Wm. Clopton, Cl. to ye Vest'r., 500 C. C., 60 | 560 |
| To Mr. Hilton, Sexton for 1 year | 540 |
| To Rob't Hughes for ye Gleabe land, 2100 C. C., 294 | 2394 |
| To Eliza. King, Wid., her acc't, 913 Cask, 72 | 985 |
| To Mr. Rob't. Napier p acc't | 300 |
| To Wm. Gardener his acc't Regulated | 1575 |
| To Idem. for Cask of 1200 of ye same | 096 |
| | 25602 |
| To Rich'd Scruggs p acc't Regulated, 545 Ca., 44 | 589 |
| To Jno. Hilton for keeping widd. Ashile, 5 mo. | 450 |
| To Geo. Austin his acc't Regulated | 749 |
| To Wm. Hughes p acc't | 300 |
| To Capt. Richard Littlepage p acc't | 030 |
| To Edw'd Morgan p acc't, 585 Ca., 68 | 923 |
| To Mr. Upshere p acc't & keeping a bastard child 12 mos. at ye 12 of Nov'r & Clothes | 1280 |
| To Capt. Rich'd Littlepage p acc't, 1200 Ca., 1000 Do, 80 | 125 |
| To Capt. Scott for a Staun. | 040 |
| To Thos. Jackson acc't | 050 |
| To Tho. Mins. for keeping wid. Faulkner 1 yr, 1000 Ca. 80 | 1080 |
| To Mr. Geo. Poindexter p acc't 653 C. C., 91 | 744 |
| To Capt. Littlepage, She'r, p acc't of fees, 60 | 660 |
| To Wm. Clopton p ball. his acc't | 709 |
| To Jno. Hilton his acc't Regulated | 300 |
| To Sam'l Smith for his Right for ye Gleabe land given by his father, Geo. Smith, to this p'sh, but to Lie in ye Collector's hands till he acknowledges ye same from him & his heirs | 1250 |
| To C. C. to Do. | 112 |
| To ye Collector to give to Coll. Lightfoot serv'ts for their trouble about ye plates, &c. | 200 |
| To Rich'd hare for Service Done to ye Church | 500 |
| | 34721 |

To Capt. Richard Littlepage for building one house 20 feet long & 16 feet wide w'th an Inside Chimney 8 foot Pitch with a Shead on one Side & a Partition in ye Same w'th two doores, ye house to be   *   fled w'th Clapboard w'th a Lock & Key & hinges to ye outward Doore, all to be done w'th Strong & workman like & to be finished by ye last day of Jan'r next, & Capt. Littlepage asumes to enter into bond w'th ye Ch'r W'ns for ye due p'formance of ye same .................................. 1500
    910

36431

To Sall'r of 4797 at 5 p cent. ........................ 238
To Sall. of 36431 at 5 p Ct. ........................ 1821

C'r. 38490
P. Thos. Jackson ................................. 1000
P. Capt. Jno., S'r to pay Mr. Levermore for rent 1000 C. C., 140 ......................................... 1140
P. Capt. Jno., Sr., part of w't was left in his hands for a bal 570
P. 533 Tytha's at 69 lb. p. polo ..................... 36777
Pa. Deposito. to be p'd ye Collector next year .......... 143

The p'sh Levy being Proportioned am'tt to 69 lb. Tobo. p polo with Sume of 69 lbs tobo Capt. Rich'd Littlepage is hereby impowered to Collect according to Law & make paym't thereof to ye Severall p'sons for whom it was Levied ......................................... 39630

Geo. Poindexter, Wm. Bassett, Ch'r War.
Rich'd Littlepage, Jno. Scott, Tho. Butts, Rich'd Allen, Tho. Massie, Wm. Waddill, Wm. Clopton.

At a Vestry held for St. Peter's parish in New Kent County ye 31st Dec'r, 1705.
PRESENT:

Capt. Jno. Scott, Mr. Tho. Butts, Mr. Rich'd Allen, Mr. John Parke, Jun'r, Mr. Wm. Waddill, Wm. Clopton.
Mr. Wm. Bassett, Mr. Geo. Poindexter, Chu'r wardens.
This vestry doe order & agree yt Mr. Rich'd Squire be Con-

tinued minister of this p'sh for this Ensuing year & be paid as formerly.

Ordered that Mr. Wm. Norris, Co. Clerk of this p'sh & Vestry & to be paid at ye rate of one Thous'd Three hundred pounds of Tobacco & Cask, Ct., p annum, but if ye S'd Mr. Wm. Norris doth not come to live in this p'sh by Easter day next then this agreement to be Void.

Mr. Wm. Bassett, Mr. Geo. Poindexter, Mr. Jno. Scott, Tho. Butts, Rich'd Allen, Mr. Parke, Jr., Wm. Waddill, Wm. Clopton.

At a Vestry held for St. Peter's Parish in New Kent County ye 16th day of March, 1705|6.

PRESENT:

Jno. Lightfoot, Esq., Mr. Jno. Scott, Mr. Jno. Forster, Mr. Rich'd Allen, Mr. Tho. Massie, Mr. Jno. Parke, Jun'r, vestrymen.

Mr. Wm. Bassett, Churchwarden.

Whereas, there has been an order of Court dated Jane'y 28th, 1705|6, for processioning according to Law, & for dividing the p'shes into precincts.

The Vestry having met accordingly have ordered ye Church of the Vestry to give notice to the people of this p'sh to procession as has been usuall ordered that Mr. William Bassett & Mr. Thomas Massie give notice to two g'n the Vestry of the upper pa'sh to meet them about processioning of this P'ish Line, & that they give timely notice to bring their Children to see the S'd processioning. Ordered that Mr. Thomas Butts & Mr. Geo. Poindexter give notice to two of the Vestry of the Lower P'ish to meet them ab't processioning of the P'sh line & yt ye give timely notice to bring their Children to See the procession. Geo. Poindexter.

Ordered that a Vestry is to be held for this p'sh ye 25th of this instant March, it being Easter munday aft nine of the Clock in the morning.

Registered p          WM. NORRIS, Clk Vestry.

At a Vestry held for St. Peter's P'ish in New Kent County, May ye 4th, 1706.

90          VESTRY BOOK OF ST. PETER'S PARISH.

Geo. Poindexter, Rich'd Allen, Church wardens.
Jno. Scott, Wm. Bassett, Wm. Clopton, Wm. Waddill, Jno. Parke, Jun'r.

Ordered that Mr. Geo. Poindexter & Mr. Rich'd Allen are chosen & elected Church wardens for the ensuing year & to Expire next Easter, but that Mr. Rich'd Allen shall continue a year longer, & also that every Vestryman w'c shall be chosen from this ensuing time shall continue two years.

Ordered that the Church wardens so provide necessary ornaments for the Church, according to Law.

Registered p                    WM. NORRIS, Clk of Vestry.

At a Vestry held for St. Peter's P'ish New Kent County, October ye 11th, 1706.

Mr. Rich'd Squire, min.

PRESENT:

Capt. Rich'd Littlepage, Capt. John Scott, Mr. Wm. Bassett, Mr. Wm. Waddill, Mr. Wm. Clopton, Mr. Tho. Butts, Mr. Jno. Parke, Mr. Thos. Massie.

Mr. Geo. Poindexter, Mr. Rich'd Allen, Ch. Wardens.

| ST. PETER'S PARISH, | Dr. |
|---|---|
| To Mr. Rich'd Squire, min'r, for 1 year | 16000 |
| To C. C., for Do. | 240 |
| To Wm. Norris, Cl'k of the Church. & Vestry | 1300 |
| To C. C., to Do. | 182 |
| To Jno. Hilton, Sexton, for 1 year | 570 |
| To Wid'o Austin for keeping Wid. Ashley ½ year, Ca. | 540 |
| To Jno. Hilton's acc't | 228 |
| To Do. acc't for keeping & burying Mary Wilkinson | 400 |
| To Do. acc't for fetching & Carrying ye Plate from Mr. Poindexter | 100 |
| To Rich'd Scruggs for keeping a sick child ½ year Ca | 540 |
| To Tho. Hughes' acc't regulated | 200 |
| To Capt. John Scott's acc't | 290 |
| To Mr. Walker for keeping Fem'e Berass from ye parish | 100 |
| To Jno. Upshear for keeping a p'ish child 1 year | 1188 |
| To Tho. Wm's for keeping wid'w faulkner us. p | 1080 |
| To Peter Lespleete for keeping & burying El. Tomson | 200 |
| To Rich'd Harvey for service to ye Church | 114 |

| | |
|---|---|
| To Mr. Geo. Poindexter's acc't to 13 L., 12s 9d., at 10 p. c. | 2707 |
| To Do. Assignee of Rob't Napier | 200 |
| To Do. Assignee Eliz. King | 590 |
| To Do. Assignee of Wm. Gardiner | 300 |
| To Do. for Services Done | 145 |
| To C. C. to his acc'ts | 531 |
| To Mr. Tho. Massie for Liquor in giving ye procession | 16 |
| To Mr. Wm. Bassett for Services done | 170 |
| To Capt. Cloughan acc't fees | 970 |
| To Capt. Moss, Shr. acc't | 50 |
| To Capt. Littlepage, Shr. accts | 30 |
| | 30211 |

Built in y'r 1703 The Brick Church Cost Building above 146073 Lbs. of Tobo. as may be found by Examining ye accounts when ye Severall payments were made.

JAMES TAYLOR, Reader.

The agreement between Mr. Rich'd Squire and the Vestry of St. Peter's parrish ye 25th 8br. 1706.

Agreed that Mr. Rich'd Squire be paid four thousand pounds of Tob'o, C. C., viz.: two thousand pounds of Tob'o, C. C., to be paid at ye next Levy in 1707, & two thousand lbs. Tobo. more C. C., to be p'd at ye Laying of ye nevt Levy in 1708, for w'ch paym't to be duly made to ye S'd Mr. Squire, Do hereby acquit ye S'd parish forever from providing any glebe or Leasing any plantation for him During his time of being min'r, but if the S'd Mr. Squire Should die or leave the p'ish before the expiration of four years, then to refund to the S'd p'ish ye S'd Sume of four thousand pounds of Tobo. C. C., after ye proportion of one thousand lbs. of tobo, C. C., p ann'm to the true intent of this agreem't it yt Mr. Squire is only to refund proportionably according to his continuance.

Ordered that Wm. Norris be continued Clk of the Church & Vestry this ensuing year & yt he be p'd Eighteen hundred pounds of tob'o C. C., for his S'd Service.

Richard Squire, Thos. Butts, Wm. Clopton, John Parke, Jun'r, Thos. Massie, Wm. Waddill, Wm. Bassett.

Geo. Poindexter, Rich'd Allen, Chu'h Wardens.

Recorded by　　　　WM. NORRIS, Clk of the Vestry.

At a Vestry held for St. Peter's p'ish in New Kent Count, May ye 8, 1707.

PRESENT:

Mr. Jno. Forster, Mr. Geo. Poindexter, Mr. Will. Bassett, Mr. Jno. Parke Jun'r, Mr. Will Waddill, Mr. Tho. Massie.

Mr. Rich'd Allen, Chr. Warden.

Mr. Wm. Clopton is elected churchwarden to assist w'th Mr. Richard Allen this ensuing year, according to an order of Vestry, &c.

Whereas, Mr. Charles Fleming by an order of Court was appointed Surveyor for making rodes to his mill & to apply himself to ye vestry of St. Peter's p'ish for Assistance to make ye S'd rodes, the Vestry therefore, in p'sance to sd order, has appointed help for clearing ye said rodes, viz.: Capt. James Moss, Sam'll Jordan, William Norris, Tho. Ashcroft, Capt. Wyatt, Jr., Tho. Henderson, Jno. Ashburton, they and all their male tithables to assist in making ye S'd rodes.

Whereas, Jno. Hilton petitioned to ye vestry for being acquitted from paying ye parish Levy the S'd John Hilton's petition is granted according to ye order of Court to ye Same effect October 25th, 1707.

Ordered that James Austin, Peter Elmore & Elmore, David Bell & John Bacon, they & all * added to his former help David Claxton, appointed by an order of Court Surveyor for Clearing ye ridge rode & applying himself to this vestry for help it was accordingly granted or to Collo. Forster, Mr. Wm. Smith, Mr. * Jr., Mr. Jno. Butts, Mr. Jno. * & the Surveyors own hands they & all those male tithables to assist in Clearing ye ridge rode.

Whereas Tho. Minns complains that his allowance for keeping wid. Faulkner is too little, the vestry have ordered it increased for ye future 1100 lbs. tobo. C C & * * if she lives.

Thos. Ashcroft being allowed 600 lbs. tobo. C C according to agree'mt for keeping a bastard child a year * * S'd child die before time expire proportionable to ye time.

Whereas there is 5000 lbs. Tobo. C C Levyed for Mr. Geo. Poindexter in part of pay toward ye plate ornament sent for by him for the Church's use upon w'ch he is to advance but 50 per cent. & to allow 10 p ct. for ye tobo. so Levyed, its ordered to take the tobacco aforesaid out of ye Collector's hands this year & to Discount it when ye p'sh receive ye things so Sent for.

Thos. Butts, Geo. Poindexter, Thos. Massie, Jno. Forster, Wm. Waddill, Wm. Bassett.
Rich'd Allen, Wm. Clopton, Church wardens.
Registered. WM. NORRIS, Clk. Vest.

The agreement between Mr. Daniel Taylor, mins'r & the vestry of St. Peter's p'sh of 30th xbr., 1707.

Agreed that Mr. Taylor officiate as minister of this p'sh for three months, viz.: ye three first Wednesdays in Januery, February, & March & to be allowed 500 lbs. tob'o C. C. for each sermon he shall preach on those days, but if shall officiate after ye sd time of 3 mos. be expired then for each time so officiating to receive after ye rate of ye annuall Sallary of 16000.

Reg'r p WM. NORRIS, Clk. Vest.

---

At a Vestry held for St. Peter's Parish in New Kent County at the Brick Church February the 4th, 1707.

PRESENT:

Coll. Joseph Forster, Mr. George Poindexter, Mr. Jno. Parke, Jun'r, Capt. Jno. Forster, Capt. Jno. Scott, Mr. Tho. Massey, Mr. Wm. Bassett, Mr. Wm. Waddill.

Mr. Rich'd Allen, Mr. Wm. Clopton, Chu'r Wardens.

Ordered that James Taylor officiate as Reder and Clerk of the Vestry, and to be paid at the usal Rate Excepting Cask.

RICH'D ALLEN,
WM. CLOPTON, Church Wardens.

Jno. Forster, Thos. Massie, Jo. Forster, Wm. Bassett, Jno. Parke, Jun'r, Wm. Waddill, Jno. Scott, Geo. Poindexter.

Reg'd p JAMES TAYLOR, C. V.

---

At a Vestry held at the Brick Church of St. Peter's p'sh, in New Kent County, Feb'ry the 15th, 1707.

PRESENT:

Capt. John Forster, Mr. Jno. Parke, Jun'r, Mr. Wm. Bassett, Mr. Wm. Waddill, Mr. Geo. Poindexter.

Mr. Rich' Allen, Church Warden.

Ordered that Mr. Rich'd Allen, Church warden and Mr. Wm. Waddill Shall forthwith go Down to the President with a Complaint that the p'sh Church Doore were Shut up Against the Vestry & the Parishioners. Rich'd Allen, Ch. Ward.

Jno. Parke, Jun'r, John Scott, John Forster, Wm. Waddill, George Poindexter, Wm. Bassett.

Reg'd JAMES TAYLOR, Clk. Vest.

At a Vestry held for St. Peter's Parish at the p'sh Church in New Kent County March the 3rd, 1707-8.

PRESENT:

Capt. John Scott, Mr. Geo. Poindexter, Mr. Jno. Parke, Jun'r, Capt. John Forster, Mr. Wm. Bassett, Mr. Wm. Waddill; Mr. Richard Allen, Church Warden; Capt. Jno. Scott, one of Her Maj'ties Justices of the Peace for this County, Administered this day the oaths Appointed by Law to Coll. Joseph Forster one of the gentlemen of the Vestry of St. Peter's Parish.

Reg'd p JAMES TAYLOR, Clk. Vest.

Jno. Parke, Jun'r, Wm. Waddill, George Poindexter, Jno. Forster, Jno. Scott, Wm. Bassett.

Rich'd Allen, Ch'r Warden.

At a Vestry held at St. Peter's Parish Church in New Kent county April the 2nd, 1708.

PRESENT:

Coll. Joseph Forster, Mr. Tho. Butts, Mr. Wm. Waddill, Capt. Jno. Forster, Mr. Wm. Bassett, Mr. Tho. Massie,

Mr. Rich'd Allen, Mr. Wm. Clopton, Ch. Wardens.

Whereas Mr. Daniel Taylor hath Complyed with a former Agreem't made with their Vestry. It's further Agreed with the S'd Mr. Daniel Taylor to Continue Preaching once a fortnight. To begin on Sunday the Eighteenth Day of the Instant Aprill and So on. Are to be paid for his so preaching Proportionable to 16,000 lbs of Tobo. p Annum and Cask.

Mr. Jno. Parke, Jun'r, is Elected Church warden to Assist Mr. Wm. Clopton this Ensuing year as usual.

Tho. Massie, Rich'd Allen, Tho. Butts, Jno. Forster, Wm. Waddill, Jo. Forster, Will Bassett.

Wm. Clopton, Ch. Warden.

Reg'd by JAMES TAYLOR, Cl. Vestry.

At a Vestry held at St. Peter's Parish Church in the County of New Kent, May ye 19th, 1708.

VESTRY BOOK OF ST. PETER'S PARISH. 95

PRESENT:

Mr. Geo. Poindexter, Mr. Tho. Massie, Coll. Joseph Forster, Capt. John Scott, Mr. Tho. Butts, Mr. Wm. Waddill, Capt. Rich'd Littlepage, Capt. Jno. Forster, Mr. Wm. Bassett, Mr. Rich. Allen. Mr. Jno. Parke, Jun'r, Ch. warden.

Whereas, Mr. Sam'll Grey, min'r, at the Request of the vestry, has Preached A Sermon at St. Peter's Parish Church, And being unanimously Liked of, Wee the S'd vestry doe Agree with the S'd Mr. Sam'll Grey to Entertain him as our Min'r on the first Sunday after the Tenth of October next Ensuing upon the Same Terms which wee agreed with Mr. Rich. Squire.

Ordered That There be a vestry held at St. Peter's p'sh Church on Monday next, being ye 24th of this Instant. And Likewise ye Clerk is ordered to Give Notice on the next Sunday that there is a Dwelling house to be Built upon the Gleeb Land, And if any undertakers are Designed to undertake it, they are Desired to be at ye S'd vestry.

Jno. Parke, Jun'r, Ch. Warden.

Wm. Bassett, Wm. Waddill, Rich'd Allen, Rich'd Littlepage, Jno. Forster, Geo. Poindexter, Tho. Massie, Jo. Forster, Jno. Scott, Tho. Butts.

Reg'd p JAMES TAYLOR, Cl. V.

At a Vestry held at ye Schoolhouse at ye Brick Church for St. Peter's Parish in ye County of New Kent, May ye 24th, 1708.

PRESENT:

Coll. Jos. Forster, Mr. Tho. Butts, Mr. Wm. Bassett, Mr. Wm. Waddill, Capt. Jno. Scott, Mr. Geo. Poindexter, Mr. Rich'd Allen, Mr. Tho. Massie.

Mr. Wm. Clopton, Mr. Jno. Parke, Jun'r, Ch. wardens.

Whereas Mr. Sam'll Gray, Min'r, hath p a former Order of Vestry made an Agreem't with this Vestry to be Entertained as Min'r in October next ensuing. The S'd Mr. Gray appearing at this vestry. And Agreed with this vestry to Begin to Preach in our Parish on Sunday ye 13th of June next Ensuing.

Whereas, Capt. Rich. Littlepage hath Agreed with this vestry to Build upon ye Gleeb Land a Dwelling house whose Dimensions are as followeth, viz.: Thirty-six feet in length, eighteen feet wide. Eight feet cleer from ye uper part of ye Cell. to ye uper part of ye Plate, Two Inside Chimneys, A pair of Stairs to go up in ye Clossett in ye Hall & a Closset in ye Chambers all ye frame to be Sawn & framed such as ye new way of Building is.

The Hall to be fourteen feet & ye Chamber twelve feet, two Rooms above & a Closset in ye inner Room, above, the floors to be laid above & below with Plank & Wainscotted above & below with Plank w'th Doors & Mantelpieces & in ye Hall two Transom windows, in ye Chamber one Ditto. In ye Chamber above each one Dormer window, three lights & a light at each end of ye house above Stairs & a small light in ye Closset below. To be weather boarded w'th featheredge plank & a Gable ended & Covered w'th Plank & Shingles w'th Cypress Shingles ye Covering & weatherboards to be well Tarred. The Chimney to be close larthed & plastered w'th Lyme & hair. The Backs & hearths Brick and ye house underpinned with Brick & Cornished each Side under ye eves. And to find Nayles, Lathes, Catches, Hinges, Locks, Glass & Casements & to finish all workmanlike, Turn & Go by ye last day of October next ensuing. For ye w'ch Building of ye S'd house according to ye Dimension aforesaid, Wee ye s'd vestry do agree with ye Capt. Rich'd Littlepage to pay him Thirty-two thousand pounds of sweet sented Tobo., Caske & Convenience with Proviso ye S'd Capt. Rich'd Littlepage Enter into a Bond with the Supervisers to finish the house According to ye Dimensions afores'd by ye Last day of October next ensuing.

Mr. Geo. Poindexter & Mr. Wm. Waddill are elected & chosen Supervisers to see the Gleeb house built, according to ye Dimensions in ye above order. And also are Requested to take Bond of Capt. Rich'd Littlepage for ye Performance of ye above Agreement.

Wm. Bassett, Tho. Massie, Jno. Scott, Wm. Waddill, Sam Gray, Tho. Butts, Rich'd Allen, Jos. Forster, Geo. Poindexter. Wm. Clopton, Jno. Parke, Jun'r, Ch. wardens.

Reg'd p JAMES TAYLOR, Clk. Vest.

At a Vestry held at St. Peter's Parish Church, in New Kent County, Aug't 13th, 1708, &c.

VESTRY BOOK OF ST. PETER'S PARISH. 97

Whereas, Mr. Peter Massie being appointed Surveyor of the highways he Complaining to this vestry that the Assistance which he hath allowed is not sufficient to Clear the S'd Roade. It's therefore ordered that Mr. Tho. Massie's Male Tithables, Jno. Spheares, Edm. Harris & Charles Massie Give their Allowance in Clearing the S'd Surveyors Roads belonging to his Precincts.
Reg'd JAMES TAYLOR, C. V.

---

At a Vestry held at the Gleebs House in St. Peter's Parish in the County of New Kent, October ye 30th, 1708.

PRESENT:

Mr. Sam'l Gray, Min'r; Mr. Wm. Waddill, Coll. Joseph Foster, Capt. Jno. Scott, Mr. Thos. Butts, Mr. Geo. Poindexter, Capt. Rich'd Littlepage, Capt. Jno. Foster, Mr. Wm. Bassett, Mr. Rich'd Allen, Mr. Tho. Massie.
Mr. Jno. Parke, Jun'r, Ch. Ward.

St. Peter's Parish. Dr. L. Tobo.
To Mr. Sam'l Gray, Min'r, from ye 18th of June to ye last of 8br 23 Serm. .................................. 6461
To C C to Ditto ..................................... 0911
To Mr. Gray More p Agreement .................... 0500
To C C to Do....................................... 0070
To Mr. Dan. Taylor, Min'r, for 3 Sermons at 500 p Agreem't ........................................ 1500
To C C for Do. .................................... 0210
To Mr. Dan Taylor for 3 Sermons more Proportionable, &c 0922
To C C to Do ..................................... 0129
To James Taylor Read'r & Clerk of ye Vestry for 9 Mon 1350
To Conveniency to Do. ............................. 0035
To Jno. Hillon, Sexton, for one year ................ 0570
To Capt. Clough's Acct. Allowed .................... 0186
To Geo. Bradby ................................... 0300
To Wm. Gardner for keeping A B Child 13 Mon. ........ 1100
To C C to Do ..................................... 0154
To Tho. Mines for keeping ye Wid'w Faulkner 12 mon.. 1100
To C C to Do. .................................... 0154
To Sam'l Bugg Allowed for work done at the Gleeb Plantation ........................................ 0500

| | |
|---|---|
| To Rich. Crump, Acco. Allowed .................... | 0300 |
| To Mr. Rich. Alllin & Mr. Wm. Waddill, Allowed for Expences going to Town, Two Journeys, Each 100 p Journey ...... ..................................... | 0400 |
| To Mr. Rich. Allin for 3 Bottles of Wine ............. | 0090 |
| To Jno. Helton's Acco. Allowed ..................... | 0325 |
| | 17313 |
| To Capt. Littlepage's Acco. Allowed ................. | 00231 |
| To Capt. Littlepage for building the Gleb House as by Agreement p an Order of Vestry ................... | 32000 |
| To Ditto for an Addition to the House by Agreem't..... | 01200 |
| To C C to ye whole 332,000 of Tob'co................ | 04648 |
| To Geo. Poindexter Acco. Allowed ................... | 00440 |
| To Mr. Geo. Poindexter Acco. Allowed for Plate and Ornaments for ye Church ........................... | 14260 |
| To C C for 14700 pd of Tob'co...................... | 02058 |
| To Sallary of 72150 pd of Tob'co at 5 p cent.......... | 03617 |
| To Peter Warren's Acco. ........................... | 00040 |
| To Sallary for 3420 hds of Tob'co Cr at 5 p cent....... | 00171 |
| To Dar. Clark for going for ye Min'r ................ | 00200 |
| To Capt. Littlepage for Biulding a Stable upon the Glebe as p Agreem't by Mr. Gray ..................... | 00700 |
| To C C to Do. ..................................... | 00098 |
| To Sallary for 998 pds of Tob'co at 5 p cent ........... | 00049 |
| | 77025 |
| | 3420 |
| | 73605 |

| Com. Cr. L. Tob. | L. Tob. | 77025 |
|---|---|---|
| p Madam Levermore .......... | 1000 | |
| To C. C. to Do. .............. | 140 | |
| To Capt. James Morse......... | 1000 | |
| To C. C. to Do. .............. | 140 | |
| p Madam Squires ............ | 1000 | |
| To C. C. to Do. .............. | 140 | |
| | 3420 | |

p 551 Tythables at one hundred and thirty-three pounds
of Tob'co p poll .................................. 73283
To A Deposit to pay the Collector next year .......... 322
                                                    -----
                                                    73605

The Parish Levy being proportioned amount to one hundred Thirty three pound of Tobacco p Poll. Which sum of 133 pd of Tob'co Capt. Rich. Littlepage is Ordered to Collect and pay it to those for whom it is Levyed upon Proviso; the S'd Rich. Littlepage Enter into Bond with the Church wardens according to Custom.

Ordered that Mr. Samuel Gray, Min'r, be continued as by a former order of Vestry.

Ordered that James Taylor be Continued Clerk of the Church and Vestry for the Ensuing year. And to be paid as usual.

Ordered that Jno. Hilton be Continued Sexton, and to be paid as usual.

Ordered that Mr. Thomas Massie furnish the Widow Morriss with such necessaries as he Shall think fitt. And bring in his charge at the next Levy Laying. This Vestry doth Agree with Capt. Littlepage to pay him Tob'co C C at one peney the pound at the next fall, For what Lead and oyl he shall think fit to use about the Gleeb house.

S. Gray, Wm. Bassett, Rich. Allin, Jno. Scott, Geo. Poindexter, Wm. Waddill, Tho. Massie, Jo. Forster, Rich. Littlepage, Tho. Butts, Jno. Foster.

                    Registered p JAMES TAYLOR, Cl. Vest.

At a vestry held at the School house for St. Peter's Parish in ye County of New Kent March ye 9th, 1708-9.

Mr. Samuel Gray, Min'r; Coll. Jos. Foster, Capt. Jno. Scott, Mr. Rich. Allin, Mr. Wm. Waddill, Mr. Jno. Parke, Jun'r, Capt. Rich. Littlepage, Mr. Wm. Bassett, Mr. Thos. Massie, Mr. Wm. Clopton, Ch. Wardens.

Ordered that Mr. John Parke, Jun'r, Continue Church warden, And Mr. William Waddill is Elected Church warden to Assist him this ensuing year as usuall.

Whereas, John Hilton Petitioned to this Vestry for an Addition to his Sallary, This Vestry has Considered his Condition. And hath Added to his Sallary Three hundred pounds of Tobacco C C.

Capt. Rich'd Littlepage hath agreed with the vestry to Build upon the Glebe A Two and Thirty feet Tobacco house, Sixteen feet wide, And a twelve feet Square Milk house with Plank Shelves and Plank doors, And to find two Locks for the Doors, And to find Nayles and everything for the finishing of ye above s'd houses, Also to find two Locks for the Doors, And to make a Curb and Windless for the well, and a Shed over the Well, And to find Iron hooks and Hinges for the Doors, And to be paid for the S'd Building Two Thousand pounds of Tobo. C C And the work to be finished forthwith.

Whereas this Vestry has Considered the Great Charges which Mrs. Catherine Squires is like to be at in Repairing the house which was formerly Rented for Mr. Squires. They have ordered one Thousand pounds of Tob'co C C to be Levied at the Next laying of the Parish Levy Toward ye Repairs of the said house.

Sam Gray, Mr. Bassett, Rich'd Allin, Rich. Littlepage, Wm. Clopton, Tho. Massie, Jos. Foster, Jno. Scott.

Jno. Parke, Jun'r, Wm. Waddill, Ch. wardens.

Reg'd p JAMES TAYLOR, Cl. V.

At a Vestry held at the School house at ye Brick Church for St. Peter's Parish, in ye County of New Kent, Sept'r ye 30th, 1709.

Mr. Sam'l Gray, Min'r; Coll. Jos. Foster, Capt. Jno. Foster, Mr. Geo. Poindeter, Mr. Rich. Allin, Mr. Tho. Butts, Capt. Rich. Littlepage, Mr. Wm. Clopton, Mr. Wm. Bassett, Capt. Jno. Scott.

Mr. Jno. Parke, Jun'r, Mr. Wm. Waddill, Church wardens.

| St. Peter's Parish, Dr. | L. Tobo. |
|---|---|
| To Mr. Sam'l Gray, Min'r for 1 year ending ye 30th of October | 16000 |
| C C to Ditto | 02240 |
| To James Taylor, Reader for 1 year 01800. To Conveniency to Do. 00108 | 01908 |
| To Jno. Helton, Sexton for 1 year | 0570 |

| | |
|---|---|
| To Tho. Minnes for keeping ye wid'd Faulkener 12 months 1100 C C to Do 154 | 1254 |
| To Mad'm Squires p Order of Vestry 1000 lb C C | 1140 |
| To Capt Clough's Acct Allowed | 0156 |
| To Jno. Helton Added to his Sallery p Od'r of Vestry 300 L C C | 0342 |
| To James Sanders for helping A B child 12 mon. p Agreem't, 1000 L C C | 1140 |
| To Mr. Dan. Taylor Min'st Acco't Regulated—500, C C, to Do, | 0530 |
| To Capt Keelings Acc'o of sher: fees allowed | 0115 |
| To James Sanders allowed for Cloathes for A B. Child... | 0150 |
| To James Sanders Jr Agreem't wth ye Ch. Wardens for keeping Wm Gardner | 0600 |
| To C C. to Do | 0014 |
| To Mr. Wm Cloptons Acct' Ballanced | 0299 |
| To Mr. Grays acco Allowed, James Taylors acco Allowed, Convt to Do | 1093 |
| To Jno. Heltons Acc'o allowed for washing Surplace & Table Linnen | 0150 |
| & for Extraordinary Service & fetching ye plate | 0210 |
| To Jno. Howles Acco. Allowed | 0100 |
| To Jno. Hilton allowed for his Boy looking after ye Cattle. | 0050 |
| To Pelham Moore for a Well Bucket for ye Gleeb | 0050 |
| To Capt. Rich. Littlepage Acco. Allowed | 0914 |
| To Mr. Wm. Waddill for Building a Tobo. house & Milk house on ye Glebe, C C to Do | 2052 |
| To Mr. Wm. Waddill, Assinee of Cha. Waddill, Tho. Jackson Acco. Allowed | 0831 |
| To Capt. Thompson Acco. Allowed | 0136 |
| To Matt. Gardinar for Keeping 2 p'sh children 3 weeks.. | 0100 |
| To Wm. Martin for Keeping Daniel Mack Daniel | 0600 |
| To * Ragland for Keeping Rich. Coolam | 0300 |
| To Mr. Geo. Poindexter Acco. Allowed | 0320 |
| To James Taylor, Recording ye Odr for Processioning & their Return, Conv't to Do | 0636 |
| To Sallary for L-34120 of Tobo. at 5 p Cent. | 1706 |
| | 35826 |

p Con'tr                    Cr.
p Madam Levermore L-1000 C C....   1140
p Capt. Rich. Littlepage for ye Stocks  0340
p 597 Tythables at 57 L of Tobo. p
   Tythable ...... ................  34029
To a Dipositum to pay ye Collector
   next year ..................... 00317
                                   ─────
                                   35826

The Parish Levy being proportioned Amount to fifty seven pounds of Tobo. per Tythable, Besides a Fraction to pay the Collector ye next year of Three hundred and seventeen pounds of Tob'co, which sum of 57 Lbs of Tobo. Capt. Geo. Keeling, High Sheriff for this county, this present year is hereby Order'd to Collect and pay it to those for whom it is Levyed. The S'd Capt. Geo. Keeling Entering into Bond with ye Church Wardens as is usuall, &c., Wm. Bassett, Tho. Butts, Rich. Allin, Jno. Foster, Geo. Poindexter, Sam. Gray, Jo. Foster, Wm. Clopton, Rich. Littlepage, Jno. Scott.

Jno. Parke, Jun'r, Wm. Waddill, Chu. Wardens.

Whereas Capt. Rich. Littlepage at a vestry held for St. Peter's Parish at ye School house at ye Brick Church on May ye 24th, 1708, Did then and there Agree with ye S'd Vestry to Build upon ye Gleeb Land a Dwelling house according to ye Dimentions mentioned at Large in ye S'd order of that Vestry, for which Building ye S'd Capt. Richard Littlepage was to be paid Thirty two thousand pounds of Tobo. Cask & Conv't, as doth appear by ye s'd Order With Proviso ye s'd Capt. Rich. Littlepage did enter into Bond with ye Superadvisers to finish ye S'd house according to ye Dimentions in ye S'd Order, by ye last day of October last past, And ye S'd Capt. Rich. Littlepage having fully Rec'd ye Consideration for ye S'd building, It's thought fitt and accordingly ordered by the Vestry That Mr. Jno. Parke, Jun'r, & Mr. Wm. Waddill ye Present Church wardens shall view and Inspect ye s'd Building whether it be pformed & finished according to ye Tenor of ye s'd Agreement. But if not, that they Demand & Require ye S'd Capt. Rich. Littlepage fully to perform ye same. And if he refuseth, Then they are Impowered forthwith to Commence Suit against him for his Non-performance thereof & to act & do therein as they shall see fitt and Proper, which shall be Ratified & allowed by this Vestry.

Jno. Foster, Will. Bassett, Jo. Foster, Jno. Scott, Tho. Butts, Rich. Allin, Geo. Poindexter, Wm. Clopton.

Jno. Parke, Jun'r, Wm. Waddill, Chu. Wardens.

Registered p JAMES TAYLOR, Cl. Vest.

---

Sept. ye 30th, 1709, New Kent County, At a Vestry held at ye School house, near St. Peter's Parish Church Feb'y ye 9th, 1709.

PRESENT:

Coll. Jos. Foster, Capt. Jno. Scott, Capt. Jno. Foster, Mr. Thomas Butts, Mr. Geo. Poindexter, Mr. Wm. Bassett, Mr. Wm. Clopton, Mr. Rich. Alin, Mr. Tho. Massie (3 Sermons preached before this Agreem't).

Mr. Jno. Parke, Mr. Wm. Waddill, Church Wardens.

Whereas this Parish being Destitute of a Min'r by ye Death of Mr. Samuel Gray, late Deceas'd, Wee ye S'd Vestry do in behalf of ye S'd Parish Agree with Mr. Benjamin Goodwin, Min'r, To Officiate Till ye Eighth Day of January next Ensuing as our Min'r of St. Peter's Parish. Every other Saterday And every other Sunday in ye after noon, And to pay ye S'd Mr. Benj. Goodwin for his so officiating, According to Law, And then to become our Min'r Intire, And that Mr. Goodwin have forthwith Possession of ye Gleeb Given to him by the Church wardens.

Geo. Poindexter, Wm. Bassett, Benj. Goodwin, Rich. Alin, Wm. Clopton, Tho. Massie, Jo. Foster, Jno. Scott, Jno. Foster, Tho. Butts.

Jno. Parke, Wm. Waddill, Ch. Wardens.

Regist'd p JAMES TAYLOR, Cl. Vest.

---

New Kent County, At a Vestry held at ye Gleeb for St. Peter's Parish Apr. 11th, 1710.

PRESENT:

Mr. Benj. Goodwin, Clk., Capt. Rich. Littlepage, Capt. Jno. Scott, Mr. Geo. Poindexter, Mr. Wm. Clopton, Mr. Wm. Bassett, Mr. Rich. Alin, Mr. Thomas Massie.

Mr. Wm. Waddill, Ch. Warden.

Ordered that Mr. Wm. Waddill Continue Church warden for

ye Ensuing year, And Mr. Thomas Massie is Elected Church warden for this Ensuing year to assist Mr. Wm. Waddill as is usual.

Wm. Clopton, Rich. Alin, Rich. Littlepage, George Poindexter, Wm. Bassett, Benj. Goodwin, John Scott.

Wm. Waddill, Tho. Massie, Ch. wardens.

Regis'd p JAMES TAYLOR, Cl. Vest.

New Kent County. At a Vestry held at ye Schoolhouse for St. Peter's Parish May 14th, 1710.

PRESENT:

Coll. Joseph Forster, Capt. John Scott, Capt. Jno. Foster, Mr. Geo. Poindexter, Mr. Jno. Parke, Mr. Rich'd Alin, Mr. Wm. Clopton.

Mr. Wm. Waddill, Ch. Ward'n.

Whereas The Hon'ble Mr. President and Mr. Commissary, By Their Letters of Recommendations hath Recommended The Reverend Mr. William Brodie to this Parish as a Minister fully Qualified. Therefore, wee ye S'd Vestry Doe in behalf of ye S'd Parish, Covenant & agree with the S'd Mr. Wm. Brodie to Entertain him as our Minister till ye last day of December next. And to Pay him as the Law Direct.

Ordered that Mr. Goodwin's Letter Directed to Mr. President, which his Honour Sent to the Vestry, Be entered in ye Register Book. Wm. Brodie, Clerk.

Rich. Alin, Wm. Clopton, Jno. Parke, Jos. Foster, Jno. Scott, Jno. Foster, Geo. Poindexter.

Wm. Waddill, Ch. warden.

Mr. Goodwin Letter Ap'l ye 7th, 1710.

In Obedience to yo'r Hon'rs Command, I Doe Desist in my Claim of farther right to St. Peter's Parish N. K. I am S'r y'r Most obedient & Humble serv't. B. GOODWIN.

To ye Hon'ble Edmund Jennings, Esq'r, President of Virginia Vera Copia.

Reg'd p JAMES TAYLOR, Clk. Vest.

At a Vestry held at ye Schoolhouse at ye Brick Church for St. Peter's Parish in New Kent County, 9br ye 6th, 1710.

PRESENT:

Mr. Wm. Brodie, Min'r; Coll. Jos. Foster, Capt. Jno. Foster, Mr. Jno. Parke, Mr. Geo. Poindexter, Mr. Rich'd Allin, Mr. Tho. Butts, Mr. Wm. Clopton.
Mr. Wm. Waddill, Mr. Tho. Massie, Ch. Wardens.

St. Peter's Parish.    Dr. 1710.

| | |
|---|---|
| To Mr. Sam'l Gray, late Min'r, C. C. to Do. | 2692 |
| To Mr. Daniel Taylor, Min'r, an Error last year | 0040 |
| To Mr. Wm. Brodie, Min'r till ye last Day of December, Convenience to do. | 10458 |
| To James Taylor, Reader for one year, 1300 Conv't | 1908 |
| To Jno. Helton, 570 lbs. Tobo. & 300 C C added in all.. | 0912 |
| To Thos. Mims for keeping ye Wid. Faulkner & Burying her | 0655 |
| To Wm. Walker for keeping Ellen Gibbes & Burying her | 0300 |
| To Wm. Waddill, Ch. Warden, Ball. his Acco. | 0093 |
| To Mr. Wm. Clopton, Sen'r, his Acco. Allowed | 0150 |
| To ye Wid'w Millington for Rent for Wm. Gardner.... | 0220 |
| To Mr. Jno. Parke, Assignee of Matt. Gardner | 0570 |
| To Mr. Geo. Poindexter, Assignee of Do. | 0570 |
| To Matt'w Gardner, Ballance of Acct. | 0942 |
| To Mr. Wm. Waddill for keeping Dan'l Mack Daniel 15 Days | 0514 |
| To Mr. Geo. Poindexter acct allowed C C added | 0937 |
| To Evan Raglin for keeping Rich. Coolam 1 year | 1000 |
| To Mr. Wm. Clopton, Jun'r, his Acct. Allowed | 0633 |
| To James Taylor, dec't Acct. Allowed Conv't | 0316 |
| To Jno. Helton's Acct. Allowed Conv't | 0423 |
| To Jno. Helton for Keeping Ruth Harvey 3 mon. Conv. | 0265 |
| To Jno. Helton's Boy for looking after ye hors's | 0050 |
| To James Alford's Acct Allowed for keeping a p'sh Child | 0420 |
| To Sallary of 24233 pound of Tobo. at 5 per Cent | 1214 |
| To Ball. Due to ye Parish next year from ye Collecter.. | 0023 |
| | 25530 |

P. Cont. Cr.

p 555 Tythables at 46 lb. Tob. p Poll is............... 25530

We ye Vestry of this Parish having this Day meet Do find the Parish Debts to amount to fourty Six pound of Tob'co p Tythable Excepting 23 L of Tob'co ye Collecter is to be Accountable for to ye Vestry next year. The which Sum of 46 lbs. of Tobacco, Coll. Jos. Foster high Sheriff is hereby ordered to Collect from Every Tythable Person in this Parish, and in Case of non payment to make * according to Law & pay it to those for whom it is Levyed. He ye S'd Coll'l Foster Entering into Bond with the Church wardens as is usual.

Ordered That Mr. Wm. Brodie, Clk., Continue Min'r of this Parish & to be paid as ye Law directs.

Ordered that the Church wardens forthwith give Mr. Wm. Brodie, Min'r, Possession of ye Gleeb.

Ordered that James Taylor Continue Reader & Clerk of the Vestry and to be paid as usual.

Wm. Brodie, Clk.; Jos. Foster, Tho. Butts, Jno. Foster, Geo. Poindexter, Wm. Clopton, Rich. Allin, Jno. Parke.

Wm. Waddill, Tho. Massie, Ch. Wardens.

Registered p JAMES TAYLOR, Cl. Vest.

At a Vestry held at ye Brick Church for St. Peter's Parish April ye 22nd, 1711.

PRESENT:

Mr. Wm. Brodie, Min'r; Capt. Jno. Scott, Capt. Jno. Foster, Mr. Tho. Butts, Mr. Wm. Bassett, Mr. Geo. Poindexter, Mr. Wm. Clopton, Mr. Rich. Allin, Mr. Jno. Parke.

Mr. Wm. Waddill, Ch. warden.

Ordered that Mr. Thomas Massie Continue Church warden for the Ensuing year, And Capt. Jno. Foster is Elected Church warden for ye Ensuing year in stead of Mr. Wm. Waddill.

Geo. Poindexter, Wm. Clopton, Rich. Allin, Jno. Parke, Wm. Waddill, Will Brodie, J. Scott, Tho. Butts, Wm. Bassett.

Jno. Foster, Church warden.

At a Vestry held for St. Peter's Parish at ye Brick Church July ye 30th, 1711.

Mr. Wm. Clopton, Mr. Wm. Bassett, Mr. Rich'd Allin, Mr. Jno. Parke, Mr. Wm. Waddill, Mr. Tho. Massie, Capt. John Foster, Chu. Wardens.

Charles Winfry being Appointed Surveyor of ye High Ways from ye upper Side of Capt. Richard Littlepage's mill to ye lower Side of Stone's Swamp Bridges. He applying himself to this vestry for help, It is ordered That Mr. John Major Male Tythable, Rich'd Austin, Sam'l Smith, Mr. Jno. Mens, Tithables, Give there Attendance on ye S'd Surveyor or when Required.

Thomas Jackson being Appointed Serveyor of ye highway in Capt. Jno. Scott's Precincts. He applying himself to this vestry for Assistance, It is ordered that Madam Lightfoot, Mr. Sherwood Lightfoot, Wm. Jackson & James Taylor, Tythables, Give their Attendance on ye S'd Serveyor when Required.

Wm. Bassett, Wm. Clopton, Wm. Waddill, Jno. Parke, Rich'd Allin.

Tho. Massie, Jno. Foster, Chu. Wardens.

At a Vestry held for St. Peter's Parish at ye Schoolhouse near ye Brick Church, 8br 15th, 1711.

PRESENT:

Coll. Jos. Foster, Mr. Geo. Poindexted, Mr. Tho. Butts, Mr. Wm. Waddill.

Mr. Thomas Massie, Capt. Jno. Foster, Church Wardens.

| St. Peter's Parish. | Dr. | L Tob'co. |
|---|---|---|
| To Mr. Wm. Brodie, Min'r, for 12 Months Conv't to Do. | | 16960 |
| To James Taylor, Reader & Clerk for 1 year, Conv't to Do | | 1908 |
| To Jno. Helton, Sexton 70 Lb Tob. & 300 Lb. Tob. Added C C. | | 0870 |
| To C C to 300 L. Tob. | | 0042 |
| To Thomas Moss for Keeping Rich. Colam 1 year | | 1000 |
| To ye Widow Millington for 1 year's Rent ending ye 25th of March | | 0200 |
| To Capt. Jno. Scott, part of his Account allowed, Conv't to Do. | | 0343 |
| To Mad'm Clough omitted last year | | 0060 |
| To ye Wid'w Hawle for Keeping & Tending on Mary Wild 10 month ending ye last October C C to Do. | | 4332 |
| To Alex. Strange for Keeping Mary Wild 10 days | | 0106 |
| To Martha Gardner for 1 year p Agreement C C to Do.. | | 1140 |
| To Martha Gardner, omitted last year | | 0200 |

| | |
|---|---:|
| To Coll. Foster, Acct. Allowed | 0249 |
| To James Taylor, part of his Acct. | 0096 |
| To Mr. Tho. Massie, Chu. Warden, his Acct. | 0140 |
| To Wm. Walker for Keeping Elinor Dene 1 Month | 0100 |
| To Mr. Poindexter, Accomp allowed | 0923 |
| To John Helton, for Acct. allowed | 590 |
| To Jno. Helton for Keeping Ruth Harvey 1 year | 1000 |
| To Sallary of 30764 L. Tobo. at p cent. | 1533 |
| | 32302 |

| P. Cont. | Cr. |
|---|---:|
| p Jno. Askew | 0615 |
| p A fraction from ye Collector last year | 0028 |
| p 573 Tythables at 55 L Tob. per poll | 31515 |
| p A fraction Due to ye Collector next year | 0144 |
| | 32302 |

Wee ye Vestry of St. Peter's Parish have this day mett & do find ye Parish Debt amount to Thirty two thousand, three hundred & two pounds of Tob'co, which being divided by five hundred, seventy three Tythables ye Number in our Parish this year amounts to fifty five pounds of Tob'co p poll besides a fraction, to pay ye Collecter next year at One hundred fourty & four pounds of Tob'co, Which Sum of 55 L of Tob'co Collect'r Jos. Foster, high Sher., is ordered to Collect from Tythable persons in this p'sh & in Case of non payment to make Distress. Provided ye S'd Coll'r Jos. Foster, enter into Bond w'th ye Church wardens to pay ye same to whom it is Levyed according to their Claim.

Ordered that ye Church wardens Agree with Some Doctor to Cure Mary Wilde of her Ailement, & if she think herself able to undergo a Course of Phisic, The Church wardens are to agree w'th ye Doctor for ye same.

Jos. Foster, Geo. Poindexter, Wm. Waddill, Tho. Butts, Wm. Clopton.

Tho. Massie, Jno. Foster, Chu. Wardens.

VESTRY BOOK OF ST. PETER'S PARISH. 109

At a Vestry held for St. Peter's Parish at the Dwelling house of James Taylor, Clerk of ye Vestry, March ye 31st, 1712.

PRESENT:

Capt. John Foster, Mr. Wm. Clopton, Mr. Rich'd Allin, Mr. Geo. Poindexter, Coll. Joseph Foster, Mr. Jno. Parke, Mr. Wm. Bassett.
Capt. Jno. Foster, Mr. Tho. Massie, Church Wardens.

Wee the Vestry of St. Peter's Parish, having this day met to Take in and Receive Such Returns as shall be Return'd with ye Order for Processioning according to Law And find that Capt. Rich'd Littlepage, Mr. Thomas Butts, Tho. Mitchell, Alex'r Strange, Jno. Aldridge, & Jno. Brothers, have not yet Returned their orders for Processioning.

Tho. Massie, John Foster, Chu. wardens.
Jos. Foster, Jno. Scott, Geo. Poindexter, Wm. Clopton, Rich'd Allin, Jno. Parke, Wm. Bassett.

Registered p JAMES TAYLOR, Cl. Vest.

---

At a Vestry held at the Brick Church for St. Peter's Parish May 18th, 1712.

PRESENT:

Mr. Wm. Brodie, Min'r; Coll. Joseph Foster, Capt. Jno. Scott, Mr. Wm. Bassett, Mr. Geo. Poindexter, Mr. Wm. Clopton, Mr. Jno. Parke, Mr. Rich. Allin, Mr. Wm. Waddill.
Mr. Jno. Foster, Mr. Tho. Massie, Church Wardens.

Ordered that Capt. Jno. Foster Continue Church Warden for the ensuing year. And Mr. Thomas Butts is Church Warden in ye stead of Mr. Tho. Massie. Wm. Brodie, Clk.

Jo. Foster, John Scott, Will Bassett, Geo. Poindexter, Wm. Clopton, John Parke, Rich. Allin, Wm. Waddill, Tho. Massie. John Foster, Church Warden.

Registered p JAMES TAYLOR, Cl. Vest.

---

At a Vestry held at the Brick Church for St. Peter's Parish, 8br 23rd, 1714.

PRESENT:

Mr. Wm. Brodie, Min'r; Coll. Jos. Foster, Capt. Jno. Scott. Mr. Wm. Bassett, Mr. Wm. Clopton, Mr. Geo. Poindexter, Mr. Rich. Allin, Mr. Wm. Waddill, Mr. Tho. Massie.

## VESTRY BOOK OF ST. PETER'S PARISH.

Mr. Tho. Butts, Church Warden.

| St. Peter's Parish, Dr. | Lbs. Tob'co. |
|---|---|
| To Mr. Wm. Brodie, Min'r, for 12 Months | 16000 |
| To C C to Ditto. The Cask being allowed in Consideration there is no Gleeb house | 2240 |
| To James Taylor, Reader & Clerk for 12 Mon. Con'vt to Do. | 1908 |
| To Jno. Helton, Sexton, 570 L Tob'co & 300 C C added | 0870 |
| To the Widow Millinton for 1 year's Rent Wm. Gardner | 0200 |
| To Mr. Atkison for Expenses at Town L4, G5, d8, at 1 peney p L, C C to Do | 1160 |
| To Jno. Helton C C to 300 L Tob'co | 0042 |
| To Tho. Moss for Keeping Rich. Colam 1 year & finding Clothes | 1200 |
| To C C to 200 L Tob'co p Agreem't | 0028 |
| To Jno. Helton for Keeping Rich. Harvey 1 year & Clothes | 1200 |
| To C C to 200 L Tob'co p Agreem't | 0028 |
| To Mr. Jno. Thornton Acct Allowed | 0382 |
| To Jos. Baughn, &c. | 0025 |
| To Capt. Jno. Scott for Keeping Mary Wild | 4057 |
| To Capt. Littlepage for Maj'r Holloway C C, C to Do 112 | 0912 |
| To Coll. Jos. Foster for Delinq't | 0402 |
| To Mr. Geo. Poindexter for Mat. Gardner | 1294 |
| To C C to Do. | 0181 |
| To Rich. Brookes for Keeping Mary Wild | 0400 |
| To Col. Foster for Sher. fees | 0380 |
| To Nath'l Brothers for Keeping Margaret Watkins' Child | 0750 |
| To Capt. Foster, allowed for wine furn'shing ye same | 0102 |
| To Wm. Timson for Keeping Mat. Gardner | 0200 |
| To Mr. Tho. Massie's acct. | 0626 |
| To Jno. Helton's Acct. Allowed | 0480 |
| To James Taylor for Tending at Wm'burgh, &c. | 0500 |
| To Cha. Waddill ye same | 0500 |
| To Mr. Benj. Goodwine, Judgment | 4900 |
| To C C Convt. to Do The Cask overcharged to be paid ye p'sh next year past | 0686 |
| To Mr. Wm. Waddill for Carting Mat. Gardner | 0050 |

To Coll. Foster allowed for going to Wm'burgh 200 Capt.
Littlepage the same .................................. 0400
To Sallary of 41559 L Tob'co at 5 p Cent.............. 2177
To A fraction Due to ye Parish from ye Collecter....... 0040

44320

Wee the Vestry of St. Peter's Parish, having this day mett and Do find the Parish Debts amount to Fourty four Thousand Three hundred and Twenty pounds of Tobacco, Which S'd Sum being Divided by 576 Tythables Amount to 76 L per Tithable only a fraction Due to ye Parish next year from ye Collector of 40 L of Tob'co, The Which Sum of Tobacco Mr. Thomas Butts, Church warden, is hereby impowered to receive of every Tithable person in St. Peter's Parish and pay the same to those Persons which it is Levyed for, And if in case of non payment to make Distress according to Law.

Robert Wood appeared at this Vestry and agreed with ye S'd Vestry to keep Martha Gardner one year at ye Rate of 150 l of Tob'co p Month, and to keep Wm. Gardner at 75 L. of Tob'co p mon. And to keep Mary Wild at 150 L. Tob'co p month.

Richard Ross appeared at this Vestry and agreed to keep Richard Harvey one whole year for 500 pounds of Tob'co.

Mr. Wm. Waddill agreed to keep Richard Collam one Whole year for 600 pounds of Tob'co.

Wm. Brodie, Clk.; Wm. Bassett, Rich. Allin, Wm. Waddill, Tho. Massie, Jos. Foster, Jno. Scott, Wm. Clopton, Geo. Poindexter.

Registered p JAMES TAYLOR, Clk.

At a Vestry held for St. Peter's Parish, at ye Brick Church April ye 19th, 1713.

Mr. Wm. Brodie, Min'r; Capt. Jno. Scott, Mr. Geo. Poindexter, Mr. Wm. Clopton, Mr. Jno. Parke, Mr. Rich. Allin, Mr. Wm. Waddill, Mr. Tho. Massie.

Capt. Jno. Foster, Chu. Warden.

Ordered that Mr. Thomas Butts Continue Church Warden for the ensuing year, And Coll. Joseph Foster is Elected Church Warden for ye ensuing year in Capt. Jno. Foster's Place.

Test: p JAMES TAYLOR, Clk. Vest.

At a Vestry held for St. Peter's Parish at ye Dwelling House of James Taylor, May ye 4th, 1713.

PRESENT:

Mr. Wm. Brodie, Min'r; Capt. Rich. Littlepage, Mr. Wm. Clopton, Mr. Rich. Allin, Mr. Tho. Massie, Capt. Jno. Scott, Mr. Geo. Poindexter, Mr. Wm. Bassett, Mr. Wm. Waddill. Mr. Tho. Butts, Coll. Jos. Foster, Chu. Wardens.

Ordered that ye Clerk give Public Notice Two Severall Sundays at the Church; That There is a Gleeb house to be Built with Brick and all undertakers are desired to appear at the vestry on Wednesday in Whitson week To undertake ye Building.

Ordered that Mr. Rich'd Allin shall be paid five hundred Pounds of Tob'co for keeping Mary Holt one whole year.

Tho. Butts, Jo. Foster, Chur. Wardens.
Tho. Massie, Wm. Waddill, Wm. Clopton, Rich. Allin, Wm. Bassett, Rich'd Littlepage, Jno. Scott, Geo. Poindexter.

---

At a Vestry held for St. Peter's Parish at the Dwelling house of James Taylor on May ye 27th, 1713.

PRESENT:

Mr. Wm. Brodie, Min'r; Capt. Ric'd Littlepage, Capt. Jno. Scott, Mr. Geo. Poindexter, Mr. Wm. Clopton, Mr. Rich. Allin, Mr. Wm. Waddill.

Mr. Tho. Butts, Chu. Warden.

Persuant To an Order of Vestry Baring Date the 4th of this Instant May, appointing all undertakers to appear at a Vestry to be held for St. Peter's Parish on the Wednesday in Whitson week to undertake the Building and finishing of a Gleeb House whose Dementions are as followeth, viz.: Fourty two feet in Length, Twenty feet wide, A Seller Three Feet in the Ground and three feet above, nine feet Pitch from floor to floor, The Hall to be Eighteen feet Long, The Chamber to be fourteen feet in Length, A Chemney at each end five feet Deep, The Stairs to go up in ye Hall by ye Chemney & a Light at ye Gable end & a Clossett by the Chemney in ye Chamber. In the Clossett, under the Stairs a way into the Seller and at the other end under ye Clossett a way into ye seller out of Doors, two Windows in ye Seller, Two Outward Doors in ye Hall & two Transem Windows, and in ye Chamber one outward Door & one Transum Window, and a Window in each Clossett. The Wall to be two Brick thick to the Water Table & then a Brick & half, The outward Room above Stairs fourteen feet, The Inward Room Eighteen feet and a Chemney & a Clossett in ye Inward Room above. Two Three light Dorman Windows in each Room above Stairs, And to be Lathed & Plaistered above Stairs & Plaistered below Stairs, A Good Grit Roof Covered with Sawn Larths & Shingled & well Tarred and each floor to be Rabbitted & Good Steeps at each outward Door & a Brick Petition between the two Lower Rooms from ye foundation to ye second floor, And ye Cornish Doors & Window frames & Mantle Pieces & Door frames to be Primed with Lincett oyl & Spanish Brown, hinges, Glass, Locks, Keys & finish all workmanlike, Turn Key and Go. Mr. Thomas Jackson appeared at this Vestry and Agreed with ye Sd Vestry to Build the above s'd house according to ye s'd Dementions for fourty nine Thousand five hundred pounds of good, sound, sweet scented Tob'co & Cask and Conveniency and to be paid unto ye S'd Tho. Jackson or Order one half of ye s'd 49500 L. of Tob'co C C the next fall, and the other half to be paid in the year 1714. The S'd Gleeb house to be finished according to ye S'd Dementions by ye Tenth Day of October in ye year 1714. Mr. Thomas Jackson to Inter into Bond with ye Church wardens with good & Sufficient Security to Perform such Articles as ye s'd Vestry or Church wardens shall think fit to Draw, And ye s'd Tho. Jackson to gett all ye frame sawn & Brick made & Burnt this fall & to get all Plank & other Timber Sawn by the Tenth day of October next ensuing the Date of the Order.

Wm. Clopton, Rich'd Allin, Wm. Waddill, Wm. Brodie, Rich'd Littlepage, John Scott, George Poindexter.

At a Vestry held for St. Peter's Parish, at the Dwelling house of James Taylor, November ye 16th, 1713.

Mr. Wm. Brodie, Min'r; Capt. Rich'd Littlepage, Capt. Jno. Scott, Capt. Jno. Foster, Mr. Wm. Bassett, Mr. Wm. Clopton, Mr. Geo. Poindexter, Mr. Rich'd Allin, Mr. Jno. Parke, Mr. Tho. Massie, Mr. Wm. Waddill.

Mr. Tho. Butts, Coll. Jos. Foster, Church Wardens.

St. Peter's Parish, Dr. L Tobo.

| | |
|---|---:|
| To Mr. Wm. Brodie, Min'r, C C to Do. 2240 | 18240 |
| To James Taylor, Reader, &c., 1800 Conv'y 108 | 1908 |
| To Jno. Helton, 870 C C to 300, is 42 | 0912 |
| To Thos. Jackson to lie in ye Church warden's hands CC | 24750 |
| To C C to Ditto | 3465 |
| To James Taylor's Acct. | 0715 |
| To Capt. Jno. Thornton's Acct. | 0110 |
| To Capt. Jno. Foster's Acct. | 0095 |
| To Mr. Tho. Butt's Acct. | 0991 |
| To Wm. Jackson's Acct. | 0130 |
| To Mr. Geo. Poindexter p Mr. Butt's note | 0100 |
| To Mr. Wm. Waddill Ball. | 0505 |
| To Capt. Littlepage acct. 212 C C added 29 | 0241 |
| To James Sanders for keeping Wm. Gardener 2 mo. & ½ | 0250 |
| To Rich'd Ross Ball. | 0185 |
| To Natt'l Brothers for keeping A. B. Child 11 mon. | 1100 |
| To Mrs. Alford for Keeping Mary Delign & her Child 4 mon. | 0400 |
| To Wm. Major for writing a Bond | 0050 |
| To Jno. Helton's Acct. | 0460 |
| To Mr. Jno. Meas for 1 Gall. Wine | 0100 |
| To Mr. Rich'd Allin for 6 mon. Keeping Mary Holt | 0250 |
| To James Taylor, &c. | 0300 |
| To Sett. Walker for Keeping Collam 1 mon. | 0060 |
| To Sallary of 54241 L Tob'co at 6 p cent | 2712 |
| | 58029 |

P. Cont. Cr.

| | |
|---|---:|
| p James Alford's Bill | 350 |
| p A fraction due to ye p'sh last year | 40 |
| Mr. Butts for C C Levy last year to Mr. Goodwin's Tob'co | 686 |
| p 587 Tythables at 97 L pTythable | 56939 |
| p A fraction Due to ye Collector next year | 14 |
| | 58029 |

Wee the Vestry of St. Peter's Parish having this Day meet and do find that ye Parish Debts do amount to Fifty six thousand nine hundred, fifty & Three pounds of Tobacco, which ye Sum of 56953 L of Tob'co being Divided Between 587, The Number of Tithables this year Amount to Ninety Seven pounds of Tob'co p Tythables, Besides a fraction of 14 L of Tob'o Due to ye Collector next year. The which Sum of 97 lbs. of Tobo. Mr. Tho. Butts, Church warden, is Hereby Impowered to Collect from every Tithable Person in St. Peter's Parish, And pay it to those Persons according to there Severall Claims, And in case of non-payment, to make distress according to Law.

Selvanus Walker appeared at this Vestry and Agreed w'th the s'd Vestry to Keep Rich'd Coollam one whole year for seven Hundred pounds of Tobacco.

John Helton appeared at this Vestry and Agreed to Keep Rich'd Harvey one year for 900 pound of Tobacco.

Mr. Wm. Waddill Agreed with this Vestry to keep Wm. Gardner one year for 1000 pounds of Tobacco.

By the Motion of Capt. Jno. Foster, In behalf of John Bacon Serveyor of ye highways, It is Ordered That Mr. Jno. Parke and Anthony Waddys Tythables be added to his Precinct.

W. Brodie. John Scott, John Foster, Rich. Allin, Geo. Poindexter, Rich'd Littlepage, Will. Bassett, Wm. Clopton, Tho. Massie, Wm. Waddill, Jno. Parke.

Registered p JAMES TAYLOR, Cl. Vest.

At a Vestry held for St. Peter's Parish, at ye House of James Taylor, May ye 14th, 1714.

PRESENT:

Wm. Brodie, Min'r; Capt. Rich'd Littlepage, Capt. Jno. Scott, Mr. Geo. Poindexter, Mr. Rich'd Allin, Mr. Jno. Foster, Mr. Wm. Waddill.

Mr. Tho. Butts, Coll. Jos. Foster, Ch. Wardens.

Ordered, That Coll. Jos. Foster Continue Church warden for the ensuing year and Capt. Rich'd Littlepage is elected Church warden in ye stead of Mr. Tho. Butts.

Ordered that there be a Vestry held at ye Gleeb house on Munday next, ye 17th Day of this Instant. And ye Gentlemen are Desired to meet there by Ten of ye Clock in ye afternoon.

Likewise It's Ordered That Capt. Littlepage and Mr. Geo. Poindexter be Supervisers to see ye work well Done.
Jno. Parke, Wm. Brodie, Clk.; Tho. Butts, Rich'd Allin, John Scott, Wm. Waddill, Geo. Poindexter.
Jos. Foster, Rich'd Littlepage, Ch. Wardens.

At a Vestry held for St. Peter's Parish December ye 7th, 1714. Mr. Wm. Brodie, Min'r; Capt. Jno. Scott, Mr. Wm. Clopton, Mr. Jno. Parke, Mr. Tho. Butts, Mr. Rich'd Allin, Mr. Wm. Waddill.
Coll. Jos. Foster, Capt. Rich'd Littlepage, Ch. Wardens.

St. Peter's Parish,    Dr.      L Tobo.

| | |
|---|---:|
| To Wm. Brodie, Min'r, for 12 months, Cask to Ditto, at 42½ p Cent. | 16720 |
| To James Taylor, Reader for 12 months & Cask | 1872 |
| To Jno. Helton, &c. | 0894 |
| To James Sanders for Keeping Wm. Gardner & Cask | 1417 |
| To Mr. Tho. Jackson, Cask to Do at 4 & ½ p Cent. 1110. | 25869 |
| To Mrs. Alford for Keeping Mary Design & Child, &c. | 1400 |
| To Robt. Wood for Keeping Mary Wild five & forty days, &c. | 0375 |
| To Capt. James Massie for Acct. Allowed | 0583 |
| To Ame'a Morgan to lie in ye Church warden's hands till she brings Testimony from a Justice that her acc. is Just | 0233 |
| To Sett. Walker for Keeping Rich'd Collam 12 months | 0700 |
| To Jno. Helton's acct. | 0415 |
| To Ditto for Keeping Rich'd Harvey 1 year | 0900 |
| To Nath. Brothers for Keeping Anne Watkins | 0950 |
| To Mr. Tho. Jackson Allowed for a Double Door | 0100 |
| To Capt. Littlepage's Acc. Allowed | 1111 |
| To Mr. Menx for 2 Gall. Wine | 0200 |
| To ye Church warden 4 days to Settle & Receive ye Agent's Notes | 0800 |
| To lie in Mr. Brodie's hands Toward Cloathing ye poor, Cask to Do. at 4½ p cent. | 1045 |
| | 55584 |

VESTRY BOOK OF ST. PETER'S PARISH. 117

P Conta.  Cr.
p 603 Tithables at 92 L of Tobo. p Tithable............ 55476
p A fraction Due to ye Church wardens next year........ 108
                                                      _____
                                                      55584

The Parish Levy being proportioned, wee find ye Parish Debts to amount to 55584 lb. of Tobo., which being divided by 603 ye number of Tithables this year amounts to 92 lbs. of Tobo. p Tithable, besides a fraction of 108 lb. of Tobo. to pay ye Chu. Wardens next year. And ye Church wardens are ordered to Collect ye s'd sum of 92 lb. of Tobo. from each Tithable in St. Peter's p'sh, And if in Case of non payment to make Distress. And ye Chu. Wardens are to enter into Bond with ye S'd vestry according to Law.

Whereas, Mr. Tho. Jackson Did agree with this Vestry to Build a Brick house on ye Gleeb Land as p a former order of Vestry. The S'd vestry having this Day met at ye Gleeb house. And find ye s'd Gleeb house to be fr'nished according to Agreement. And having this Day Take Possession of ye s'd House and Delivered ye Key to Mr. Wm. Brodie, Min'r, And have ordered That Mr. Tho. Jackson's Bond be Delivered to him, so that he may be Discharged from ye afores'd Agreement.

At ye motion of Mr. Charles Fleming, perveyor of ye highway to this Vestry, It is ordered that ye Tithables of Esq'r Lewis at Will's Quarter, Jno. Turner, Thomas Bassett and Wm. Greens Tithables shall be added to his Precincts to assist ye said Charles Fleming in Clearing ye s'd Road and making Bridges when thereunto Required.

Whereas, Mr. Thomas Jackson assumed to this Vestry That he would, with James Henderson, Enter into Bond with ye Church Wardens to Keep ye Parish Endemnified and Clear from all manner of Charge which may accrue by Reason of James Henderson, Jun'r, Coming into St. Peter's Parish, & from this time forever.

Wm. Brodie, Jno. Scott, Tho. Butts, Jno. Parke, Rich'd Allin, Wm. Clopton, Wm. Waddill.

Jos. Foster, Rich'd Littlepage, Chu. Wardens.

Registered p JAMES TAYLOR, Cl. Vest.

At a Vestry held at James Taylor's Dwelling House for St. Peter's Parish, April ye 27th, 1715.

PRESENT:

Mr. Wm. Brodie, Min'r; Col. Jos. Foster, Ch. Warden; Capt. Jno. Scott, Capt. Jno. Foster, Mr. Rich'd Allin, Mr. Wm. Clopton, Mr. Wm. Waddill.

Ordered that Capt. Rich'd Littlepage Continue Church warden for ye ensuing year and Capt. Jno. Scott is Appointed Church warden in stead of Coll. Jos. Foster for ye next ensuing year.

Ordered that Jno. Hitchcock Take Wm. Gardiner into his Care from this Day And to find him in Sufficient Diet for ye ensuing year, for which this Vestry doth agree w'th ye S'd Hitchcock to pay him six hundred pounds of Tobacco, Provided James Sanders will not keep him for ye same.

Ordered that Jno. Guilam shall Keep Rich'd Collam for five hundred pounds of Tobacco one year, Provided Sell. Walker will not keep him for ye same.

William Vaughn appeared at this Vestry and agreed to Keep Rich'd Harvey one year for four hundred & fifty pounds of Tobacco. Provided Jno. Helton will not keep him for ye same.

Richard Brooker appeared at this Vestry and Agreed to Keep Mary Design for one year for Three hundred pounds of Tob'co, Provided Mrs. Alford do not Keep her for ye same.

Wm. Brodie, Jas. Foster, Jno. Foster, Wm. Clopton, Rich'd Allin, Wm. Waddill.

Jno. Scott, Ch. Warden.

Registered p JAMES TAYLOR, Cl. Vest.

At a Vestry held at ye Gleeb house for St. Peter's Parish November ye 21st, 1715.

PRESENT:

Mr. Wm. Brodie, Min'r; Coll. Jos. Foster, Mr. Geo. Poindexter, Mr. Wm. Clopton, Mr. Tho. Butts, Mr. Rich'd Allin, Mr. Tho. Massie, Mr. Wm. Waddill.

Capt. Rich'd Littlepage, Capt. Jno. Scott, Ch. Wardens.

St. Peter's Parish,         Dr.                       L Tob'co.
To Mr. Wm. Brodie, Min'r, for 12 Mon. and Cask.... 16720
To James Taylor, Read'r and Clark for 12 Mon. ...... 01872

VESTRY BOOK OF ST. PETER'S PARISH.    119

To Jno. Helton, Sexton, &c. .......................... 00894
To Sett. Walker for keeping Richard Collam ..........00496½
To Tho. Martin for keeping Alex'r Johnson's Child ...... 00100
To Mr. Tho. Butt's Acct. Allowed .................... 01093
To Capt. Jno. Scott's Acct. Allowed................... 01795
To Jno. Helton's part of his 2 acct. .................. 00285
To Tho. Winfield's act. .............................. 00160
To Mr. Jno. Thornton, part of his acct. for 2 years ...... 00120
To Richard Brook's acct. ............................ 00050
To Tho. Jackson allowed ............................ 00300
To Mrs. Alford for keeping Mary Design ............. 00688
To Jno. Helton for Keeping Richard Harvey ......... 00700
To James Smith for Keeping Elis. Osling ............. 00725
To Capt. Littlepage's acct. .......................... 00475
To Edward Osling part of his acct. ................... 00292
To Jno. Guilam for Keeping Elis. Johnson's Child ...... 00250
To James Sanders for Keeping Wm. Gardners to this day 00731
To James Taylor's acct. ............................. 00322
To Wm. Clopton, Jun'r, Acct. Allowed .............. 00539
To Coll. Foster, Acct. 4 Delinqu't Step. Crump * Ld... 00368
To Cha. Waddill for Wm. Timpson ................... 00072
To ye Church Wardens for 4 days Settling at 200, &c.... 00800
To Mr. Brodie, &c. .................................. 00200
To Wm. Jackson for Keeping A B Child 3 weeks...... 00075
                                                    ─────
                                                    30122½

  P Cont.   Cr.
p 584 Tythables at 51 lb. tobo. p poll ................. 29784
p A fraction to pay ye Ch. Wardens next year..........00338½
                                                    ─────
                                                    30122½

At a Vestry held at James Taylor's house for St. Peter's Parish, November ye 18th, 1717.

PRESENT:

Coll. Jos. Foster, Mr. Wm. Bassett, Mr. Rich'd Allin, Mr. Jno. Parke, Mr. Tho. Butts, Mr. Wm. Clopton, Mr. Tho. Massie, Mr. Wm. Waddill.
Capt. John Scott, Church Warden.

St. Peter's Parish,    Dr.                    L Tobo.
To Mr. Wm. Brodie for 12 months, Conveniency to Do..  16960
To James Taylor for 12 mon. Conveniency to Do. 108...  1908
To John Helton for all offices & Keeping Harvey 1 year,
  500 .......  .......................................  1400
To Tho. Winkfield for Keeping Geo. Ross ............  210
To Mr. G. Lightfoot for Keeping Wm. Gardner........  770
To Mr. Wm. Waddill for Keeping Collam..............  117
To James Smith for Keeping Elisabeth Johnson........  860
To Mr. Thornton's acct. ...........................  060
To Mr. Rich'd Allin for Keeping Mary Holt 10 mon.....  300
To Tho. Moore for making ye Parishioners, &c.......  050
To Tho. Jackson for Clerk's fees, &c................  210
To Jos. Boughon for Expences when marking ye parsture  50
To Mr. John Parker for Keeping Wm. Mallett..........  400
To Capt. Scott's Account, 136—James Taylor's acct., 250  386
To Mr. Geo. Poindexter's acct. allowed ..............  337
To Tho. Winkfield for Geo. Ross funerall, &c..........  150
To Jno. Alford for Mary Design, &c. .................  300
To Jno. Alford for Carrying away Robb. Barber ........  600
To Rich'd Brookes for Keeping Jery White ...........  245
To Edw'd Ossling for Keeping Do. .................  225
To Samuel Ossling for 1 Barrell·Corn ...............  125
To Mr. Wm. Clopton, Jun'r, allowed ................  204
To Sam'el Bugg for Keeping Edm'd Bedford 45 days,
  Coll. Foster's Ball. 60 ............................  360
To Anne Major for Keeping Jno. Cooke's child ........  170
To Wm. Waddill for burying Collam, &c., Capt. Little-
  page's acct. allowed, 645 .......................  915
To Mr. Tho. Butts Levy V p Clear at 97 ct., Ditto for Jno.
  Fennell's 2 Levy, 194 ...........................  582
To Ditto for Wm. Green 2 Levy, 194, Capt. Scott for
  Upshear, 53 ....................................  247
To Sallary of 28141 lb. of Tobo. at 5 p cent. ...........  1407
To Ballance from ye Collector next year ..............  153
                                                    ———
                                                    29701
       P. Cont.            Cr.
P the Collector Ballance last year, 56; p 605 Tythables at
  49 lb. Tobo. p Poll. ............................  29701

## VESTRY BOOK OF ST. PETER'S PARISH.

Wee, the Vestry of St. Peter's Parish, having this Day mett and find the Parish Levy amount to forty nine pounds of Tobacco p poll Besides a fraction of 183 lb. of Tob'co, The Collector is to be accountable to ye Parish next year. The which sum of 49 lb. of Tobo. Capt. John Scott is hereby ordered and Impowered to Receive from every Tythable Person in St. Peter's Parish. And if in Case of non-payment to make Distress according to Law.

|  | Lbs. Tobo. |
|---|---|
| John Helton for Keeping Rich'd Harvey 12 months.... | 500 |
| James * for Keep Elisabeth Johnson 12 mon., 550; Edw'd Ossling Keep Jeremiah White 12 mos. ............. | 1000 |
| Sam'el Bugg Keep Edm'd Bedford 12 mon. ............ | 900 |
| Capt. Scott to sallavate Lydiate Parker & Discharge her from the Parish this year........................ | 1000 |
| John Spear Keep Jno. Cooke's Child 12 months........ | 500 |
|  | 3900 |

Wm. Clopton, Tho. Massie, Wm. Waddill, Jos. Foster, Wm. Bassett, Jno. Parke, Rich'd Allin, Tho. Butts.

At a Vestry held for St. Peter's Parish at the Brick Church ye 11th Day of June, 1718.

Mr. Wm. Clopton, Mr. Wm. Bassett, Mr. Jno. Parke, Mr. Rich'd Allin, Mr. Wm. Waddill.

Capt. John Scott, Mr. George Poindexter, Chu. Wardens.

Mr. Richard Allin and Mr. Wm. Clopton are Elected and Chosen Church Wardens Instead of Capt. John Scott and Mr. George Poindexter.

Mr. Ebenezer Adams is Elected a Vestryman instead of Capt. Rich'd Littlepage, Dec'd, And the Clerk is Ordered to Give him Notice, That he may appear at the Next Vestry To take the oaths of a Vestryman Enjoyned by Law, And allso to Sign the Test, &c.

Ordered, That the Church Wardens are Impowered to Repair ye Church Pales; And also to Repair the Church Where there is a Necessity, &c.

George Poindexter, Will Bassett, John Scott, Wm. Waddill. John Parke.

Rich'd A. Allin, Wm. Clopton, Church Wardens.

Registered p JAMES TAYLOR, Cl. Vest.

## 122  VESTRY BOOK OF ST. PETER'S PARISH.

At a Vestry held for St. Peter's Parish at the Brick Church September ye 29th, 1718.

PRESENT:

Mr. Wm. Brodie, Min'r; Coll. Joseph Foster, Capt. John Foster, Capt. John Scott, Mr. John Parke, Mr. George Poindexter. Mr. Thomas Massie, Mr. Wm. Waddill, Mr. Ebenz. Adams added.

Mr. Rich'd Allin, Mr. Wm. Clopton, Chur. Wardens.

| St. Peter's Parish, | Dr. | L Tobo. |
|---|---|---|
| To Mr. Wm. Brodie, Min'r, 16000, Conv'e to Do., 960.... | | 16960 |
| To James Taylor, 1800 Conv'y, 108 ................. | | 1908 |
| To John Helton acct. Ditto for Rich'd Harvey 6 months and Burying him, & Extraordinary Trouble ........ | | 1400 |
| To Mr. Littlepage's acct, 228200 C C 28 Do. C C for 645 lb. omitted last year .............................. | | 1318 |
| To Mr. Thomas Massie Acct. Allowed, 55 Elizabeth Wicker for keeping George Baizey ................. | | 0605 |
| To Elis. Harris for Keeping Elis. Watkins to this Day.... | | 0400 |
| To Capt. Jno. Scott, Acct. Ballanced 1441½, James Smith for Keeping Elis. Johnson ..................... | | 1691½ |
| To Edw'd Ossling for Jeremy White, 6 mon., 250 Samuel Bug for Edm'd Bedford, 1 year ................... | | 1150 |
| To John Spear for Jno. Cookes 1 year ................ | | 0500 |
| To Mr. Wm. Clopton for Charles Harper's funeral 420 &c., Mrs. Thornton's acct. ....................... | | 0480 |
| To Robt. Clopton for 47 feet of plank 47, Wm. Jackson's Acct. Allowed .................................. | | 0504 |
| To Mr. Geo. Poindexter's Acc. C. C. added 1026, Edm'd Moore, 15 ....................................... | | 1041 |
| To Sallary of 269 lbs. & 70s Tob. at 5 p ct. A fraction due from ye Coll. & cler. next year, 178 ............... | | 1525 |
| | | 28482 |

P Cont'a.  Cr.

p 609 Tythables at 47 pounds of Tobo. p Poll .....28482

The Parish Levy being Proportioned amount to fourty seven pounds of Tobacco p poll (Except a fraction due from ye Collector next year of 178 lbs. of Tobo.), The which sume of 47 lb. of Tobo. The Church Wardens are Ordered to Collect from

Every Tythable in this Parish and pay to those persons for whom it is Levyd. Provided ye Church Wardens Enter into Bond with the Vestry as usuall.

Capt'n John Scott Administered the Oaths of A Vestryman to Mr. Ebenezer Adams this Day, who also Signed the Test, Who is added to the Vestry.

Ordered, that Mr. Thomas Butts and Mr. Wm. Waddill are Desired to Divide ye Tythables in Each of ye Lower Precincts Between Thomas Jackson and James Alford, Serveyre of ye Highways.

Ordered that Mr. William Waddill Keep James Raymond till the next Vestry.

Will Brodie, Clk.; Jos. Foster, George Poindexter, John Foster, John Parke, Wm. Waddill, Tho. Massie, Eben. Adams. Richard Allin, W. Clopton, Chu. Wardens.

Registered p JAMES TAYLOR, Clk. Vest.

---

December ye 17—1718.

Mem'm: This Day Elisabeth Wicker Agreed with these Gentlemen of the Vestry, viz.:

Mr. Richard Allin, Mr. Wm. Clopton, Church Wardens, and Mr. Wm. Waddill and Mr. Eben. Adams to keep George Baisey for five hundred pounds of Tobo. one year, &c.

Wm. Sanders to have Jno. Cooke's Child bound to him and to be paid four hundred pounds of Tobo. next fall.

Samuel Bugg to Keep Edmund Bedford Proportional to Nine hundred pounds of Tobacco p year, &c.

James Smith to Keep Elisabeth Ossling Proportionable to six hundred pounds of Tobo. one year, &c.

Mr. Allin Keep Mary Holt for one year at Three hundred pounds of Tobo. and so proportionable, &c.

Charles Waddill to Keep James Raymond and to bring in his Charge at the Next Levy Laying, And this Vestry to allow him what is Reasonable, &c.

Test p JAMES TAYLOR, Clk. Vest.

---

At a Vestry held for St. Peter's Parish at ye Brick Church 7br ye 29th, 1179.

PRESENT:

Coll. Joseph Foster, Mr. Wm. Bassett, Mr. John Parke, Capt.

124        VESTRY BOOK OF ST. PETER'S PARISH.

John Scott, Mr. Thomas Butts, Mr. Wm. Waddill, Mr. Eben Adams.
   Mr. Richard Allin, Mr. William Clopton, Chu. Wardens.

|  | St. Peter's Parish, Dr. | L Tobo. |
|---|---|---|
| To Mr. Wm. Brodie, Min'r, for 12 months, Conveniency to Do., 960 | | 16960 |
| To James Taylor for Reader, &c., for 12 mon. Conv'cy to Do., 108 | | 1908 |
| To John Helton for 12 mon., 900—Mr. John Thornton, 100 | | 1000 |
| To William Sanders for Keeping Jno. Cooke's Child | | 0400 |
| To Elis. Wicker for Keeping Geo. Baisey 12 mon., Ending ye 18th of 9bo | | 0500 |
| To James Smith for Keeping Elis. Atkinson, &c. | | 0625 |
| To Mr. Rich'd Allin for Keeping Mary Holt, &c., Elisabeth Clarkson, 62 | | 0362 |
| To Mad'm Littlepage 518 Conv'y, 31, Cha. Waddill for James Raymond, 150 | | 0699 |
| To Thomas Weaver for Jane Price, Walter Clopton, &c., 275--Elizabeth Harris, 458 | | 0964 |
| To Mr. Merriwether, Conv'y added 155, Mr. Thomas Massie acct. Do., 238 | | 0393 |
| To Sam'el Bugg for Dinah Bedford, 150, Sam'el Smith for Do., 150 | | 0300 |
| To William Bourn for Wm. Druman 250, John Helton 30, James Taylor 157½ | | 0437½ |
| To Ly. in the Church Warden's hands C C 1000, C C to Do., 140 | | 1140 |
| To Sallary of 26588½ pounds of Tobo. at 5 p ct., A fraction Due to the Parish, &c., 131 | | 1460 |
| | | 28149 |

        P Conta.        Cr.

p Mrs. Sarah Poindexter's Bill 500, 643 Tythables at 43 lbs. of Tobo. p Poll .................... 28149

   The Parish Levy being this Day Proportioned, And wee find the Parish Levy Do amount to 43 pounds of Tobacco for Each Tithable Person in St. Peter's Parish, Except a fraction Due from the Church Wardens of 131 pounds of Tobo. to be accounted for next year. The which sum of 43 pounds of Tobo. the Church Wardens are hereby Impowered to Receive from Every Tithable, And pay it to those Persons, which it is Levyed for: Provided the Church Wardens Enter into Bond with the Vestry as usuall.

Ordered that Walter Clopton Deliver unto Mr. Rich'd Allin and Mr. William Clopton, Church wardens, The Servant man's mare, which come out of Esex County, And that the Said Church wardens Detain ye s'd Mare untill Such time as ye owners of her make Satisfaction unto ye Parish for the Sum of Two hundred and Seventy five pounds of Tobacco, Which was allowed ye S'd Walter Clopton by the Vestry for Burying and other Charges of Thomas Burdenwin, or Else to pay Cash for the S'd 275 pounds of Tobo. at 20 Shillings p Hundred.

Ordered That the Clark Draw out an Order and Publish it Three Several Sundays in the Church, To Give Notice to all Persons which Live in St. Peter's Parish, That they shall not entertain any person that is a Jobber or a Traviler in his or her house above Eight and fourty hours without giving notice thereof, unto the Church Wardens upon pain of Inflicting Such Penalties as the Law injoyns against Such Persons, &c., as shall Entertain any such.

Whereas, Mr. Eben. Adams has Applyed himself to this Vestry, &c., that his Gang which is allowed him in his precinct is too small, that they are not able to clear the Roads and Repair the Bridges in his precincts. It is ordered that Thomas Massie and William Massie, Tithables, shall be added to his former Gang.

Ordered that ye Widow Amos is to go along with Mr. Thomas Massie and he to provide some person to take Care of her for the Ensuing year, and to allow them 300 pounds of Tobacco ye year.

Ordered that Madam Littlepage's Tithables at Touze hill be added to Stephen Mitchell's Precinct, to Clear the Roads and Repair the Bridges when thereunto Called by the S'd Stephen Mitchell, Serveyer.

Whereas, Capt. John Scott has made an offer To take all the Poor People of this Parish: It is ordered That he shall Receive all the poor people which shall be sent him by the Church Wardens, And to provide for them all such Necessaries as Shall be

Convenient (Except Apparrell) As the Church Wardens and he can agree.

Ordered that the Clerk give Notice that there will be A Vestry held at this Church on the 18th Day of November next, And that there is a Brick Wall to be made Round the said Brick Church. Therefore all Persons that are minded to undertake the said work are Desired to appear at the s'd Vestry.

Jos. Foster, John Scott, Will Bassett, Wm. Waddill, Tho. Massie, John Parke, Eben Adams, Tho. Butts.

Richard A. Allin, William Clopton, Church Wardens.

Registered p JAMES TAYLOR, Clk. Vest.

---

At a Vestry held for St. Peter's Parish at the House of James Taylor, November ye 18th, 1719.

Mr. Wm. Brodie, Min'r; Mr. Richard Allin, Mr. William Clopton, Chu. Wardens; Coll. Joseph Foster, Mr. George Poindexter, Mr. John Parke, Mr. William Waddill, Mr. Tho. Massie, Mr. Eben'r Adams.

Elisabeth Wicker hath this Day Agreed with this Vestry to keep George Baisy to the 18th Day of November next for four hundred and fifty pounds of Tobacco.

James Smith have this Day Agreed with this Vestry to Keep Edward Bedford and Elisabeth Johnson for the ensuing year, And to be paid for Each of them six hundred pounds of Sweet Scented Tobacco, and if in case of Mortality to be paid in Proportion.

Jarvis Austin, At his Motion to this Vestry, is appointed Sexton of this Parish instead of John Helton, and to be Paid five hundred Pounds of Tobacco p'r Annum for all Officers belonging to the Church. And Likewise he is to be allowed half a Crown for Digging of a Grave, &c., And John Helton is ordered to Deliver him the Key of the Church. Capt. John Foster added.

Whereas There is a Brick wall to be Built about the Brick Church, whose Dimentions are as followeth, Viz.: One hundred feet square, To be fourteen Inches thick, four feet & a half above Ground, And four feet and half high in the Lowest Place, all Levell, And the Bricks Laid upon a Good foundation with a handsom Coopin Brick upon the Top And Genteely Rompt at each side of the Gates. The Bricks to be according to the Statute something Less than Nine Inches in Length, two Wide Handsom Gates made after the form of Iron Gates w'th Handsom Square Peares (or Posts) for the Gates, with a hollow Spire, a Top and Good Hinges for the two Gates, with Hasps, Bolts and Locks as Good as can be got and in fashion, and to allow 16 bushels of Lime to a Thousand Bricks. The s'd wall to be in all Respects as well Done as the Capitol wall in Williamsburgh. And the Church to be repaired with Shingles wherever there is any wanting, And to Lay two Course of Shingles on each side to enclose the Rough, And to make a pair of New Doors and Door Cases at the West End of the Church.

James Skilton appeared at this Vestry and Agreed with the s'd Vestry to Build the within mentioned Brick wall according to the within Dementions. And to Do the other work mentioned in Repairing the Church, &c., for which Brick woll & other work The Vestry Doe agree to pay unto ye s'd James Skelton at the next fall Twenty Six Thousand pounds of Sweet Scented Tobacco, and Cask, Provided the s'd James Skilton Enter into Bond with Security with the Church warden for the true Performance of the above agreement & that the S'd Brick Wall and other work may be finished by the Last day of August next.

Whereas, Madam Francis Littlepage hath out of her Generous Inclination offered to this Parish a Bell, Wee the s'd Vestry, in behalf of ye Parish Doe Desire the Reverend Mr. William Brodie to Return her Thanks for her kind and Generous offer.

---

At a Vestry held for St. Peter's parish at ye Brick Church April 29th, 1720.

PRESENT:

Coll. Foster, Maj'r Scott, Mr. Massie, Wm. Waddill Mr. Poindexter, Mr. Adams, Capt. Foster, Mr. Allen, Mr. Park, Mr. Clopton. Mr. Tho. Sharp, Min'r.

Whereas, this parish of St. Peter's being destitute of a minister by ye Death of ye Late Rev'd Mr. Wm. Brodie, Deceas'd, & Mr. Thomas Sharp (now minister) of St. Paul's parish has offered himself to Supply ye Said parish of St. Peter's (as minister) in ye room of ye late Rev'd Mr. Wm. Brodie. We ye Church wardens & vestry of this parish are willing to accept & Entertain ye Said Mr. Thomas Sharp to preach on Every other Friday for 3 months & to be paid in proportion for that time and afterwards to Continue Entirely our minister & to be paid yearly as ye Law directs.

Registered p CHA. GORE, Clk. V.

At a Vestry held at ye Glebe house on Monday ye 11th day of July for ye Parish of St. Peter's, in ye County of New Kent.

PRESENT:

Maj'r Scott, Mr. Geo. Poindexter, Mr. Rich'd Allen, Capt. Massie, Mr. Wm. Waddill.

Mr. Wm. Clopton, Mr. Eben'r Adams, Church wardens.

Ordered, that Mr. Geo. Poindexter do put 2 Substantial posts on each side of ye Cellar door of ye Glebe house, and to make a new door on ye outside flush with a Shed over it, which is to be Shingled, also to find a bolt for ye Inside of ye Cellar Door and a new Lock for one of ye doors of ye house, and to nail Clap boards on ye windows round about ye house, and to be paid for ye same three hundred pounds of Tobacco.

Regis'd p CHA. GORE, Clk. V.

At a Vestry held at St. Peter's Church, in New Kent County, Octo'r ye 20th, 1720.

PRESENT:

Maj. Scott, Capt. Tho. Massie, Mr. Jno. Parke, Mr. George Poindexter, Mr. Tho. Butts, Mr. Wm. Waddill, Mr. Rich'd Allen.

Mr. Wm. Clopton, Mr. Eben'r Adams, Church wardens.

Mr. Bromscale agr'd with this vestry Septem'r 29 to preach on every other Wednesday & to be paid for every sermon at ye usual rate of 16000 lb. of Tobo p an'm.

Order'd yt Edw'd Moore be allow'd 400 lb. of Tobacco p ann. for keeping Wm. Drummond.

Order'd yt John Hilton be allow'd 400 lb. of Tobacco p ann.

Order'd yt Benj. Wicker be allow'd 350 lb. of Tobacco p ann. for keeping Geo. Baisey.

St. Peter's Parish,     Dr.

To Mr. Wm. Brodie, Minist'r for 6 months & 16 days,
    Conveniency to Ditto, 516 .......................... 9116
To James Taylor for 4 months, Conveniency to Do. 36..   636

| | |
|---|---|
| To Maj'r Thornton, Clk fees. 184, Ed. Moore on acct. Sarah Poindexter | 234 |
| To Ind. Doran on acct. Ditto 40. ye Exec. Tho. Sharpe, Conveniency to Ditto | 2160 |
| To Cha. Gore for 8 months, Conveniency to Do., 72 Rich'd Crump, 100 Wm. Clopton, 73 | 1445 |
| To Tho. Weaver for Serving a War't, 10; James Smith for keeping Ed. Bedford & Eliz. Johnson & Charges in making Clothes | 1145 |
| To Benj. Wicker for keeping Geo. Baisey 392, Mad'm Littlepage's acct. for ye Church use 365 | 757 |
| To Jarvis Austin, Ditto for Cleaning ye Church yard 50 | 520 |
| To Mr. Skelton for building ye Church wall & Cask | 26580 |
| To Eliz. Weaver on acc. of Sarah Poindex'r, Ed. Moore for Sumoning Eliz. Weaver, 10 | 189 |
| To Tho. Moore for ye burial of Jam'e Durfey 150, Ditto for piloting & procession'g ye p'sh Line 50 | 200 |
| To Mr. Poindexter for repairing ye Glebe house 300, Sallary of 43282 lbs. of Tobo at 5 p ct | 2164 |
| | 45446 |

The Parish Levy being this day proportioned we find yt it amounts to 45446 lbs. Tobacco, being 76 of Tobacco p poll f'·· 593 tithable persons in St. Peter's parish, besides a fraction of 163 lb. Tobo., which ye Collector is acomptable for which Said Quantity of Tobo. ye Church wardens are hereby Impower'd to Receive from every tithable person & to pay it to those persons for whom it is Levy'd, provided the Church Wardens enter into bond with ye Vestry as usual.

Registered p CHARLES GORE, Clk. Vest.

| Contra. | Cr. | lb Tobo. |
|---|---|---|
| p 593 Tithables at 76 lb. of Tobacco p poll, with a fraction of 163 lb. Due from the Collector | | 45446 |

At a Vestry held at St. Peter's Church, in New Kent, May ye 10th, 1721.

PRESENT:

Mr. Zacharias Brooke, Minis'r; Coll. Foster, Maj'r Jno. Scott,

Capt. Tho. Massie, Mr. Rich'd Allen, Mr. Tho. Butts, Mr. Geo. Poindexter, Mr. Jno. Parke, Mr. Jno. Foster, Mr. Wm. Clopton, Sen'r.

Mr. Ebenezer Adams, Mr. Wm. Waddill, Church wardens.

Whereas ye Rever'd Mr. Zacharias Brooke has offer'd himself to supply this parish as Minister, we ye Church wardens & vestry, in behalf of ourselves & ye parish with ye Houn'ble ye Governour's approbation are willing to accept & Entertain ye S'd Reverend Mr. Brooke, as our Minister & do agree to pay him ye yearly Sallary as ye law directs.

Ordered yt Mr. Wm. Waddill be Church warden in ye room of Mr. Wm. Clopton, Sen'r.

Order'd yt ye Widdow Morris be allow'd after ye rate of Six hundred pounds of Tobacco p ann: for keeping of Rebecca Spurlock. Recorded p Chas. Gore, Clk. Vest.

June 10th, 1721.

Ordered yt Ed. Nash be allow'd 500 lbs. Tobo. to keep Francis Ellis * till ye age of eighteen years.

---

At a Vestry held for St. Peter's, at St. Peter's Church, September ye 29th, 1721.

PRESENT:

Maj'r Scott, Capt. Massie, Rich'd Allen, Mr. Geo. Poindexter, Mr. Wm. Waddill, Sen'r.

Mr. Ebenez'r Adams, Mr. Will'm Waddill, Church wardens.

St. Peter's Parish,                     Dr.

To Mr. Bromscale for 4 Sermons, Conveniency to Ditto, 258½ .... ....................................4570½
To Mr. Brooke for 6 months, it being due Novem'r 10 next, C to Ditto ................................. 8480
To Charles Gore for 12 months & C to Ditto ........... 1908
To Jarvis Austin, Sexton, for 12 months, 500; Mr. Rich'd Allen for keeping a bastard child till of age .......... 1600
To Ed. Nash for keeping a parish Child till its 18 yrs old   500
To Maj. Jno. Thornton's acct. 458; James Smith for keeping Ed. Bedford & Eliz. Johnson .................. 1658
To Ed. Moore for keeping Wm. Drummond, 400; Ditto for a Delinq't of ye Widdow Jackson, 76½.......... 476½

To Ditto for Quit rents for ye Glebe Land, 1720 & 1721,
72; Benj. Wicker for keeping Geo. Baisey .......... 467
To Jno. Hilton to be p'd to ye Church wardens, 400;
Richard Crump for work, 100 & 300 ft. of inch plank 950
To Madam Field for keeping ye Widdow Amess 9 mon... 300
To ye Widow Morriss for keeping Rebecca Spurlock,
280; Mr. Mems for keeping a child of from ye parish 780
To Mr. Wm. Clopton, Sen'r, his ballance, 90; Mr. Wm.
Waddill, Sen'r, for tarring ye Church & wall ...... 590
To Tobacco lying in ye Church warden's hands, 700;
Capt. Massie for Sending ye widow Amiss to Dover.. 800
To James Alford for an Overlist, 76; Wm. Waddill, Jun'r,
for going to Mr. Bromscale ....................... 101
To Madam Littlepage's Acct., 1568; To Sallary of 23903
lbs. Tobacco at 5 p cent. ........................ 2764

25945½

p Fines due to ye parish ........................... 736

p 655 Tithables at 38½ lb. p poll, 25209½ ............25209½

The Parish levy being this day proportioned, we find it to be 38 lbs. of Tobo. p poll for each tithable person in this parish, there being 655 which said Tobacco ye Church wardens are hereby Impower'd to receive from every tithable person & to pay it to those for whom it is levyed, provided ye Church wardens enter into bond with ye vestry as usual.

Ordered yt Jno. Guillam be allow'd 800 lbs. Tobacco for keeping Eliz. Johnson 1 year.

Ordered yt Samuel Bugg be allow'd 700 lb. Tobo. for keeping Edw'd Bedford one year.

Ordered yt Wm. Waddill, Jun'r, be allow'd 450 lb. Tobacco for keeping George Baisey one year.

Ordered yt Mr. Meux be allow'd 500 lb. Tobacco for keeping a bastard child & taking it of ye parish, which said Tobacco was levy'd for him in the last levy.

Order'd yt Mr. Sherw'd Lightfoot be allowed 500 lbs. Tobacco for keeping a Molatta Child & taking it of ye parish.

Order'd yt Cha. Gore be clerk of ye church & vestry for ye ensuing year & to be paid as usual.

Order'd yt Jarvis Austin be Sexton for the ensuing year & to be paid as usual.

---

At a Vestry held at the Parish Church of St. Peter's, in the County of New Kent, on Wednesday the 10th of Jan'ey, 1721-2.

Order'd that Charles Noden be Clerk of the Church and Vestry and to be paid as Usual and Entered the 10th Day of Dec'r.

Ordered by the Church Wardens and Vestry of the parish of St. Peter's that they, with the Consent of the Governour, do receive Mr. Francis Fontaine as Minister of the aforesaid parish.

Eben. Adams, Wm. Waddill, Jo. Foster, George Poindexter, John Parke, Thos. Massie, Rich'd A. Allen, Wm. Clopton.

---

At a Vestry held at Major Scott's on Friday the 26th of Jan'ey, 1721-2.

Ordered that the Clerk do give Notice to Capt. Charles Lewis to attend at the next Vestry in Order to take the usual Oath, Being Elected in the Room of Capt'n Foster.

Ordered that there be Notice given that there will be a Vestry on Thursday ye 15th of Feb'ry, 1721-2, at the Brick Church where those persons that are willing to Undertake to build a Substantial Bellfry at the West End of the Church are desired to appear and make their proposals to the said Vestry and if at that time, there be not a sufficient Vestry, It is Ordered yt ye Church Wardens be Impowered to agree w'th the said Workmen. Ordered that the Rev'd Mr. Forbess have 1000 lb. of Tobacco for the two Sermons that He has preach'd at the Parish Church of St. Peter's.

Ordered that the Church Wardens and Vestry do in the Behalf of the parish ac. * the Rev'd Mr. Forbess if he should come to preach any more that * willing to Entertain him his Voice being so Low that the * * people cannot Edifie.

John Scott, George Poindexter, Wm. Clopton, Rich'd Allen, John Parke.

Ordered that * * * feet have 800 lb. of Tobacco for keeping a Molatto child of ye parish.

---

At a Vestry held at the Brick Church in St. Peter's Parish June * 1721-2.

Ordered that Mr. Jno. Parke be Church Warden in the Room of Mr. Adams being present.
Wm. Waddill, Jno. Parke, Chu. Wardens.
Jo. Forster, Ebenezer Adams, John Scott, Wm. Clopton, Richard Allen.

At a Vestry held at the Parish Church of St. Peter's on the Second day of September, 1722.
Whereas the Reverend Mr. Henry Collings has offered himself to Supply this parish as Minister, We the Church Wardens and Vestry, in behalf of ourselves and the parish, with the Hon'ble the Governour's Approbation are willing to accept & entertain the said Reverend Mr. Henry Collings as our Minister, and do agree to pay him the yearly Sallary as the Law directs.
John Scott, Tho. Massie, Rich'd Allen, Eben. Adams, Wm. Waddill.
Wm. Waddill, John Parke, Church Wardens.

At a Vestry held for St. Peter's parish on Saturday the 29th of Sep'tr, 1722.
Ordered that Marg't Guillam have 600 lb. of Tobacco for keeping Rebecca Spurlock.
Ordered that Eliz. Scruggs have 600 lb. of Tobacco for keeping Mary Amoss.
Ordered that Edward Oslin have 350 lb. of Tobacco for keeping George Baizey.
Ordered that Jno. Guillam have 800 lb. of Tobo. for keeping Eliz. Johnson.
Ordered that Thos. Howle have 700 lbs. of Tobo. for keeping Edmund Bedford.
Ordered that Mr. Edward Moore have 400 lbs. of Tobo. for keeping Wm. Drummond.
Ordered that Capt. Wm. Macon be Chosen Vestryman in the Room of Mr. Wm. Bassett, who desires to be Excused & that he appear to take the Oath at the next Vestry.
Ordered that Charles Noden be Continued Clerk for the year following, and be paid as usual.
Ordered that Mr. Edward Moore Collect the Tobo. due to the Parish and that he pay the Sev'll Creditors to whom it is As-

signed and Enter into Bond and Security for the performance of the Same.

Ordered that Jarvis Austin be Continued Sexton & to be paid as Usual.

Test Pret't by Eben. Adams, Hen. Collings, Wm. Clopton, Tho. Massie, John Scott, Rich'd Allen.

| | |
|---|---:|
| Bro't from ye Other Side | 24437 |
| To Madam Littlepage. 444; To Rob't Cade for making a Coffin for Johannah Johnson & Day's Attendance.... | 569 |
| To Mr. Thos. Weaver for serving a warr't Mr. Wm. Waddill, 584 | 1198 |
| To Mr. Wm. Clopton, Jun'rs, acct., 543; For the widow Taylor for 2 Delinqu'ts in 1720 | 696 |
| To Mr. Wm. Waddill for keeping George Baisey & for Hanging ye Bell | 2460 |
| To Sallary of 29360 at 5 p cent. | 1420 |
| | 30780 |

The Parish Levy being this day proportioned, we find it to be 46 lb. of Tobo. p poll for Each Tithable person in this parish, there being 670 Tithables besides a fraction of Tobo. due to ye Collector from the parish w'th Said quantity of Tobo., Mr. Edward Moore is hereby Impowered to receive from every Tithable person & to pay it to those persons for whom it is Levyed, provided that He enter into a Bond with the Vestry as usual.

Whereas the Church wardens of this parish have begun to erect a Bellfry at the Church, It is ordered that 3 lbs. of Tobo. p poll be Levyed for the defraying the Charge thereof & that the said Tobo. do Lye in the hands of the Collector till the said Bellfry be finished if the Bell be hung Workmanlike.

---

At a Vestry held at Mr. Taylor's, in St. Peter's Parish, in New Kent County, on Monday the 19th of November, 1722.

A kitchen at the Glebe to be built by John Johnson & John Careless 20 feet long & 16 foot wide, the Chimney 5 foot out and Ten in the width of the House, Closett **6 and 5, 7½ foot** pitch, and a 14 foot Rafter above the Jett of the Joyce, 9 inch Joyce and Rafter Loft laid with Clapboards for the building of which House the Vestry above agreed to pay the said Workmen the Just and full Summ of One Thousand pounds of Tobo., with Conveniency as usual, & all Nails found them.

Ordered that Mr. Thos. Pinchback and wardens are Impowered and desired to come and view the Bellfry and to make a true and Just report of the Value of the whole work, and that Next Saturday be the appointed day & if they can not agree they are Impowered and desired to pitch upon a Third and that the Vestry do allow them for their Trouble and that neither Church Wardens nor Vestry are to have any Conference with them.

Ordered that Jarvis Austin have an addition of 200 lbs. of Tobo. p ann. to his Sallary for his Trouble in Ringing the Bell.

Ordered that Capt. Thos. Massie have 200 lbs. of Tobo. for finding Nails for building the Kitchen at the Glebe.

Test: Henry Collins, George Poindexter, Thos. Massie, Eben. Adams. The Mark of I, Richard Allen.

Wm. Waddill, John Parke, Church Wardens.

---

At a Vestry held at Mrs. Taylor's, in New Kent County, on Thursday, Dec'r ye 20th, 1722.

Ordered that Mr. Sherwood Lightfoot have 500 lbs. of Tobo. for keeping a Molatto Child of the parish; In Consideration of which Mr. Sherwood Lightfoot for his part doth promise never to bring any claim of the like Nature for the future nor Any One else for him.

Ordered that Mary Epperson have 1000 lbs. of Tobo. for keeping Susannah Henderson, Daughter of Thos. Henderson, of the parish.

Ordered that Mr. John Dodd and Mr. Stephen Moore, by the Joynt Consent of the Vestry and Church Wardens are Impowered and desired to come and view the Bellfry and to make a True and Just report of the value of the whole Work, and that the time appointed be on or before the Saturday the 29th day of this present Dec'r, and if they cannot agree they are Impowered and desired to Pitch upon a Third person, and that the Vestry do allow them for their Trouble and that neither Church Wardens nor Vestry are to have any Conference with them.

Test: Hen. Collings, Thos. Butts, Eben. Adams, Charles Lewis, John Scott. (The mark of A) Richard Allen. Will'm Waddill, John Parke, Chu. Wardens.

At a Vestry held for the parish of St. Peter's on Tuesday, the 30th day of July, 1722.

Ordered that Mr. Tho. Butts be Church warden for the year ensuing in the Room of Mr. Wm. Waddill.

Mr. Wm. Macon and Mr. Walter Clopton having first taken the oaths according to Law were appointed Vestrymen of the s'd parish, having taken the oaths in that Case appointed.

Ordered that Eliza Taylor do provide a person to officiate as Sexton to ye parish, to be paid as usual for the same.

Ordered that Robt. Walton be chosen Reader of ye s'd parish in the Stead of Charles Noden, provided he becomes an Inhabitant of the s'd parish on or before ye last day of December next and Clerk of the s'd Vestry.

Ordered that the Clerk of the Vestry do draw & issue the Severall orders for processioning Land to ye persons Nominated by the Vestry.

Ordered that the Tithables belonging to Mad'm Littlepage at Tong Hill be removed from Setph. Mitchell's Gang & added to Evan Ragland's.

Ordered that Richard Brooke's, Eliza Taylor's, Mary Jackson's, Wm. Burk's, Jno. Ross's, Sam'l Bugg's, & Charles Smith's Tithables do Clear the Roads whereof Jno. Jackson is overseer.

Ordered that Henry Scruggs, Sen'r, & his Tithables be added to Mr. Adams' precincts for clearing the highway.

Test: Hen. Colling, John Scott, Tho. Massie, Rich'd Allen, Wm. Clopton, Eben'r Adams, Wm. Macon, Wm. Waddill, Will Clopton.

---

At a Vestry held for St. Peter's Parish Sep'r 30th, 1723.

Mr. Henry Collings, Min'r; Maj'r John Scott, Mr. George Poindexter, Mr. Tho. Massie, Mr. Eben Adams, Mr. Wm. Macon, Wm. Clopton, Wm. Waddell, Walter Clopton. Mr. Jno. Parke, Mr. Tho. Butts, Ch. Wardens.

To　　　　St. Peter's Parish,　　　　Dr.　　　　L. Tobo.

To Mr. Henry Collings, with 7 mons. Conv. added..... 10176
To Cha. Noden, Clk. 9 mon. & Conv. added, 1431; Robt.
　　Walton Clk, 2 mons. Conv. added .................. 1749

To Mr. Thorp & Conv. added, 159; Jervas Austin, Sexton 2 mons., 175 ................................. 334

13259

To Eliz. Taylor, Sexton, 9 mon. & other Charges, 645; Mad'm Littlepage, 1194 ......................... 1839
To Mr. Merriwether's Acct. C. C. added, 478; Capt. Massie's own acct. & Mary Aperson's ................. 1265
To Mr. Ed. Moore acct., Mr. Sher'd Lightfoot for keeping a child ......................................... 1358
To Jno. Gilliam for keeping Eliz. Jnoson, 815; Tho. Howl for keeping Edm'd Bedford ................... 1515
To Jno. Johnson & * * To be p'd Cap. Massie, 1060; Mr. Jno. Parke * Glebe kitchen ...................... 1260
To Ed. Ossling for * * 2 mon. & Burial, Mr. Geo. Poindexter, 734; * Maj. Thornton, 40 ................ 960
To Ste. Moone, Eliz. Scruggs, * Marg't Gilliam * Mr. Wm. Waddill * * ................................. 2991
To Han. Waddill on * 100; Jno. Dodd * 25; Robt. Cade * 25; Mary Apperson * 384 ........................ 534
To Sallary on * 1199; Due to ye parish * * 204........ 1403

25384

Pr Contra.
By 668 Tythables at 38 lb. Tobo. p poll is ............. 25384

The Parish Levy being proportioned, we find it amounts to ye sum of 38 lbs. of Tobo. p poll for each Tythable person, Except a fraction of 204 lbs. Tobo. Due to ye parish from ye Collect'r, w'ch S'd Sum of Tobo. the Ch. Wardens are Impowered to receive from Every Tythable person & to pay it to those to whom it is Levyed, provided they enter into bond as usual.

Ordered that Mary Bourn Do Keep Mary Amoss and be allowed for ye same 600 lb. Tobo. pr annum.

Thos. Roper Came to this Vestry & offered 2 Children to ye Vestry, which his Serv't woman brought & he Agreed to take them himself upon other people's offering to take them.

Ordered that Sam'll Bugg be allowed 650 lb. Tobo. pr. annum for keeping Ed. Bedford.

Ordered that Wm. Perkins be allowed 650 lb. Tobo. p annum for Keeping Eliz. Johnson.

Ordered that if Tobo. w'ch is Levy'd for Mary Apperson be not p'd untill Robt. Cade appear Security to ye Child off of the parish w'ch Mary Epperson Keeps.

Mr. Adams Informed this Vestry yt Mr. Jno. Doran has 20 shill Lying in his hands Due to this parish & 5 still in ye hands of Mr. Jno. Fleming, It is ordered yt ye Church wardens Do receive ye Same.

Ordered that ye Rev'd Mr. Henry Collings be Continued min'r of this parish.

Ordered that Robt. Walton be Continued Clk of ye Church & Vestry.

Ordered Tho. Sanderson be Sexton of this parish & to be paid 700 lbs Tobo. p annum for all services.

Registered p ROBERT WALTON, Clk. Vestry.

At a Vestry held for St. Peter's Parish, April ye 7th, 1724.

Ordered that Mr. Charles Lewis be Church Warden in the Room & Stead of Mr. John Parke this present & ensuing year.

Alice Matthews came to this vestry & offered to keep herself off from being a parish Charge Eighteen months w'th what Living she has. Ordered that if she doth not give Security by the 20th Day of this month the Church Wardens are to take her & wh't Estate she has into their hands.

Ordered yt the Goods of Thos. Ashcraft be valued by Capt. Massie & George Wilkinson & yt Thos. Martin take them as they are valued (if he thinks fitt).

Test: Henry Collings, Minister; Thos. Massie, Will'm Macon, Wm. Clopton, Rich'd Allen, Wm. Waddill, Walt'r Clopton.

At a Vestry held for St. Peter's parish June 13th, 1724.

Whereas, by an act of Assembly intituled an act for ye more Effectual Emproving the Staple of Tobo. & for ye Better Discovery of frauds therein which said Act directs the Vestry of every parish in this Dominion before ye last day of June yearly to lay their respective parishes into precincts and to appoint Two persons in each precinct to Examine & Enquire of ye names & members of all persons alowed to tend Tobacco & ye crops of ye severall planters within their precincts & ye number of plants

VESTRY BOOK OF ST. PETER'S PARISH. 139

Growing on any & Every plantation & plantations within ye same.

In Obedience to the said Act this Vestry hath proceeded this day to lay out this parish into precincts & to appoint Two persons in each precinct to view & number according to the directions of the Said Act of Assembly, whose names & ye precincts are as followeth:

Mr. Charles Massie & Mr. Walter Clopton are appointed to view & number Tob'co plants according to law: from ye long bridge upon Chickehominy Swamp along ye main Road by Mr. Adams' to ye Burnt mill & so Down black creek to the mouth thereof & to ye extent of ye parish upward.

Mr. Robt. Clopton & Mr. David Pettison are appointed to View & Number Tobo. plants as afores'd from Mr. Wm. Thomas's Store along ye main road by Coll. Scott & so to Alex'r pattison's the full Bredth of the parish to Black Creek.

Mr. Wm. Waddill & Mr. John Otey are appointed to View & Number as afore'sd from Mr. Thomas's Store along ye main road by Coll. Scott's & so to Alex'r Pattison's & so to ye Extent of the parish Downwards. Signed by Henry Collings. Min'r, and Recorded by Robt. Walton, Clerk of Vestry.

Jno. Scott, Thos. Massie, Wm. Macon, Eben'r Adams, Wm. Clopton, Rich'd Allen, Wm. Waddill, Walter Clopton, Vestrymen.

---

At a Vestry held for Saint Peter's p'sh 7ber 29th, 1724.

St. Peter's Parish, Dr.

To Mr. Hen. Collings, min'r, 12 mon. Including Conv'q 16960
To Robt. Walton, Clerk, 12 mon. Including Conv'y;
   Thos. Sanderson, Sexon, 12 mon., 700 ............ 2608
To Marg't Gilliam for keeping Spurlock, Sam'l Bugg for
   keeping Edm. Bedford ........................... 1450
To Jno. Guilliam for keep Eliz. Johnson, Rich'd Crump
   for work at ye Church, 350 ..................... 1000
To Amy Morgan for keeping John Goodwin, 600; Dan'll
   Wilmore for keeping Mary Amoss, 500 ........... 1100
To Coll. Scott for Acct., Thos. Moore for piloting &
   marking parish line, 50 ........................ 1050

To Rich'd Brookes for work at ye Glebe, 300; Pelham
  Moore for a pr Shoes for Eliz. Jnson, 30 ............   330
To Mad'm Littlepage her acct. allowed 865; Mr. Moore
  his acct., 280; Capt. Massie acct., 187 ............  1272
To Maj'r Thornton fee, 40; Edw'd Morgan for keeping
  Alice Matthews ................................   140
To Thos. Martin for keeping Thos. Ashcroft, Sallary on
  26435 Lbs. Tob'co at 5 p ct. .....................  1846
                                                      ─────
                                                      27756

Pr Contra: 692 Tythables a 40 lb. p poll, A fraction due to
  ye Collector, 76 ....  ...........................  27756
This day ye parish Levy being proportioned, we find it amounts to be 40 lbs. Tobo. p poll besides a fraction Due at 76 lbs. to ye Collector.

W'ch said sum of 40 lbs. of Tobo. the Church wardens is Impowered to receive from Every Tythable person in the parish & to pay it to those for whom it is Levyed, provided ye Church wardens give Bond & Security as usual.

Ordered that Rich'd Crump & Edw'd Baily & their Tithables do work upon ye high roads w'th Wm. Crump Survey. Ordered that ye Church wardens do Contribute ye goods of Thos. Ashcroft for ye use of this parish before there be any more Tobo. Levyed for him or before they agree w'th any person for ye maintainance of him at ye Charge of this parish.

Ordered yt Amy Morgan be allowed 250 lbs. of Tobo. pr annum for keeping Jno. Goodwine.

Ordered yt Jno. Austin be allowed 80 lbs. Tob. pr annum for keep'g Mary Amoss.

Ordered yt Jno. Gilliam be allowed 495 pr an'm for Eliz. Johnson.

Ordered yt Sam'll Bugg be allowed 495 pr an'm for Edm'd Bedford.

Test: Henry Collings, min'r; George Poindexter, Tho. Massie, W. Clopton, Will'm Macon, Rich'd Allen, Walter Clopton, Vestrymen.

                    Recorded p ROBT. WALTON, Clk. Vestry.
                                                    ─────

At a Vestry held for St. Peter's Parish June 17th, 1725.

Whereas, by an Act of Assembly intituled an Act for the * * better Effectual improving the Staple of Tob'co & for * * Discovery of fraud therein which S'd Act Directs * * of Every parish in this Collony before ye Last of * * to lay their Respective parishes into precincts * * persons in each precinct to Examine & Enquire * * numbers of all persons allowed to Tend Tob'co & the * * Several planters within ye S'd precinct & ye number * * growing on any & every plantation & plantations within the same ————. In obedience to ye S'd Act of Assembly this Vestry * * this day to lay out this parish into precincts & * * persons in Each precinct to View & number Tob'co * * to ye Directions of ye S'd Act of Assembly whose * * precincts are as followeth:

Mr. Charles Massie & Mr. Walter Clopton are * * * appointed to view & number Tob'co plants according * * the Long bridge upon Chickahominy Swamp * * road by Mr. Adams's to ye Burnt mill & * * to ye mouth thereof & so to ye extent of ye parish.

Mr. Robt. Clopton & Mr. David Pattison are * * to View & Number Tob'co plants according to * Thomas's former Store along the main road w'ch leads * * Scott's & so to Alex'r Pattison's the full bredth of ye parish to Black creek ye former bounds.

Mr. Wm. Waddill & Mr. Jno. Otey are Ordered & appointed to View & number Tob'co plants according to law from Mr. Thos.'s former Store along ye main road w'ch leadeth by Coll. Scott's & so to Alex'r Pattison's, so to ye Extent of ye parish Downwards—Capt. Wm. Marston & Mr. Jno. Netherland are ordered & appointed to view & number Tob'co plants according to law, all ye New addition to this parish in James City County. Ordered that Capt. Wm. Marston, Mr. Wm. Browne, Mr. Jno. Netherland be added to this Vestry.

Mr. John Netherland was Sworn this day Vestryman of this parish and hath Assigned the Test.

Ordered yt Capt. Charles Lewis be Continued Chu. warden of this parish this year & Capt. Tho. Massie is appointed Church warden in ye room of Mr. Tho. Butts. Ordered that Capt. Charles Lewis be allowed 500 lbs. of Tobo. for keeping Mary Wazzard till ye 29th day of Sept'r Come twelve months, & to be p'd in proportion at ye laying ye next Levy. Test: Henry Collings, min'r.

John Parke, Wm. Macon, Walt'r Clopton, Eben'r Adams, Wm. Waddill, Jno. Netherland, Tho. Butts, Wm. Clopton, Rich'd Allen, Vestrymen. *, *, Church Wardens.

Registered p ROBT. WALTON, Clerk Vestry.

At a Vestry held for St. Peter's p'sh 7br 29th, 1725.
Thos. Massie, Church warden; Eben'r Adams, W. Clopton. Wm. Marston. W. Browne, Wm. Macon, John Parke, Wm. Waddill, Walt. Clopton.

Ordered yt Sam'l Ossling be allowed 450 lbs. Tob'co pr annum for keeping Eliz. Johnson.

Ordered yt Jno. Guilliam be allowed 300 lb. of Tob'co pr annum for keeping Henry Dike.

Ordered yt Wm. Pearson be allowed 500 lbs. of Tob'co pr annum for Keeping Jane Morris.

Ordered yt Amy Morgan be allowed 250 lbs. of Tob'co pr annum for Keeping Jno. Goodwin.

Ordered yt Sam'l Bugg be allowed 495 lbs. of Tob'co pr annum for Keeping Edm'd Bedford.

St. Peter's Parish,            Dr.

| | |
|---|---|
| To Mr. Hen. Collings including Con'cy Robt. Walton, Clk., including Con'cy, 1908 | 17868 |
| To Tho. Sanderson, Sexon, 12 mon. & mend surplis, Sam'l Bugg for keeping Edm'd Bedford, 495 | 1215 |
| To Jno. Gilliam for keeping Eliz. Johnson, Amy Morgan for keeping Jno. Goodman, 250 | 745 |
| To Capt. Cha. Lewis for keeping Mary Hazzard, Jno. Austin for keeping Mary Amos, 400 | 510 |
| Mad. Littlepage's acct., 675; Mrs. Eliza. Taylor's acct., 220; Mr. Math. Jouet, his acct., 38 | 933 |
| To Rich'd Crump for work at ye Ch. & hor. blocks, Capt. Wm. Marston & Mr. W. Browne 2 accts. 676 | 1076 |
| To Mr. Wm. Browne his acct. for keep Mary Haz'd 3 mon., 125; Capt. Massie Two accts added, 723 | 848 |
| To Mr. Wm. Pearson for keeping Jane Morriss, Mr. Chamberlayne's acct., 200 | 923 |

To Doct'r Greenhill his acct & for ye Burial of K. I. Richard Brooke for work at ye Glebe .................... 409
To Chas. Winfree for keeping Eliz. Hilton 2 mon., 80; Sallary on 29204 lbs. Tob'co at 5 p· ct. .............. 1340

Total ........ .......................... 26464

ut. Supra.  Cr.

By 902 Tithables at 29 pr poll, A fraction Due to ye Collector next year, 306 ............................. 26464

At a Vestry held for St. Peter's Parish Octo. ye 10th, 1725.

The Parish levy being this day proportioned, we find it amounts to 29 lb. Tobo. pr polo besides a fraction 306 lbs. Tob. Due to ye Collector next year w'ch S'd Sum of 29 lbs. of Tobo. p poll ye Church wardens are Impowered to Collect from every Tythable person in this parish & to pay it to those for whom it is Levyed, provided ye Chu. wardens enter into bond as usual.

Tho. Massie, Chu. warden; Jno. Scott, Wm. Clopton, Jno. Netherland, Wm. Waddill, Wm. Browne, Wm. Marston, Jno. Parke.

Decem'r 12, 1725. Whereas ye Rev'd Mr. Jno. Lang being recommended to this parish by ye Hon'ble Maj'ty Leu. Goven'r to be minister of this parish, we approve & willingly accept of him as such, & agree to pay him ye yearly Sallary as ye law Directs. Wm. Marston, Wm. Waddill, Eben'r Adams, Wm. Macon, Tho. Massie, Ch. warden; John Netherland.

The Governeurs Letter to this Vestry in recommending the Rev'd Mr. Jno. Lang to this parish.

W'msburgh, Dec'r 1, 1725.

Gen'n, Having lately had information of ye Death of yor Clergyman, I possess myself of ye occation of Sending this Gentleman the Rev'd Mr. Lang to Succeed him in ye parish. He's Just Arrived from England with a plenary Commission to preach ye Gospel * * long as ye Commissary who has the Inspection of those * may advise you, & he is strongly recommended to me by persons of the first Quality for his Verture that I must think him worthy of a good parish, & knowing yours to be such in all Respects I Recommend him to you & require you the Gen'r the Church wardens & Vestry to receive him among you as yo'r

Teacher; Not doubting from ye Character I have of you both, but that yee will be happy in Each Othere. I am Gent'm, Your Humble Serv't, HUGH DRYSDALE.

Registered p ROBT. WALTON, Clk.

A Copie of ye Comissary's Letter in Recommending Mr. Jno. Lang Dec. 1st, 1725:

Gentlemen, The Govourner having recommended ye Rev'd Mr. Jno. Lang to your parish now vacant by the death of Mr. Collings, I thought it my duty to acquaint you that I have seen his Deacons & presbyters orders & License from my Lord Bishop of London together with a Certificate of his Taking ye oaths to ye Government. He comes likewise mighty well recommended & as far as I can Judge by hearing him preach, & a good deal of Conversation with him, I do not at all doubt that he will prove a very worthy Clergyman & give good Satisfaction both as to his Life & Doctrine, which is ye hearty prayer of Your Most Humble Servant, JAMES BLAIR.

Recorded by ROBT. WALTON, Clk. Vest.

The Governour having recommended the Rev. Mr. Lang to y'r parish, vacant by the death of Rev. Mr. Collins, I sh'r it my duty to acquaint you that I have seen his deacons & presbyter's orders * * him to be a virtuous good man, and is well recommended to me by severall competent persons for his learning, & if I may be a Judge I * * him worthy of a good parish, which It has * ye to be therefore * * *.

---

At a Vestry held for St. Peter's Parish on Easter Tuesday, April ye 12th, 1726.

PRESENT:

Mr. John Lang, Min'r; Mr. Eben'r Adams, Capt. Wm. Macon, Mr. John Netherland, Mr. Wm. Clopton, Mr. Wm. Waddill, Mr. Walter Clopton, Vestrymen. Capt. Tho. Massie, Church Warden.

The Reverend Mr. John Lang reported to this Vestry that he hath given Capt. Mitchel thanks for his present being thereto. Requested by an Order of Vestry bearing Date ye 15th of Feb'ry Last past.

VESTRY BOOK OF ST. PETER'S PARISH. 145

Ordered that Capt. Thos. Massie be Continued Church warden this present year & Capt. Wm. Macon is Chosen Church warden in the room of Capt. Charles Lewis. Ordered that Capt. Thos. Massie & Capt. Wm. Macon, Church wardens, Do agree with Some workman to build a Dairy at ye Glebe twelve foot Square, & Repair ye Smoak house & Repair ye Tob'co house & make a partition in ye Tob'co house Eight foot and Likewise to pale in a Garden Eighty foot Square all workman Like. Ordered that the Church wardens do provide a new Surplice for this parish Church as Soon as Conveniently they can.
John Lang, Wm. Clopton, Jno. Netherland, Eben'r Adams, Wm. Waddill, Walt. Clopton. Tho. Massie, * *, Church wardens.
Registered by ROBT. WALTON, Clk. Vestry.

---

At a Vestry held for St. Peter's Parish June 19th, 1726.
Tho. Massie, Wm. Macon, Chu. Wardens; Mr. Wm. Clopton, Geo. Poindexter, Wm. Waddill, Eben'r Adams, Walt. Clopton, Vestrymen.
Mr. Charles Massie & Mr. Walter Clopton are ordered & appointed to view & number Tob'co plants according to Law from ye Long bridge upon Chickahominy Swamp along ye main road by Mr. Adams's to the burnt mill & so Down Black creek to the mouth thereof & so to ye extent of the parish upwards.
Mr. Robt. Clopton & Mr. David Pattison are ordered & appointed to view & number Tob'co plants according to Law from Mr. Thomas's former Store along ye main Road by Col. Scott's & so to Alex'r Pattison's. So to ye extent of ye parish downwards.
Capt. Wm. Marston & Mr. Jno. Netherland are ordered & appointed to view & number Tob'co plants according to law, all ye new Addition to this parish in James City County.
Registered pr. ROBT. WALTON, Clk. Vestry.

---

At a Vestry held for St. Peter's Parish, 7ber ye 29th, 1726.
Mr. Jno. Lang, Min'r; Mr. Wm. Brown, Mr. Jno. Netherland, Capt. Wm. Marston, Mr. Wm. Clopton, Mr. Wm. Waddill, Mr. George Poindexter, Vestrymen. Capt. Tho. Massie, Capt. Wm. Macon, Ch. Wardens.

St. Peter's Parish, Dr.

| | |
|---|---:|
| To Mr. Jno. Lang, minister from ye 12th Decem'r to ye 12th of Decem'r, Conveniency to Do., 960 | 16960 |
| To Robt. Walton, Clk. for a year, Including Conveniency, Thos. Sanderson, Sexon for 1 year, 700 | 2608 |
| To Amy Morgan for Keeping Jno. Goodwin, Sam'l Ossling for keeping Eliz. Johnson & for her burial, 340 | 950 |
| To Jno. Guilliam for keeping Hen. Dike & for his burial, 230; Major Thornton's fees, 220 | 450 |
| To Sam'l Bugg for Keeping Ed'd Bedford, To be paid to Epa'e Guilliams, Mr. Wm. Waddill his acct., 79 | 574 |
| To Wm. Pearson for keeping Jane Morris, 500; Pridgin Waddill for work at ye Glebe | 1860 |
| To Capt. Charles Lewis for keeping Mary Hazard, 390; Capt. Thos. Massie, his acct., 1889 | 2279 |
| To Mr. Jno. Lang for necessaries for ye Glebe, 274; Mad'm Littlepage's acct., 192 | 466 |
| To Capt. Wm. Macon his Acct., Mr. Wm. Chamberlayne his Acct., 60 | 276 |
| To Mr. Thos. Thorp Adm'r of Mr. Henry Collings, Conveniency to Do., 139 | 2462 |
| To Mrs. Taylor her charge for making ye Surplice, Math Jowet his Acct., 854 | 794 |
| To Rich'd Crump for work at ye Church, Wm. Clopton Jun'r, his Acct., 172½ | 372½ |
| To Rob't Vaiden for keeping Hannah Richardson 25 Days, 50; James Moore for ye burial of Peter Davis | 200 |
| To Peter Beer for mending ye Glebe windows | 100 |
| To Edw'd Baily for Keeping Sarah Tunson 60 Days | 250 |
| To Epa'r Guilliam for making Clothes for Bedford, 40; Mr. Geo. Poindexter his acct. | 180 |
| To Sallary on 30421½ at 5 p cent. | 1521 |
| Total | 31942½ |

P Contra Cr.

By 899 Tithables at 35 p poll, 31465, A fraction due to ye Collector next year, 477½ ...... 31942½

The Parish Levy being this day proportioned, wee find it

amounts to the Sum of 35 lbs. Tob'co p poll on 899 tythables, besides a fraction of 477½ to be paid ye Collector next year, w'ch said 35 lbs. Tobo. p poll ye Church wardens are Impowered to collect from Every Tythable person in this parish & to pay it to those persons for whom it is Leveyed, provided ye Church wardens Enter into bond with ye Vestry as usual.

Ordered that Sam'l Bugg have Twelve Hundreds pounds of Tob'co Levyed next year in this parish, for which ye said Sam'l Bugg doth promise to give bond & Security to this Vestry to keep Ed'd Bedford off from being a Parish Charge.

An allowance made to Jno. Brothers of 300 lbs. Tob'co for keeping Anne Watkins.

Wm. Pearson to have the usual allowance for keeping Jane Morris.

Amy Morgan to have her usual allowance for keeping Jno. Goodwin.

Signed by the Rev'd Mr. Jno. Lang, minister; Tho. Massie, Will'm Bacon, Ch. Wardens; Wm. Clopton, Wm. Brown, Wm. Marston, Geo. Poindexter, Jno. Netherland, Wm. Waddill, Vestrymen.

Registered p me, ROBT. WALTON, Clk. Vestry.

---

At a Vestry held for St. Peter's Parish, June 24th, 1727.

PRESENT:

Coll. Jno. Scott, Capt. Wm. Marston, Mr. Wm. Browne, Mr. Jno. Netherland, Mr. Wm. Waddill, Mr. Wm. Clopton, Mr. Walter Clopton, Vestrymen. Capt. Tho's Massie, Capt. Wm. Macon, Church Wardens.

Whereas the Rev'd Mr. David Mossom being recommended to this Vestry by ye hon'ble ye president of this Colony to be minister of this parish, Wee ye Church wardens & Vestry do approve and willingly Accept of him as Such & do agree to pay him ye yearly Sallary as ye law Directs.

A Copy of the president's Letter in recomendacon of Mr. Mossom:

Williamsburgh, June 13th, 1727.

Gentlemen,—The Reverend Mr. David Mossom, bearer hereof, hath show'd me Sufficient Testimonials of his admission into priest's orders and of his Qualifications to Exercise his Ministerial function in the plantations, And being a person not unknown among you, I cannot provide better for you & him than by Sending him to Supply your Vacant parish, where I hope his Conduct will render him agreeable to you.  I am, Gentlemen, Your most Humble Servant,

ROBERT CARTER.

Ordered that Several Viewers of Tob'co plants in this parish be Continued to number Tobo. plants in their usual precincts.

Ordered that Capt. Wm. Macon Continue Church warden this present year, And Mr. Wm. Brown is chosen Church warden in ye Room of Capt. Tho. Massie.

Upon the petition of Edward Parish to this Vestry to be Levy free, Ordered that he be Exempted from paying any Levey in this parish.

David Mossom, Min'r; Jno. Scott. Wm. Marston, Jno. Netherland, Wm. Clopton, Tho. Massie, Wm. Waddill, Walt'r Clopton. Will'm Macon, Wm. Browne, Ch. Wardens.

Registered p me, ROBT. WALTON, Clk. Vestry.

---

At a Vestry held for St. Peter's Parish 7ber 29th, 1727, And further Continued by Adjournment to ye 14th of 8ber, 1727.

Mr. David Mossom, Min'r; Capt. Tho. Massie, Mr. Wm. Clopton, Mr. Eben'r Adams, Mr. Wm. Waddill, Capt. Wm. Marston, Mr. Jno. Netherland, Mr. Walter Clopton, Vestrymen. Capt. Wm. Macon, Mr. Wm. Browne, Church wardens.

St. Peter's Parish, Dr.

| | |
|---|---:|
| To the Rev'd John Lang from ye 12th of Decem'r abating 9 sermons & 140 L of Tobo. for 7 tithes not listed for last year | 5098 |
| Conveniency to Do. at 6 per cent | 306 |
| To ye Rev'd Mr. David Mossom, min'r, from ye 18th of June and Levyed to ye first day of January | 8559 |
| Conveniency to Do. at 6 p cent., 513; Robt. Walton, Clk. for a year Including Conveniency | 2421 |
| To ye Exec'ix of Thos. Sanderson. Sexon. to ye 24th of Feb'ry. Richard Brookes. Sexon. from ye 26th of Feb'y | 700 |
| To Sam'l Bugg for taking Edm'd Bedford off from ye parish. 1200: Amy Morgan. for keeping Jno. Goodwin | 1450 |

To Wm. Pearson for keeping Jane Morris, 500; Rich'd
Booker for boarding of workmen & for other services   1246
To Capt. Wm. Macon his acct., 3323; Charles Hughes
his acct., 123 ..................................   3446
To John Barkwell for digging ye Glebe well, 2800; Ed.
Barley for keeping Sarah Timson 2 mon. & for her
burial ...........................................   496
To Jno. Brothers his allowance for Anne Watkins, 300;
Ed. Parish his acct., 140 .........................   440
To Capt. Tho. Massie, his acct. for wine & Lawyer's fees,
342; Mr. Wm. Browne his acct., 93 .................   435
To Jno. Dennet his Charge for carrying a poor man of ye
p'sh ..............................................   50
To Hugh Grimley for keeping of Sarah Timson, 232;
Maj'r Thornton, his Acct., 104 ....................   336
To ye fraction w'ch was due to ye Collector last year abating 105 l Tob'co for 7 tiths not listed last year ......   372½
To Sallary on 25804½ at 5 p cent. is ................   1290
                                                    ──────
                                                      26970
P Contra      Cr.

By 899 Tithables at 30 p ct. is 26770, A fraction Due to ye
Collector next year, 124½ .......................27094½

The Parish Levy being this day proportioned we find it amounts to the sum of 30 lb. Tobo. p poll on 899 tythables besides a fraction of 124½ pounds of Tobo. to be paid ye Collect'r next year, which said sum of Thirty pounds of Tobo. the Church wardens are Impowered to Collect from Every Tythable person in this parish & to pay it to those persons for whom it is Levyed, provided the Church wardens enter into bond with the Vestry as usual.

Ordered that the Clerk draw of the several orders for processioning of Lands as usual, And deliver them to the persons nominated by the Vestry.

Jno. Dodd proposeth to keep Jno. Goodwin provided the Vestry find him Clothes. Ordered that the said Jno. keep him this ensuing year, and that the Church wardens find him with Clothinge.

───────

At a Vestry held by Adjournment the 14th Oct'r, 1727.

150        VESTRY BOOK OF ST. PETER'S PARISH.

PRESENT:

Mr. David Mossom, Min'r; Mr. Eben'r Adams, Mr. Tho. Butts, Mr. Wm. Waddill, Capt. Wm. Marston, Mr. Wm. Clopton, Mr. Walt'r Clopton, Vestrymen. Capt. Wm. Macon, Mr. Wm. Browne, Church wardens.

Robt. Walton is this day Sworn Clerk of the Vestry.

Ordered that Eliz'eth Taylor be allowed 700 l of Tobacco p annum for keeping Mary Hazzard.

Signed by David Mossom, Min'r; Eben'r Adams, Wm. Marston, Tho. Butts, Wm. Clopton, Wm. Waddill, Walt. Clopton, Vestrymen. Will Macon, W. Browne, Ch. wardens.

---

At a Vestry held for St. Peter's parish April the 23rd, 1728, Mr. David Mossom, min'r; Capt. Thos. Massie, Capt. Wm. Marston, Capt. Chas. Lewis, Mr. Jno. Netherland, Mr. Wm. Clopton, Walter Clopton, Mr. Wm. Waddill, Mr. Geo. Poindexter, Vestrymen.

Capt. Wm. Macon, Church Warden.

Ordered that Mr. Wm. Browne be Continued Church warden this Ensuing year, And Capt. Tho. Massie is Chosen Church warden in the room of Capt. Wm. Macon.

Mr. Wm. Clopton being Very aged & not of ability to attend on Vestrys, Declineth ye office of a Vestryman.

Ordered that the Church wardens provide a new Common prayer Book for St. Peter's Church by ye first Opportunity Recorded p Robt. Walton, Clk. Vestry.

---

At a Vestry held for St. Peter's Parish June ye 15th. 1728.

PRESENT:

Mr. David Mossom, Min'r Mr. Eben'r Adams. Mr. Jno. Netherland, Mr. Geo. Poindexter, Mr. Walter Clopton, Mr. Tho. Butts, Mr. Wm. Waddill, Capt. Wm. Marston, Vestrymen. Capt. Tho. Massie, Mr. Wm. Browne, Church wardens.

Whereas, by an act of Assembly Entitled an act for ye more & better Effectual inproving ye staple of Tobo. which Said Act Directs ye Vestry of every parish within this Colony on ye fifteenth Day of June yearly During the Continuance of this Act To lay their respective parishes into precincts & appoint Two persons in Each precinct to View, Examine & Number Tob'co

VESTRY BOOK OF ST. PETER'S PARISH.   151

plants, & to Cut up & destroy or Cause to be cut up & Destroyed all Tob'co Stalks, Strips & Suckers above ye heighth of nine Inches from ye Ground on any and Every plantation or plantations within ye same.

Persuant to ye Said Act of Assembly this Vestry hath proceeded this day to Lay this parish into precincts according to the directions of the S'd act of Assembly whose Names & the Bounds of the precincts are as followeth:

Mr. Charles Massie & Mr. Walter Clopton are Nominated & appointed to View & Number Tob'co plants according to the directions of ye Act of Assembly from the Long bridge on Chickahominy Swamp along the main Road which Leadeth by Mr. Adams his plantacon to Thos. Pinchback's Mill, thence to the mouth of Black Creek & so the Extent of ye parish upwards.

Mr. David Patteson & Mr. Robt. Clopton are nominated & appointed to View & number Tob'co plants according to the Directions of the Act of the Assembly from Mr. Thomas his former Store along the main Road, which leadeth by Coll. Scott's plantacon to Martha Patteson's ye full breadth of the parish to Black Creek ye former bounds.

Mr. Wm. Waddill & Mr. Jno. Otey are Nominated to View & number Tob'co plants according to the Direction of ye Act of Assembly from Mr. Thomas's his former store along the main Road which Leadeth by Coll. Scott's to Martha Pattison's so to the Extent of the S'd parish Downwards.

Capt. Wm. Marston & Mr. Jno. Netherland are nominated & appointed to View & number Tob'co plants According to ye Directions of ye act of Assembly that part of this parish which lies in James City County.

Agness Tudora, poor Infirm Girl, being put upon this parish for a Charge And Rich'd & Sarah Brookes being willing to take the said Girl, Ordered vt ye Church wardens bind the said Agnes Tudor to the Said Rich'd & Sarah Brookes for Seven years.

Peter Clark applying himself to this Vestry to be Levy free, Ordered that the Said Peter Clark be Exempted from paying any parish Levy in this parish.

Signed by Mr. David Mossom, Min'r and Tho. Butts, Geo. Poindexter, John Netherland, Wm. Marston, Eben. Adams, Wm.

Waddill, Walt'r Clopton, Vestrymen. Wm. Browne, Tho. Massie, Ch. Wardens.

Recordede p me, ROBT. WALTON, Clk. Vestry.

At a Vestry held for St. Peter's parish Octob'r ye 8th, 1728.

PRESENT:

Mr. David Mossom, Min'r; Capt. Wm. Macon, Mr. Eben'r Adams, Mr. Wm. Waddill, Mr. Tho. Butts, Mr. Walt'r Clopton, Mr. John Netherland, Vestrymen.

| St. Peter's Parish, | Dr. |
|---|---|
| To ye Rev'd Mr. David Mossom for his Ministerial function to ye 29th of 7ber. | 12000 |
| Cask & Conv'cy to Do. & Cask for 4000, paid Last year, 2000, Robt. Walton, Clk, 1908 | 3908 |
| To Rich'd Brookes, Sexton, 200; Eliz. Taylor for keeping Mary Hazzard, &c., 760 | 1460 |
| To Capt. Wm. Macon his acct., 1145; Maj'r John Thornton his acct., 120 | 1265 |
| To Robt. Walton for work done on the Glebe | 1261 |
| To Jno. Brothers his allowance for keeping Anne Watkins | 300 |
| To Wm. Pearson for keeping Jane Morris 6 mon. & 20 days, & for her burial | 357 |
| To Rich'd Brookes his charge for work at ye Glebe & Church | 244 |
| To Stephen Brooker for work at ye Glebe | 48 |
| To John Barkwell for Cleaning ye Glebe well | 80 |
| To Jno. Dodd for a pr of shoes for Jno. Goodwin | 40 |
| To Clem't Read for Q't R'ts of ye Glebe land for ye years 1726 & 1727 | 60 |
| To Mr. Wm. Waddill for 2 Delinq'ts in ye year 1724, 40; Mr. Wm. Browne for 1 qu't of wine, 24 | 64 |
| To Sallary on 21087 lb. of Tob'co a 10 p ct. | 2108 |
|  | 23195 |
| To a fraction Due from ye Collect'r to ye parish | 109 |
| Pr Contra, Cr. | 23304 |
| By 971 Tithables a 24 p poll ............ 23304 | |

VESTRY BOOK OF ST. PETER'S PARISH. 153

The Parish Levy being this day proportioned, we find it amounts to ye Sum of 24 lbs. of Tob'co p poll on 971 tithables, besides a fraction of 109 l of Tob'co to be paid to ye parish next year, Which said Sum of 24 l of Tob'co Capt. Thos. Massie is appointed & impowered to Collect from Every Tithable person in this parish, And to pay it to those persons for whom it is levyed, provided the said Capt. Thos. Massie Enter into bond with the Vestry as ye Law directs.

Ordered that Eliz. Taylor be allowed 756 l of Tob'co for keeping of Mary Hazzard this Ensuing year.

Signed by David Mossom, Min'r, and Tho. Butts, Eben'r Adams, Wm. Waddill, Will'm Macon, Jno. Netherland, Walt'r Clopton, Vestrymen.

---

At a Vestry held for St. Peter's Parish June ye 23rd, 1729.

PRESENT:

Mr. David Mossom, Min'r; Mr. Eben'r Adams, Capt. Wm. Marston, Mr. Jno. Netherland, Mr. Wm. Waddill, Mr. Walt'r Clopton, Vestrymen. Capt. Tho. Massie, Warden.

Pursuant to an Act of Assembly Instituled an act for the more & better improving the Staple of Tob'co, this Vestry hath proceeded this day to lay out the parish into precincts, & to Appoint two persons in each precinct whose names & the bounds of the precincts are as followeth:

Mr. Charles Massie & Mr. Walter Clopton are Nominated & appointed to View & number the Tob'co plants According to ye Directions of ye Act of Assembly from the Long bridge upon Chickahominy Swamp Along the main Road which leadeth by Mr. Adams's plantation to Thomas Pinchback's mill, thence to the mouth of black Creek, And so to the extent of the parish upwards.

Mr. David Patteson & Mr. Robert Clopton are nominated & appointed to View & number Tob'co plants according to the Directions of ye Act of Assembly from Mr. Thomas's former Store along the Main Road. Which Leadeth by Coll. Scott's to Martha Patteson's the full bredth of ye parish to black Creek, the former bounds.

Mr. Wm. Waddill & Mr. John Otey are Nominated & appointed to View & number Tob'co According to the Directions of the Act of Assembly from Mr. Thomas' former Store along the main road which leadeth by Colo. Scott's to Martha Patteson's, so to the Extent of ye s'd Parish, in New Kent County, Downwards.

Capt. Wm. Marston and Mr. John Netherland are Nominated and appointed to View & number Tob'co plants According to the Direction of the Act of Assembly, All that part of this parish which lies in James City County.

Ordered that Capt. Thomas Massie be Continued Ch. Warden this present year, And Mr. Jno. Netherland is Chosen Church Warden in the room of Mr. Wm. Browne.

Capt. Charles Lewis voluntarily resigning the office of a Vestryman by his Letter to ye Vestry, Mr. David Patteson is Chosen & Elected a Vestryman in his room, And it is ordered that the Clerk give him Notice to appear at the Next Vestry in order to take the Oaths According to law.

Mr. John Netherland hath this day taken the Oath of a Church warden. Mr. John Netherland hath agreed with this Vestry to Digg, make the bricks & brick a well at ye Glebe and to Compleat the same on or before the last day of December next for the Sum of three Thousand pounds of Tob'co one half to be Levved at ye Laying of the next Levy and the other half the year' following. For the performance of which he hath given Bond & Security to the Vestry.

Wm. Apperson, a poor Lad with a sore Legg, Applying himself to this vestry for relief, Ordered that Richard & Sarah Brookes do take ye S'd Lad and keep him untill the Laying of the next Levy & Endeavour to Cure his Legg, & that the S'd Brookes' be paid for the Same at the laying of the next parish Levy.

D. Mossom, Min'r; Tho. Massie, Jno. Netherland, Wardens; Eben'r Adams, William Marston, Wm. Waddill, Walt. Clopton, Vestrymen.

---

At a Vestry held for St. Peter's Parish Sept'r ye 29th, 1729.

PRESENT:

Mr. David Mossom, Min'r; Capt. Wm. Macon, Mr. Walter Clopton, Mr. Wm. Waddill, Mr. David Patteson, Vestrymen; Tho. Massie, Jno. Netherland, Wardens.

## VESTRY BOOK OF ST. PETER'S PARISH.

St. Peter's Parish,              Dr.

To the Rev'd Mr. David Mossom for his ministerial function C. C. to Do. .................................... 18240
To Robt. Walton, Clerk, including Conveniency, 1908; Richard Brookes, Sexton, 700 ..................... 2608
To Jno. Brothers his Allowance for Anne Watkins, 300; Capt. Wm. Macon his acct., 262 .................. 562
To Mr. Jno. Netherland his first paym't for ye Glebe well, 1500; Capt. Massie his acct., 794 ................. 1294
To Jno. Turner for the burial of Wm. Dikes, 150; Rich'd Brookes for keeping Wm. Apperson, 300 ............ 450
To Do. for a pr of Gates & for 48 foot of plank, 98; Salary on 24045 lb. Tob., a 10 p Ct. ................. 2504

Total ................................. 27549

P Contra,              Cr.
By 971 Tithables at 28 p poll is 27188, A fraction due ye Collector next year, 361 .............. 27549

The Parish Levy being this day proportioned, we find it Amounts to the Sum of twenty eight pounds of Tob'co p poll on 971 tithables in this parish besides a fraction of 361 pounds of Tob'co to be paid to the Collector next year, Which Said Sum of twenty eight pounds of Tob'co Capt. Wm. Macon is appointed and impowered to Collect from Every tithable person in this parish to pay it to the Several Creditors for whom it is Levyed. Provided the s'd Wm. Macon gives bond & security to ye Vestry for ye performance of the Same as the Law Directs. Mr. David Patteson hath this day taken the Oath of a Vestryman and subscribed to the Test.

Ordered that Robt. Allen be allowed 250 lbs. of Tob'co for keeping Anne Watkins this ensuing year.

Signed by D. Mossom, Min'r; Tho. Massie, Jno. Netherland, Wardens; Wm. Macon, Wm. Waddill, Walt'r Clopton, David Patteson, Vestrymen.

---

At a Vestry held for St. Peter's Parish 7ber 29th, 1730.

Mr. David Mossom, Min'r; Mr. Jno. Netherland, Church Warden; Mr. Eben'r Adams, Mr. Thos. Butts, Mr. Wm. Waddill, Mr. David Patteson, Mr. Walter Clopton, Vestrymen.

156        VESTRY BOOK OF ST. PETER'S PARISH.

St. Peter's Parish,                 Dr.

| | |
|---|---:|
| To Mr. David Mossom for his Ministerial function, 16000; C C to Do., 2240 | 18240 |
| To Rob't Walton, Clerk, Including Conveniency, 1908; Richard Brookes, Sexton, 700 | 2608 |
| To Mr. Jno. Netherland his last paym't for ye Glebe well | 1500 |
| To Jos. Waddill for keeping Mary Hazzard & for a pr shoes | 796 |
| To Robt. Allen for Keeping Ann Watkins & her burial.. | 205 |
| To Maj'r Thornton for a Copy of 2 lists of Tythables in 1729 & 1730 | 80 |
| To Rob't Walton his acct., 486; Richard Brookes his acct., 625; Jno. Netherland his acct., 1266 | 2377 |
| To Jno. Finch for keeping of Chas. Parker, 166; Hugh Grinly for work for the Glebe, 160 | 326 |
| To Sallary on 26132 l of Tob'co a 10 p Ct. | 2613 |
| | 28745 |

P Contra,            Cr.

By 973 Tithables a 29½ p poll, 28703½, A fraction due to the Collector 41½ ...................... 28745

The Parish Levy being this day proportioned, we find it amounts to the Sum of 29½ pounds of Tob'co p poll on 973 Tithables in this parish, besides a Fraction of 41½ pounds of Tob'co to be paid to the Collector next year, which Said Sum of 29½ of Tob'co Capt. Tho. Massie is apointed & Impowered to Collect from Every tythable person in this parish, & to pay it to the Several Creditors for whom it is levyed, provided the Said Capt. Thos. Massie gives bond & security to the Vestry for the performance of the Same as the law directs.

Mr. Wm. Chamberlayne & Mr. Charles Massie are Chosen & appointed Vestrymen in the Stead of Col'l John Scott, Deceased, and Mr. Wm. Browne who hath declined the office of a vestryman by his letter to this Vestry. And the Clerk is Ordered to give them Notice to Appear at the Next Vestry to take the Oaths of Vestrymen.

Mr. Jno. Netherland hath promised to pay the fine of Eliz'th Peare, it being five hundred pounds of Tob'co or fifty shillings

Curr't money, And Likewise he hath * * in his hands for the fine of Eliz'th Ingoe by a bill from Sam'l Buxton.

Mr. John Netherland hath agreed w'th this Vestry to Build on the Glebe a Barn 24 foot long & 16 foot wide, framed work wide planked below with Inch & ½ plank, the Roof lathed & Shingled with good Cypress Shingles; Good plank doors. Nine foot between the lower floor & the under part of the plate, to find all nails & Everything else Necessary for which work he is to have two Thousand pounds of Tob'co & Cask to be levyed at ye laying the Next Levy for the performance of which the Said Mr. Netherland is to give bond & Security to the Vestry. The work to be Completed workman like by the last day of March Ensuing.

Signed by D. Mossom, Min'r; Jno. Netherland, Chu. warden; Tho. Butts, Wm. Waddill, Eben'r Adams, Walt. Clopton, Vestrymen.

Recorded by ROBERT WALTON, Clk. Vestry.

At a Vestry held for St. Peter's parish Ap'l 20th, 1731.

PRESENT:

Mr. David Mossom, Min'r; Capt. Wm. Macon, Mr. Wm. Waddill. Mr. Eben'r Adams, Mr. Da'd Patteson, Mr. Wm. Chamberlayne. Vestrymen.

Mr. Wm. Chamberlayne hath this day taken the Oath of a Vestryman before Mr. Eben'r Adams & hath also Subscribed the Test. Mr. Richard Littlepage is Chosen a Vestryman in the Stead of Capt. Wm. Marston, Deceas'd, and the Clerk is ordered to give him warning to appear at the next Vestry to take the Oath of a Vestryman.

Mr. Wm. Chamberlayne hath this day taken the oath of a Church warden.

Upon the petition of Charles Richardson to this Vestry, Setting forth that his son, Charles, is impotent in one of his leggs & Knees, It is ordered that he pay no levy in this parish during his infirmity.

Upon the petition of Phillis Moone for to gett her Son John Moone Levy free, Setting forth in her petition that her S'd Son is troubled with Convultion fitts & much burnt, It is ordered that the Said Jno. Moone be Exempted from paying of parish Levy During his Infirmity.

Mr. Wm. Chamberlayne hath agreed with this Vestry to tarr the Roof of the Church & to put in what Shingles is wanting & to find nails & Tarr to do the same for Eight hundred pounds of Tob'co to be levyed at the laying the Next Levy.

Richard Brookes hath agreed to Sett up three horse blocks at the Church with a Rail to Each of them for Eighty pounds of Tob'co, to be levyed at the laying the next levy.

Mr. Wm. Chamberlayne hath agreed with this Vestry to send for a Communion Table Cloth of Green Velvet three yeards Long & two yards wide, with a Silver fringe for which he is to Charge but fifty p Cent. upon the prime Cost, & to be pd in Tob'co at money Price, the Tob'co to be Levyed at the Laying the next levy. And if the Vestry & Mr. Chamberlayne can not agree upon the price, Then the Tob'co to be Sold to the best bidder for Cash.

It is ordered that the Clerk give publick Notice the Two Ensuing Sundays that there will be a Vestry held at this Church the second Saterday in May, which is the eighth day, And that Likewise give Notice that there is Carpenters, plaisterers & painters work to be Done at the Church & Glebe, and any person willing to undertake the same are Desired then to meet the Vestry & agree for the same.

Signed by D. Mossom, Min'r; Wm. Chamberlayne, Church warden; Will'm Macon, Eben'r Adams, Wm. Waddill, David Patteson.

Recorded by ROBERT WALTON, Clk. Vestry.

At a Vestry held for St. Peter's Parish May ye 8th, 1731.

PRESENT:

Mr. David Mossom, Min'r; Capt. Thos. Massie, Mr. Eben'r Adams, Mr. Wm. Waddill, Mr. David Patteson, Mr. Charles Massie, Vestrymen; Mr. Wm. Chamberlayne, Mr. Walter Clopton, Church wardens.

Mr. Walter Clopton hath this day taken the oath of a Church warden. Mr. Charles Massie hath this day been sworn a Vestryman before Eben'r Adams, Gent., and hath Subscrib'd the Test.

Ordered that Wm. Waddill be allowed 2-6 for fixing up the Dial post. Mr. James Nance hath agree with this Vestry to take up the plank in the Chansil & the Men's side & the Isle of the Church, And to lay the same with good seasoned pine plank Inch & a quarter thick upon good Saw'd White oak Sleepers Six Inches one way and four Inches the other, And put the pews down again, And to find all plank & Nayles & all other Necessaries. Also to do what Carpenter's work is wanting to the Doors of the Church. All the said work to be done workman Like by the last day of March Next Ensuing, For which he is to have Twenty pounds Curr't money, to be paid by the last day of March next Ensuing. The said Nance to give bond & Security to the Vestry for the performance of the same.

Ordered that the Church path from the Ridge road through Thomas Davis's Land be Added to Mr. Adams's & Mr. Walter Clopton's precincts, They to be Equally Concern'd in Keeping the Said Path in repairs and making a bridge & Cosway over the branch and keeping the same in repair.

Daniel Veere hath agreed with this Vestry to do all the painting work which is needfull to be done to the Church & Glebe, And Also to make good white oak plank Steps with Rails to Each Out Door to the Glebe house & fix a Sell to Each Door Case, all to be Done workman like by the last Day of June next and to find all paint, oyl, plank & nails & all other necessaries, For which he is to have the Sum of four pounds two Shillings and Six pence Curr't money to be paid by the tenth Day of March Next Ensuing. The Said Daniel Veere to give bond & Security to the Vestry for the performance of the Same.

Mr. Wade Netherland hath agreed with this Vestry to Double Cover ye Kitchen at ye Glebe and to post it with three good posts to Each Side & to repair what is wanting to the weather boards and to find boards and Nails to be done workmanlike by the last Day of June next, For which he is to have forty shillings Curr't money by the tenth Day of March next, the said Netherland to give bond & security for the performance of the same.

Mr. Wade Netherland hath agreed with this Vestry to find

160    VESTRY BOOK OF ST. PETER'S PARISH.

Tarr and Tarr the Glebe, The great house, the Kitchen & the Barn. The great house is to be tarr'd by the Last day of June Next, the other two by the Last day September next, for which he is to be paid three pounds Curr't money by the tenth Day of March Next Ensuing.

Signed by D. Mossom, Min'r; Eben'r Adams, David Patteson, Cha. Massie, Vestrymen; Wm. Chamberlayne, Walt. Clopton, Church wardens.

Recorded p ROBT. WALTON, Clk. Vestry.

At a Vestry held for St. Peter's Parish August ye 14th, 1731.

Mr. David Mossom, Min'r; Mr. Eben'r Adams, Mr. David Patteson, Mr. Charles Massie, Mr. Rich'd Littlepage, Mr. Tho. Butts; Mr. Wm. Chamberlayne, Mr. Walter Clopton, Church wardens.

Mr. Richard Littlepage hath this day taken the Oath of a Vestryman and Subscribed to the Test.

Ordered that the Clerk Draw out the Several orders for processioning of Land & Deliver them to the persons Nominated in the Said Orders to see the processioning performed.

Signed by D. Mossom, Min'r; Tho. Butts, Eben'r Adams, Chas. Massie, David Patteson, Rich'd Littlepage. Vestrymen; Wm. Chamberlayne, Walt'r Clopton, Church wardens.

Recorded p ROBERT WALTON, Clk. Vest.

At a Vestry held for St. Peter's Parish Septem'r ye 29th, 1731.

Mr. David Mossom, Min'r: Capt. Thos. Massie, Maj'r Wm. Macon, Mr. Jno. Netherland, Mr. Cha. Massie, Capt. Eben'r Adams, Mr. David Patteson, Mr. Rich'd Littlepage, Vestrymen; Mr. Wm. Chamberlayne, Mr. Walter Clopton, Church wardens.

St. Peter's Parish,            Dr.

| | |
|---|---:|
| To the Rev'd Mr. David Mossom for his ministerial function | 16000 |
| To An Allowance of 10 p Ct. retained by ye planters, 1777; Cask on 16000 at 4 p Cent., 640 | 2417 |
| To Collecting of 16000 at 4 p Cent., 640; And allowance of 10 p ct. retained, &c., 200 | 840 |
| To Robt. Walton, Clerk, 1800; Collecting at 4 p ct., 72; Richard Brookes, Sexton, 700 | 2572 |
| To Mr. Chamberlayne for tarring ye Church, &c. | 800 |

VESTRY BOOK OF ST. PETER'S PARISH. 161

To Mr. John Netherland for building ye barn at ye Glebe, but to Lye in ye Collector's hands untill ye S'd Netherland shall Compleat ye S'd barn workmanlike Abating out of ye sum of 2000 l of Tob'co, 500, for ye fine of Eliz'th Pearse, w'ch she has already rec'd............ 1500
To Cask for 2000 L of Tob'co at 4 p C., 80; Maj'r Dandridge for ye Copie of 2 Lists of 40 Tythables........ 120
To Mr. Wm. Chamberlayne his acct................... 328
To Edw'd Birch for ye Q't rents of ye Glebe land for ye years 1728, 1729, 1730, 1731, & for other fees........ 185
To James Moore for Keeping of Mary Hazzard........ 724
To Mr. Wm. Clopton for keeping Charles Barker...... 800
To Wm. Moss for keeping Jane Chapell 18 days & for carrying of her out of this parish..................... 100
To Robt. Walton for a mistake in Casting up ye List of Tithables & for Insolvent tiths.................... 777½
To Rich'd Brookes his acct......................... 560
To Jno. Askew for keeping Judith Weaver's Child 3½ months ........................................... 234
To Edw'd Barley for keeping Wm. Timson 3 months.... 150
To Tob'co to ly in ye Collector's hands to be sold for Cash for Defraying money Debts Chargeable to this parish 9450
Conveniency to Ditto, 1050 ......................... 1050
To Cask to Do. at 4 p Cent......................... 378

 Total ....................................... 38985½
p Contra,   Cr.
By 997 Tythables a 39 p. poll., 38883, A fraction Due to ye Collector 102½ .................. 38985½

 The Parish this day being proportioned, we find it amounts to ye Sum of 39 L Tob'co pr poll on 997 tithables in this parish besides a fraction of 102½ L of Tob'co, to be paid the Collector next year, which S'd Sum of 39 L of Tob'co p poll Mr. Wm. Chamberlayne is impowered to Collect from Every tithable in this parish (making abatements According to Law), Provided ye S'd Wm. Chamberlayne Enter into Bond with Security with this Vestry for ye performance of the Same.
 Edward Morgan by his wife hath agreed to keep Wm. Timson one year for 400 l of Tob'co. Jno. Askews' wife hath agreed

to keep Judith Weaver's child one year for 700 l of Tob'co. Mr. Wm. Clopton hath agreed to keep Charles Barker for 800 l of Tob'co

Upon petition of John Jackson, Surveyor of a high road for more help to Clear ye Road, It is ordered that there be added to his precinct the tithables of John Thompson, Martin Hulett, Edward Bettis and his son.

Ordered that the tithables of Thomas Davis & Jos. Crump be added to the precinct of Mr. Eben'r Adams to Clear ye roads.

Ordered that ye tithables of Mr. Dan'l Farell, Madam Littlepage, Charles Winfree, Rich'd Austin, Rich'd Ross, Matthew Pond, & Rich'd Littlepage do Clear ye Road whereof Rich'd Littlepage is Surveyor.

Signed by D. Mossom, Wm. Macon, Jno. Netherland, Eben'r Adams, Tho. Massie, David Patteson, Chas. Massie, Rich'd Littlepage; Wm. Chamberlayne, Walt. Clopton, Church wardens.

Recorded by ROBERT WALTON, Clk. of Vestry.

At a Vestry held for St. Peter's Parish March ye 2nd, 1731-2.

PRESENT:

The Rev'd Mr. Mossom, Min'r; Capt. Eben'r Adams, Mr. Tho. Butts, Mr. Wm. Waddill, Mr. Jno. Netherland, Mr. Rich'd Littlepage, Vestrymen; Mr. Wm. Chamberlayne, Church Warden.

Whereas at a Vestry held for this parish September ye 29th, 1731, There was Levyed on the Several tithables of this parish the Sum of 9450 pounds of Tob'co, Cask & Conveniency to be Sold for Cash for the Defraying of Money Debts Chargeable on this parish. It is ordered that Mr. Wm. Chamberlayne have the said Tob'co at Ten shillings p Cent.

Capt. Joseph Foster is Chosen a Vestryman in the Room of Capt. Thomas Massie, Decea'd, And the Clark is ordered to give him Notice to appear at the next Vestry in order to take the Oath of a Vestryman.

Mr. John Netherland having made appear to this Vestry (by the report of Richard Ross and Charles Crump) that the barn at the Glebe is finished workmanlike, It is ordered that Mr. Wm. Chamberlayne, Collector of this parish, do pay the Sd Netherland what Tob'co was Levyed for him at the Laying the Last Levy.

Ordered that Mr. Wm. Chamberlayne do take one bredth from

the Communion Table Cloth (and the S'd bredth to ly in his hands for the use of this parish) and to Line the S'd Cloth with proper Lining. Whereas there is in the hands of Mr. Wm. Browne a Silver Chalice belonging to this parish, It is ordered that ye S'd Mr. Wm. Browne Deliver it to the present Church warden ——— D. Mossom, Min'r; ——— Wm. Chamberlayne, Church Warden; Tho. Butts, Wm. Waddill, Eben. Adams, Rich'd Littlepage, John Netherland, Vestrymen.

Recorded by ROBT. WALTON, Clk. Vestry.

At a Vestry held for St. Peter's Parish 7ber 29th, 1732.

PRESENT:

Mr. David Mossom, Min'r; Mr. Wm. Macon, Capt. Eben'r Adams, Mr. Charles Massie, Capt. Jos. Foster, Mr. Wm. Waddill, Vestrymen; Mr. Wm. Chamberlayne, Mr. Walter Clopton, Church wardens.

| St. Peter's Parish, | Dr. | L Tob'co. |
|---|---|---|
| To the Rev'd Mr. Mossom his Salary, 16000; 10 out of the 100c retain'd according to law, 1777............ | | 17777 |
| To Cask a 4 p Ct. and Collection a 4 p Ct., 1280; Robt. Walton his salary, 1800 ......................... | | 3080 |
| To 10c out of ye 100c retain'd, &c., 200; Collection a 4 p Ct., 72; Rich'd Brookes, Sexton, his salary, 200...... | | 972 |
| To Exe'rs of Mr. Wm. Clopton for keeping Cha. Barker | | 800 |
| To Jno. Askew for Keeping Judith Weaver's Child, 700; Edw'd Birch his Acct., 884 ....................... | | 1584 |
| To Edw'd Morgan for keeping Wm. Timson, 400; Maj'r Dandridge his acct. Regulated, 76 ................. | | 476 |
| To Alex'r Mosse for keeping Mary Hazzard, 736; Do. for a pr of shoes for Do., 30 ..................... | | 786 |
| To Mr. Matt'w Kemp, Clk of James City, his acct., 105; Doctor Wm. Comrie his acct., 1146 ................ | | 1251 |
| To Edw'd Morris his Acct. & for ye burial of Dan'l Morris | | 550 |
| To Mr. Wm. Chamberlayne his acct., 124½; Mr. Wm. Browne for a fraction due in ys year 1727, 124½..... | | 1517 |
| To Rich'd Brookes his acct., 120; Fran'e Brookes for a Gate at ye Glebe, 45 ............................. | | 165 |

To Collection of 7799 of Tob'co a 4 p Ct. .............. 312

29270
To a fraction to ye parish .......................... 149

29419
P Contra.      Cr.
By 949 tithables a 31 p poll is 29419.

The Parish Levy being this day proportioned, we find it Amounts to the Sum of 31 l pr poll on 949 tithables in this parish, Except a fraction (due to the parish from ye Collector) of 149 l of Tob'co, Which Said Sum of 31 l of Tob'co Mr. William Chamberlayne is impowered to Collect from Every Tithable person in this parish, Provided the S'd Wm. Chamberlayne Enter into Bond with the Vestry for the performance of the Same.

Ordered that Capt. Jos. Foster, Mr. Robt. Clopton & Mr. Rich'd Crump or any two of them, do View the Glebe & make their report to ye Next Vestry of the State and Condition the houses & Garden paling at present is in. John Askew hath agreed to keep Judith Weaver's Child this Ensuing year for 400 pounds of Tob'co.

Edward Morgan hath agreed to keep Wm. Timson for 400 l of Tob'co. Robt. Clopton hath agreed to keep Cha. Barker for 800 l of Tobacco. Ordered that ye Church Wardens Agree with Some person to waynscut the East end of ye Church behind the Communion Table as high as the Window. Capt. Jos. Foster hath this day taken the Oath of a Vestryman and Subscribed to the Test. Ordered that George Pearson do keep Cha. Goodwin this Ensuing year for 200 l of Tob'co.

Mr. Charles Massie is Chosen Church Warden in ye room of Mr. Walter Clopton and taken the Oath of a Church Warden.

Ordered that Rich'd Brookes do keep John Rock this Ensuing year for 800 lbs. of Tobacco. Ordered that the Church Wardens provide a new Register Book for the use of this parish.

Signed by David Mossom, Min'r; And by Walt. Clopton, Eben. Adams, Wm. Macon, Jos. Foster, Wm. Waddill, Vestrymen; Wm. Chamberlayne, Chas. Massie, Church wardens.

            Recorded by ROBERT WALTON, Clk. of Vestry.

At a Vestry held for St. Peter's Parish 7ber 29th, 1733.

VESTRY BOOK OF ST. PETER'S PARISH. 165

Mr. David Mossom, Min'r; Mr. Tho. Butts, Mr. Wm. Waddill, Capt. Jos. Foster, Mr. Walter Clopton, Mr. David Patteson, Vestrymen; Mr. Wm. Chamberlayne, Mr. Chas. Massie, Ch. wardens.

St. Peter's Parish,     Dr.

| | |
|---|---:|
| To the Rev'd Mr. Mossom his Salary, 16000; 10c out of ye 100c retain'd, 1777 | 17777 |
| To Cask at 4 p Ct. & Collection at 4 p ct., 1280; Robert Walton his Salary, 1800 | 3080 |
| To 10c out of ye 100c retain'd, 200; Collection at 4 p Cent., 72 | 272 |
| To Rich'd Brookes, Sexton, 700; Robt. Clopton for keeping Chas. Barker and for his burial and three q'ts of rum, 972½ | 1672½ |
| To Jno. Askew for Keeping Judith Weaver's Child | 400 |
| To Ed'd Morgan for keeping Wm. Timson & making a Coat | 420 |
| To Geo. Pearson for keeping Charles Goodwin | 200 |
| To Doct'r Wm. Comrie for keeping Jno. Rock | 800 |
| To Jno. Roberts for keeping Jno. Goodwin Six months & for his burial | 425 |
| To Mrs. Judith Scott for Charges on one Catherine a poor woman from Lancaster Boughleys | 250 |
| To Alex'r Mosse for keeping Mary Hazzard | 756 |
| To Mr. Matt. Kemp, Clerk of James City County | 20 |
| To Maj'r Dandridge his Acct. Regulated | 214 |
| To Mr. Wm. Chamberlayne his Acct. | 1748½ |
| To Mr. Jno. Netherland for an Overlist last year | 31 |
| To Mr. Chamberlayne for paying Mr. Rogers a lawyer's fees | 120 |
| To Thos. Martin for keeping Wm. Goodwin Since Mar. 10th | 200 |
| To Mr. Chamberlayne for paying James Nance, 440; Salary on 7697 l a 4 p Ct., 308 | 748 |
| | 28783 |
| To Due to the parish | 210 |
| | 28993 |

P Contra, Cr.
By 967 tithables a 30c p poll is.. 29010
By Edw'd Birch ............. 17
                              ─────
                              28993

The parish levy being this day proportioned, wee find it Amounts to the Sum of thirty pounds of Tob'co p poll on 967 Tithables in this parish, Except a fraction of 210 pounds of Tob'co due to the parish w'ch Said Sum of thirty pounds of Tob'co Mr. Charles Massie is impowered to Collect from Every Tithable person in this parish, provided the S'd Charles Massie give bond & security to the Vestry for the performance of the Same.

Capt. Joseph Foster is Chosen Church warden in the room of Mr. Wm. Chamberlayne, and hath taken the Oath of a Church warden. Capt. Michael Sherman is Chosen a Vestryman in the room of Mr. John Netherland and that the Clark give him Notice to Appear at ye Next Vestry. Ordered that Doct'r Wm. Comrie have 500 l of Tob'co for keeping John Rock this ensuing year, provided the S'd Comrie puts him through a Course of Physick. Ordered that the Church wardens provide a Copie of ye body of the Virg'a laws of Mr. Parke, the minister, for the use of this parish.

Ordered that Robt. Morgan have 210 l of Tob'co (being ye fraction of ye parish proportion this year) for keeping Wm. Goodwin this year upon Consideration of having the S'd Goodwin bound to him to the age of 21 years.

Ordered that Jno. Askew have 200 l of Tob'co for Keeping Judith Weaver's Child this Ensuing year upon Consideration of having the S'd Child bound to him to the age of 21 years.

Ordered that Mr. Charles Massie have 300 l of Tob'co for keeping Wm. Timson. Ordered that Deremiah Dalton have 650 l Tob'co for keeping of Mary Hazzard. Ordered that George Pearson have 200 l of Tob'co for keeping Charles Goodwin. Ordered that the Church wardens provide a good new Surplice for the use of this parish.

David Mossom, Min'r; Walt'r Clopton, David Patteson, Tho. Butts, Wm. Waddill, Wm. Chamberlayne, laymen; Chas. Massie, Jo's Foster, Church wardens.

At a Vestry held for St. Peter's Parish September 28th, 1734.

PRESENT:

Rev'd Mr. David Mossom, Min'r; Major Wm. Macon, Capt. Eben'r Adams, Mr. William Waddill, Mr. Walter Clopton, Mr. David Pattison, Vestrymen; Capt. Jos. Foster, Mr. Charles Massie, Church wardens.

| | | |
|---|---|---|
| St. Peter's Parish, | Dr. | L Tobacco. |
| To Rev'd Mr. Mossom his Salary, 16000; 10c out of the 100c retain'd, 1777; Cask at 4 p ct., 640 | | 18417 |
| To Robt. Walton, Clerk, 1800; Richard Brookes, Sexton, 700c, 10 out of the 100c retain'd, 200 | | 2700 |
| To Maj'r Jno. Dandridge for Copie 2 Lists Tithables, 40 | | 40 |
| To Mrs. Judith Scott for keeping Mary Hamilton & her Burial | | 230 |
| To Eliz'a Taylor for keeping Mary Hamilton 6 weeks... | | 600 |
| To Edw'd Morgan for keeping Wm. Timson 5 mon. & bur'l | | 260 |
| To George Pearson for keeping Charles Goodwin | | 200 |
| To Jno. Askew for Judith Weaver's Child | | 200 |
| To Mr. Wm. Chamberlayne his Acct., 1491; Do. for Keeping Jos. Showers, 500 | | 1991 |
| To Deremiah Dalton for keeping Mary Hazzard, 218½ and for making waistcoat & petticoat Thos Dowle for Do., 152½ | | 671 |
| To Julius Barbridge for Qt. Rents Glebe Land 1734, 29; Edward Birch his acct., 120 | | 149 |
| To Mr. Mossom for making the Surplice | | 110 |
| To Richard Brookes for digging Chas. Barker's grave.. | | 15 |
| To 10 out of the 100 on 104 1 Tob'co for Mad'm Scott.... | | 10½ |
| To Collection 25596½ at 4 p Ct. | | 1023½ |
| | | 26620 |
| To A fraction due to the Parish | | 113 |
| By 938 Tithables at 28½ p poll, 26733 | | 26733 |

Mr. David Pattison is chosen Church Warden in the Room of Mr. Charles Massie and hath taken the Oath accordingly.

The Parish Levy being this day proportioned, we find it

amounts to the Sum of 28½ pounds of Tob'co p poll on 938 Tithables, besides a fraction of 113 1 Tob'co due to the parish which said Sum of 28½ pounds of Tob'co Mr. David Pattison is impowered to collect from every Tithable Person in this Parish, provided the S'd Mr. David Pattison give Bond and Security to the Vestry for the Performance of the Same.

John Davis is discharg'd from paying parish Levy. Ordered that George Pearson have 150 1 of Tob'co for keeping Charles Goodwin this ensuing year.

That Abram Alloway have 550 lb. Tob'co for keeping Mary Hazard this ensuing year.

That Eliza Turner have 500 lbs. Tob'co for keeping Mary Major this ensuing year.

Mr. David Pattison has given Bond for the Parish Collection together with his Security, Maj'r Wm. Macon and Mr. Chas. Massie.

Signed by D. Mossom, Min'r; Chas. Massie, Eben'r Adams, Will'm Macon, Wm. Waddill, Walter Clopton; Jos. Foster, David Pattison, Church Wardens.

Registered p WILL'M FORD, Clk. Vest.

At a meeting of the Vestry call'd by the Rev'd Mr. Mossom for the choosing a Parish Clerk March 5, 1734.

PRESENT:

Rev'd Mr. David Mossom, Min'r; Maj'r Wm. Macon, Mr. Wm. Chamberlayne, Mr. Rich'd Littlepage, Mr. Wm. Waddill, Vestrymen; Capt. Jos. Foster, Church Warden.

Whereas the Office of Clerk of the Parish and Vestry is become vacant by the death of the late Robert Walton and William Ford and Thomas Davis appearing as Candidates for the said office, Wm. Ford was chosen Clerk of the Parish and Vestry by the Unanimous Consent of the Minister and Vestrymen present, Provided that the said Ford become an Inhabitant of this Parish by or before Christmas ensuing.

Ordered, That the Church Wardens cause a good & substantial Pair of Stocks to be forthwith erected near the Church yard Wall for the Restraint of licentious and disorderly Persons, several such having lately appeared in the Church to the great Disturbance of the Minister and Congregation during divine Service.

Signed by D. Mossom, Min'r; Wm. Waddill, Wm. Macon, Wm. Chamberlayne, Rich'd Littlepage. Vestrymen; Jos. Foster, Church Warden.

Registered p WILL FORD, Clk. Vest.

At a Vestry held for St. Peter's Parish at the Church August 5, 1735.

PRESENT:

The Rev'd Mr. Mossom, Min'r: Maj'r Wm. Macon, Mr. Wm. Waddill, Mr. Walt'r Clopton, Mr. Charles Massie, Capt. Mich'l Sherman, Maj'r John Dandridge; David Pattison, Church Warden.

Capt. Mich'l Sherman was this day sworn a Vestryman and took the Oaths appointed by Law instead of the Oaths of Allegiance & Supremacy before Maj'r Wm. Macon, one of his Maj'tys Justices of the Peace for this County and Subscribed the Test.

Wm. Ford was this day sworn Clerk of the Vestry and took the afores'd Oaths before the S'd Maj'r Wm. Macon and subscribed the Test.

Majr John Dandridge is chosen a Vestryman in the Room of Capt. Ebenez'r Adams, dec'd, by the unanimous Voice of the minister and Vestrymen, and the Clerk is ordered to give him Notice accordingly that He may appear to take the Oaths.

Maj'r John Dandridge was call'd in by the Clerk, and according to the Order was this day sworn a Vestryman and took the oaths appointed by Law instead of the Oaths of Allegiance and Supremacy before Major Wm. Macon and subscribed the Test.

Ordered That the Order of Vestry made March 5, 1734, relating to the Church Warden's erecting a good and substantial Pair of Stocks be confirmed by this Vestry.

Ordered That John Marrohoe be discharged from paying Parish Levy.

Signed by D. Mossom, Min'r; Will Macon, Wm. Waddill, Walt. Clopton, Cha'r Massie, Mich'l Sherman, Jno. Dandridge, Vestrymen; David Pattison, Church warden.

Registered p WILL'M FORD, Clk. Vest.

At a Vestry held for St. Peter's Parish Sept'r 29, 1735.
The Rev'd Mr. Mossom, Min'r; Maj'r Wm. Macon, Mr. Wm.

170   VESTRY BOOK OF ST. PETER'S PARISH.

Waddill, Mr. Walter Clopton, Mr. Charles Massie, Capt. Mich'l Sherman, Maj'r John Dandridge, Vestrymen; Capt. Jos. Foster, Church Warden.

| St. Peter's Parish, | Dr. | L. Tob'co. |
|---|---|---|
| To the Rev. Mr. Mossom, his Salary, Cask to Do. at 4 p Ct., 840 | | 16640 |
| To the 10 out of the 100 retain'd upon Do. | | 1850 |
| To Robert Walton, late Clerk for 3 mos. & 1 week, 487½, the 10 out of 100 retained upon Do., 54 | | 541½ |
| To William Ford, Clerk, 6 months & 24 days, 1012; the 10 out of 100 retain'd, 112 | | 1124 |
| To Richard Brookes, Sexon, 700; Maj'r John Dandridge, Copy 2 Lists Tithables, 40 | | 740 |
| To Peter Butts for Quit Rents Glebe Land, 29; Maj'r Wm. Macon for Goods deliv'd Eliza Turner for the use of Mary Major, 2l:0:1½ in Tob'co at 2 p'll, 10 p C. on Do., 27 | | 246½ |
| To the Ballance of Capt. Foster's acct., 1l.0.3½ in Tob. at 122 re 2, 10 p Ct. on Do., 14 | | 136 |
| To the Rev'd Mr. Mossom for Wine L. 1. 2. 6. in Tobo. at 2l 135, 10 p Ct. on Do., 15 | | 150 |
| To George Pearson for keeping Goodwin, 150; Abraham Alloway for keeping Mary Hazzard, 550 | | 700 |
| To Elizabeth Turner for keeping Mary Major, 500; Collector for Delinquents, 370½ | | 870½ |
| To Richard Brookes for going to James City for List Tithables | | 20 |
| To Richard Brookes for digging Jos. Showers' Grave | | 25 |
| To Abraham Alloway for a Pr Shoes for Mary Hazard | | 30 |
| | | 23164½ |
| To Cornel'l Matthews for suport of his Mother last year, 300; Margret Down, 500 | | 800 |

By the Remainder due to the Parish last year, 113......23964½
To Collection at 4 p Ct., 954, the Remainder due to the Parish, 51 ........................................   413
                                                                       _____
                                                                      23851½

|  |  | 954 |
|---|---|---|
| Contra, | Cr. | 51 |
| By 956 Titheables at 26 1 Tobo. p poll, 24856½.....24856½ | | |

Ordered That John Marrhoe have 550 1 Tob'co for keeping Mary Hazard this ensuing year. That Elizabeth Turner have 500 lb. Tob'co for keeping Mary Major this ensuing year. That Wm. Perkins, Jun'r, set up new Benches made of saw'd white Oak Plank 2 inches thick, with good moul'd Blocks to support them, pinn'd down by or before the 1st of April ensuing, to be paid after the Rate of 2 lb. Tob'co p foot in length, the Benches to be 11 Inches wide.

That Robert Morgan have 400 lb. Tobo. for keeping Charles Goodwin this ensuing year. Maj'r John Dandridge is chosen Church Warden in the room of Capt. Jos. Foster. The Parish Levy being this day proportioned, wee find it amounts to the Sum of 26 lbs Tobo. p poll on 956 Titheables besides a Remainder of 51 lb. Tobo. due to the Parish, which said Sum of 26 lb. Tobo. Mr. David Pattison is impowered to collect from every Titheable Person in this Parish, provided the said Pattison enter into Bond with Security for Performance of the Same.

Mr. David Pattison has offered to give Bond with his Security * * Wm. Macon & Mr. Charles Massie, who are appointed by the * * his Performance of the Collection and is to give Bond according to Law.

Signed by D. Mossom, Min'r; Wm. Macon, Jos. Foster, Walt'r Clopton, Wm. Waddill, Cha'r Massie Mich'a Sherman; David Pattison, John Dandridge, Church Wardens.

At a Vestry held for St. Peter's Parish Oct'r 5th, 1735.

PRESENT:

The Rev'd Mossom, Min'r; Maj'r Wm. Macon, Mr. Wm. Waddill, Mr. Walt'r Clopton, Mr. Charles Massie, Vestrymen: Mr. David Pattison, Maj'r Jno. Dandridge, Church Wardens.

Ordered At the petition of Martin Hewlett an Overseer of the High Road from the Church to Mr. Chamberlayne's ferry, That he have Mr. Chamberlayne's Tithables, John Tomson & his

Prentice, John Jackson's Son, Peter Moon, John Crump at the Widow Jackson's & his own Titheables.

At the petition of Wm. Paisley, an Overseer of the High Road from the Old Church to Mr. Chamberlayne's Ordinary, That he have Wm. Atkinson's Titheables, Stephen Brookes, Lodowick Alford, Goodrick Alford and Julius Alford, Mich'a Harfield, Tith's, Rich'd Ross, Maj'r Dandridge, John Lightfoot's & Colo. Curtis's Tith's at the old Quar'r and upon the River.

Richard Crump an Overseer of an high Road, to have Thos. Davis and Joseph Crump aded to his Company.

David Pattison with his Security's, Maj'r Wm. Macon and Mr. Charles Massie hath this day given Bond for the performance of the Parish Collection.

Sign'd by David Mossom, Min'r: Wm. Macon, Wm. Waddill, Cha'r Massie, Walt. Clopton, Vestrymen; David Pattison, Jno. Dandridge, Church Wardens.

---

At a Vestry held for St. Peter's Parish September 29th, 1736,

PRESENT:

The Rev'd Mr. Mossom, Min'r; Maj'r Wm. Macon, Capt. Jos. Foster, Mr. Chas. Massie, Mr. Wm. Waddill, Mr. Walter Clopton, Mr. Rich'd Littlepage, Vestrymen; Maj'r Jo'n Dandridge, Mr. David Pattison, Church Wardens.

| St. Peter's Parish, | Dr. | Lbs. Tob'co. |
|---|---|---|
| To the Rev'd Mossom, Min'r, his Salary, 16000, Cask to Do., 4 per Ct., 640 | | 16640 |
| To the 10 out of the 100 retain'd upon Do., 1850; James Holmes his Salary, 1800 | | 3650 |
| To 10 out of the 100 retain'd, &c., 200; Richard Brokas Sexton his Salary, 700 | | 900 |
| To Maj'r John Dandridge, Copy 2 Lists Titheables & for a Copy of a Deed | | 80 |
| To John Murrahoe for keeping Mary Hazzard, 550; Peter Butts for Q't Rents Glebe Land, 20 | | 570 |
| To Eliz'th Turner for keeping Mary Major | | 500 |
| To Wm. Perkins, Jun'r, for Setting up Benches for the Church, 200 Foot of Plank a 2 l Tobo. per foot | | 400 |
| To Robt. Morgan for keeping Chas. Goodwin | | 400 |

VESTRY BOOK OF ST. PETER'S PARISH. 173

| | |
|---|---|
| To the Ex'rs of Dan'l Ferrall, Dec'd, for 12 Bottles of Wine a 2\| Per Bottle & 1 Quire Paper 1-3 £1, 5, 3 in Tobo. a 12-6 | 224 |
| To Capt. Jos. Foster for 1 Sheet Deliv'd John Gawlin to bury his Daughter -in Tob'co a 12-6 | 79 |
| To Maj'r Wm. Macon for goods Deliv'd Robt. Morgan by Order of Maj'r Dandridge for Chas. Goodwin £ 3, 13, 2½ in Tob'co a 12-6 | 592 |
| To a Stone Font bespoke of Cha'r Carter, Esq'r £8 in Tobo. at | 1420 |
| To Maj'r Kemp for 2 List Titheables, 1735 & 1736, 40; Mr. Patteson to the Ballance of his Acco't, 547 | 587 |
| To Richard Brokar his Acco't for Horse Blocks, &s. | 115 |
| To Sarah Brokar's Acco't for attending Sarah Downs, 200; Alice Ross, 39 | 239 |
| | 26405½ |
| To Collection a 4 Per Ct. | 1056 |
| | 27461½ |
| To a Remainder due to Parish | 259 |
| By 924 Titheables a 30 lb. Tobo. Per Poll, 27720 | 27720½ |

Per Contra,      Cr.

By the Ballance of Mr. Butts's Acco't, 60; Ballance remaining last year, 51 ............................. 111

Ordered that Robert Morgan have 500 lb. Tob'co for keeping Charles Goodwin the ensuing year.

That Alice Moor have 500 lb. Tobo. for keeping Mary Major the ensuing year. That John Murrahoe have 500 lbs. for keeping Mary Hazard the ensuing year.

That Sarah Brokas have 700 lb. Tobo. for taking Sarah Downe the Daughter of Marg't Downe, dec'd, & keeping her off the Parish & to be bound to her the ensuing year.

That Mr. David Pattison have 500 lb. Tobo. for taking Sarah a bastard daughter of Mary Ashberry & keeping her off the parish & the S'd Sarah to be bound to him the ensuing year.

That Tabitha Meanly be prosecuted by the Church Wardens for having a bastard child.

That Charles Smith & Jno. Baily be added to Martin Hewlett's Gang.

That Capt. Mich'll Sherman be chosen Church Warden in the room of Mr. Da. Pattison. That Mr. Ambrose Dudley be chosen a Vestryman in the Room of Mr. Wm. Chamberlayne, dec'd, & that the Clerk give him Notice to appear at the next Vestry to take the oath of a Vestryman.

That the Church Wardens, together with Maj'r Wm. Macon & Capt. Jos. Foster, do Settle the Acct. with Mrs. Chamberlayne for the Tobo. that was levied in the year 1731 & make Report to the next Vestry.

That Francis Williams be discharged from paying Levy.

That James Holmes was this day appointed Clerk of the Vestry & accordingly Sworn before Maj'r Wm. Macon, one of his Maties Justices of the Peace for this County & Subscribed the Test.

This day the Parish Levy being Proportion'd, We Find it amounts to the Sume of 30 lb. Tobo. per Poll. on 924 Titheables, besides a Rem'w of £259 of Tobo. due to the Parish w'ch S'd Sume of 30 lb. Tobo. Mr. Walter Clopton is impowered to collect from every Titheable Person in this Parish, Provided the S'd Clopton enter into Bond with Security to the Vestry for Performance of the Same, Mr. Walter Clopton has offered to give Bond with his Security's the Rev'd Mr. David Mossom, Maj'r Wm. Macon, & Capt. Jos. Foster, who are approved by the Vestry for his Performance of the Collection, & is to give Bond accordingly.

Signed by D. Mossom, Min'r; Will'm Macon, Jos. Foster, Rich'd Littlepage, Chas. Massie, Wm. Waddill, Da. Pattison, Walter Clopton, Vestrymen; Jno. Dandridge, Church Warden.

Recorded by JAMES HOLMES, Clerk of the Vestry.

---

At a Vestry held for St. Peter's Parish September 29th, 1737.

PRESENT:

The Rev'd Mr. D. Mossom, Min'r; Maj'r Wm. Macon, Capt. Jos. Foster, Mr. Walter Clopton, Mr. Wm. Waddill, Mr. David Pattison, Mr. Ambrose Dudley, Vestrymen; Maj'r Jo'n Dandridge, Capt. Mich'll Sherman, Church Wardens.

The Vestry not being able to proceed to Lay the Levy for

VESTRY BOOK OF ST. PETER'S PARISH.  175

want of the List of Tithables of that part of James City County in St. Peter's Parish.

Ordered That the Vestry be adjourned to Saturday, October the 8th, 1737.

At a Vestry held for St. Peter's Parish October the 8th, 1737.

PRESENT:

The Rev'd Mr. Mossom, Min'r; Coll. Wm. Macon, Maj'r Jos. Foster, Mr. Walter Clopton, Mr. Rich'd Littlepage, Mr. Wm. Waddill, Mr. Ambrose Dudley, Vestrymen; Maj'r Jon' Dandridge, Capt. Mith'll Sherman, Church Wardens.

St. Peter's Parish,   Dr.         Lb. Tob'co.

| | |
|---|---:|
| To the Rev'd Mr. Mossom his Salary to Sept. the 29th, 16000; Cask to Do. a 4 p ct., 640 | 16640 |
| To James Holmes his Salary to Septemb'r the 29th, Richard Brokar, Sexton, his Salary | 2430 |
| To Sarah Brookar for taking Sarah Downe, the Daughter of M. Downe | 630 |
| To Robt. Morgan for keeping Chas. Goodwin | 455 |
| To Alice Moor for keeping Mary Major | 455 |
| To John Murrahoe for keeping Mary Hazard | 455 |
| To David Pattison for taking Sarah, A Bastard of Marg't Ashberry | 455 |
| To Richard Brokar for bearing the Chain in Surveying the Glebe & 2 Days' Attendance a 18lb Tob'co p Day | 36 |
| To Peter Brokar for 1 Day's Do. a Do. * 18, Brokar for Do. a Do. 18 | 36 |
| To * Waddill for Quit Rents of 120 acres of Glebe Land | 29 |
| To Mrs. Eliz'th Farrell her acco. £2, 4, 6 a 2d p lb | 267 |
| To Maj'r John Dandridge his acco't 269; Col. Walter Clopton his acco't, 440 | 719 |
| To Coll. Wm. Macon his Acco't | 747 |
| To the Rev'd Mr. Mossom for Deficiency of Glebe, 1600 lb. Tobo., Cask to Do. a 4 p ct., 64 | 1654 |
| To Capt. Mith'll Sherman for his Trouble in keeping Thos. * a travelling man in his Sickness & for burying him | 250 |
| To Coll. Macon for Supplying Robt. Morgan with necessaries | 200 |
| To 5 lb. Tobo. upon every Tithable Person in this Parish | 4930 |

To Collection a 6 L C, Rem't in the Collector's Hands due
to the Parish .................................. 1818

32538

Per Contra,   Cr.

By 986 Tithables a 33 lbs. Tobo. p Tithable, 32538

Mr. Ambrose Dudley was sworn a Vestryman before Major Joseph Foster & accordingly Subscribed the Test.

Ordered That Francis Amos be Sett Levy free.

That Edward Nash be Sett Levy free.

That Robt. Morgan be allowed 500 lb. Tobo. for keeping Chas. Goodwin the ensuing year.

That Alice Moor be allowed 500 lbs. Tobo. for keeping Mary Major the ensuing year.

That John Murrahoe be allowed 550 lbs. Tobo. for keeping Mary Hazard the ensuing year.

That the Rev'd Mr. David Mossom be allowed 1600 lb. Tobo. & Cask for the Deficiency of a Glebe for this year & so on till such time as the Vestry consider further of the same.

That 5 !b. Tobo. p poll be Levyed upon Every Tithable person in this Parish towards Defraying the Charge of building a Vestry Room & Steeple 16 lb. Tobo. is to be paid by the Collector to the Church wardens, & to be sold by them for money at the Public Outcry to the highest bidder.

That the Order made last Vestry for Settling w'th Mrs. Elizabeth Chamberlayne be Continued & in Case she refuses to Settle, the Church Wardens are to bring suit.

Mr. George Poindexter having resigned the Office of a Vestryman by his note to the Min'r & Vestry, Mr. Joseph Marston is Chosen a Vestryman in the Room of the S'd Poindexter & that the Clerk give him Notice to attend the next Vestry in order to take the Oath of a Vestryman.

This day the Parish Levy being proportioned, we find it amounts to the Sum of 33 lb. Tobo. p poll on 935 Tithables besides a frac'n of 322 lb. Tobo. due to the Parish, w'ch S'd Sum of 33 lb. Tobo. Mr. Walter Clopton is impowered to Collect from Every Tithable person in this Parish, Provided that S'd Clopton Enter into Bond with Security to the Vestry for Performance of the Same, Mr. Walter Clopton has offered to give

Bond with his Securitys, the Rev'd Mr. David Mossom, Coll. Wm. Macon & Maj'r Jos. Foster, who are approved. That 322 lb. Tobo. Rem'd due to the Parish be sold for ready money at a publick Outcry to the highest bidder w'th the rest of the Tobo. before Levyed.

That Maj'r Jo'n Dandridge & Capt. Mich'll Sherman be Continued Church Wardens for the ensuing year.

D. Mossom, Min'r; Wm. Macon, Jos. Foster, Rich'd Littlepage, Walt'r Clopton, Wm. Waddill, Ambrose Dudley, Jno. Dandridge Mich'll Sherman, Church Wardens.

Recorded by JAMES HOLMES, Clk of Vestry.

At a Vestry held for St. Peter's Parish October 2nd, 1738.

PRESENT:

The Rev'd Mr. Mossom, Min'r; Coll. Wm. Macon, Capt. Rich'd Littlepage, Mr. Walter Clopton, Mr. Wm. Waddill, Mr. David Pattison, Mr. Ambrose Dudley, Vestrymen.

St. Peter's Parish, Dr. lb. Tobo.

To the Rev'd Mr. Mossom his Salary to Sept'r the 29th, Cask to Do. a 4 p Ct. 640 ...................... 16640
To the Rev'd Mr. Mossom for Deficiency of Glebe, 1600 lb. Tobo.—Cask to Do. a p ct. ...................... 1664
To James Holmes his Salary to September the 29th .... 1800
To Richard Brokas, Sexton, his Salary ................ 630
To Hugh Grindley for keeping Chas. Goodwin ........ 450
To Alice Moor for keeping Mary Major .............. 450
To John Murrahoe for keeping Mary Hazard .......... 495
To Sarah Waddill Quit Rents of 120 Acres of Glebe Land 29
To Maj'r Dandridge for 2 List of Tithables ............ 36
To Maj'r Matthew Kemp for a Copy of List of Tithables 18
To Mr. Walter Clopton allowed for Delinquents * .... 597
To Mr. Antho. Colt for 2 Dint & 8-2 p pound, being £1, 4s, 6d ............................................. 147
To Capt. Rich'd Littlepage for Do. a Do., being 12s.... 72
To Coll. Wm. Macon the Ballance of his Acct. being 4, 11, 6½ at 2d. ................................... 550
To Joseph Crump Acct. & for maintaining * * Warren & her bastard child .............................. 400

| | |
|---|---:|
| To Doctor Arnotto Acco't for Salivating & keeping & Supplying with necessaries & funerall expenses of Wm. Sparrow ............................................. | 1057 |
| To Sarah Waddill's Charge ag't the Parish for Arresting Stephen Sanders ................................. | 27 |
| To Arthur Cruse for keeping Marg't Grumbal Since May last to the 29th of September ................. | 300 |
| To Mr. Wm. Grey for the full Ballance of Mr. Chamberlayne's Acco't being rol, 7d., in Tobo. a 2s p Pound..... | |
| To Mr. Thomas Tarlson for 4 Acres of Land Purchased of him for the use of the Parish adjoining to that One Purchased of his Grandfather, being 40-in Tobo. a 8-2— | 240 |
| To the Collection a 6 P Ct. ........................ | 1542 |
| | 27208 |
| To Richard Brokas, for his wife, washing the Surplice.. | 50 |
| Per Contra, Cr. | 27258 |
| By 1044 Tithables a 26 lbs Tobo. p 27144 Poll. & A Rem'r, from the Parish to the Collector, 114 .............. | 27258 |

Ordered that Hugh Grindley be allowed 450 lb. Tobo. for keeping Charles Goodwin the ensuing year.

That Alice Moor be allowed 450 lbs. Tobo. for keeping Mary Major the ensuing year.

That John Murrahoe be allowed 495 lb. Tobo. for keeping Mary Hazard the ensuing year.

That Capt. Rich'd Littlepage & Mr. Ambrose Dudley be Chosen Church Wardens for the ensuing year in the Room of Maj'r John Dandridge & Capt. Mich'll Sherman, accordingly Sworn this Day before Coll. Wm. Macon.

That Arthur Cruse be allowed 495 lb. Tobo. for keeping Mary Grumball the ensuing year.

That Whereas Mr. Wm. Grey brought the Books of Mr. William Chamberlayne Dec'd, in Order to settle the Acct lying open between the S'd Mr. Chamberlayne; this parish, & it appearing upon a just Examination that there is a Ballance of ten Shillings & Sevenpence due to Mr. Chamberlayne's Estate, that sd ten Shillings & Sevenpence is this day Leveyed in Tobo. a 2d P pound & 'tis mutually agreed that this Shall be the finall Settlement of all Accounts between the Estate of Mr. Chamberlayne & this Parish to this Day.

This Day the Parish Levy being proportioned We find it amounts to Sume of 26 lbs. of Tobo. P Poll. on 1044 Tithables, which sd Sume of 26 lbs. Tobo. Mr. Walter Clopton is impowered to Collect from Every Tithable Person in this Parish Provided the Sd Clopton enter into Bond with Security to the Vestry for performance of the Same. Mr. Walter Clopton has offered to give Bond with his Securities. Capt. Rich'd Littlepage, Mr. Ambrose Dudley, who are approved by the Vestry for his Performance of the Collection, & it is to give Bond accordingly.

That there appears by an acco't under Maj'r John Dandridge's hand, dated September 29th, 1738, to be due to this Parish the Sume of forty-two Pounds, one Shilling & two Pence Curr't Money, which is Ordered to be Recorded.

D. Mossom, Min'r. (Will'm Macon, Wm. Waddill, David Patteson, Walt. Clopton.) (Rich'd Littlepage, Ambrose Dudley,) Church Wardens.

Recorded by      JAMES HOLMES, Clk. of the Vestry.

---

At a Vestry held for St. Peter's Parish September the 29th, 1739.

PRESENT:

The Rev. Mr. Mossom, Min'r; Maj'r John Dandridge, Maj'r Joseph Foster, Mr. Walter Clopton, Mr. Chas. Massie, Mr. Thomas Butts, Capt. Mich'll Shermon, Mr. Joseph Marston, Mr. David Pattison, Vestrymen; Mr. Ambrose Dudley, Church Warden.

Mr. Joseph Marston hath this Day taken the Oath of a Vestryman and Subscribed to the Test. David Mossom, Min'r; John Dandridge, Joseph Forster, Walter Clopton, Chas. Massie, Thomas Butts, Mich'll Sherman, Joseph Marston, David Patteson; Mr. Ambrose Dudley, Church Warden.

Recorded by      JAMES HOLMES, Clk of the Vestry.

---

At a Vestry held for St. Peter's Parish October the 6th, 1739.

PRESENT:

The Rev'd Mr. Massom, Min'r; Maj'r John Dandridge, Mr.

180    VESTRY BOOK OF ST. PETER'S PARISH.

Walter Clopton, Mr. Chas. Massie, Capt. Mith'll Sherman, Mr. Joseph Marston, Mr. David Patteson, Mr. Thomas Butts, Vestrymen; Capt. Rich'd Littlepage, Mr. Ambrose Dudley, Church Wardens.

| St. Peter's Parish, Dr. | Lbs. Tob'co. |
|---|---|
| To the Rev. Mr. Mossom, his Salary to Sept'r the 29th, Cask to Do. a L. p Ct. 640 | 16640 |
| To the Rev. Mr. Mosrom for Deficiency of Glebe 1600 lb. Tobo. Cask to Do. a 4 P. Ct., 64 | 1664 |
| To James Holmes, his Salary to September the 29th, Richard Broker, Sexton, his Salary | 2430 |
| To Hugh Grindley for keeping Chas. Goodwin | 450 |
| To Alice Moor for keeping Mary Major | 450 |
| To John Murrahoe for keeping Mary Hazard | 495 |
| To Arthur Cruse for keeping Marg't Grumbal | 495 |
| To Maj'r Dandridge for 2 Lists Tithables | 36 |
| To Maj'r Matt. Kemp for a Copy of List of Tithables.. | 18 |
| To Arthur Cruse for keeping Mary Grumbal in Cloathes, 40 lbs. in Tob'co a 2d p lb. | 240 |
| To Coll. Wm. Macon his Acco't £4, 19s., 0d. in Tob'o, 2d. p lb. | 594 |
| To Mr. Antho. Colt his Acco't £0, 10s., 9d., in Tobo., a Do., p Do. | 64½ |
| To Mr. Chas. Massie for keeping John Reynolds 14 days | 140 |
| To Rich'd Brokas for his wife washing the Surplice ... | 50 |
| To Mr. Walter Clopton, Allowed for Delinquents, 21 ... | 922 |
| To Capt. Rich'd Littlepage, his acca't, ten Bottles of Wine 40s. in Tobo. a 2d. | 240 |
| To George Taylor for keeping Andrew Higgins 5 Days.. | ,50 |
| To Lb. Tobo. Poll. on 1024 Tithables Leveyed as p order, Collection at 6 p Ct. | 1806 |
| Per Contra.        Cr. | 31904½ |
| By 1024 Tithables a 31 1 Tobo. P. Poll., A. Rem., due from the Parish to the Collector, 160 | 31904½ |

Ordered that Hugh Grindley be allowed 450 lbs. Tobo. for keeping Charles Goodwin the ensuing year.

That Alice Moor be Allowed 450 lb. Tobo. for keeping Mary Major the ensuing year.

That John Murrahoe be allowed 700 lb. Tobo. for keeping Mary Hazard the ensuing year.

That Capt. Rich'd Littlepage & Mr. Ambrose Dudley be Continued Church Wardens for the Ensuing year.

That the Church Wardens be impowered to Agree with Any Person for keeping Marg't Grumbal for the ensuing year.

That the Church Wardens be impowered to give Thomas Ashcraft Credit in a Store for forty Shillings towards finding him in Cloathes for the ensuing year.

That £5 of Tobo. be Leveyed on Every Tithable Person of this Parish for Carrying on the building A Vestry Room & Steeple & other Repairs of the Church, & that it be sold for ready money to the highest Bidder by the Collector.

Mr. Daniel Park Custis is Chosen a Vestryman in the Room of Mr. Waddill, Dec'd, & that the Clerk give him Notice to Attend the next Vestry to take the Oath of a Vestryman.

That the Same Processioners as were the last time of Processioning is Living be Continued, & that John Parish be appointed Processioner of the Same Precinct in the Room of Charles Hughes.

This Day the Parish Levy being proportioned, we find it amounts to the Sume of 31 lb. Tobo. p poll., on 1024 Tithables, which S'd Sume of 31 lb. Tobo. Capt Richard Littlepage is impowered to Collect from Every Tithable Person in this Parish Provided the S'd Littlepage enter into Bond with Security to the Vestry for Performance of the same. Capt Rich'd Littlepage has offered to give Bond with his Securities the Rev'd David Mossom & Mr. Walter Clopton, who are approved by the Vestry for his Performance of the Collection, & is to give Bond Accordingly.

That a Vestry is appointed to be held the first Day of December next, in Order to Agree with a Workman towards building a Vestry Room & Steeple & making good other Deficiencies of the Church, & that in the meantime the Clerk give what Public Notice he can for Workmen to come in to Agree with the Vestry accordingly for the Same. D. Mossom, M'in'r; Jno. Dandridge, Thos. Butts, Jos. Marston, Chas. Massie, Walter Clopton, David Patteson, Rich'd Sherman, Rich'd Littlepage, Ambrose Dudley, Church Wardens. JAMES DUDLEY, Clk of the Vestry.

At a Vestry held for St. Peter's Parish April the 12th, 1740.

PRESENT:

The Rev'd Mr. Mossom, Minister; Major John Dandridge, Maj'r Joseph Forster, Mr. Joseph Marston, Mr. Thomas Butts, Mr. Chas. Mallie, Mr. David Pattison; Capt. Rich'd Littlepage, Mr. Ambrose Dudley, Church Wardens.

Mr. Daniel Parke Custis was this day Sworn a Vestryman, & took the Oaths appointed by Law instead of the Oaths of Allegiance & Supremacy before Maj'r Joseph Forster, one of his Ma'ties' Justices of the Peace for this County & Subscribed the Test.

Whereas, the Minister & Vestry of this Parish have Agreed with Mr. Wm. Worthe, of the Parish of St. Paul, in the County of Stafford, Builder, to Erect & Build a Steeple & Vestry Room according to a Plan Delivered into the Vestry drawn by the S'd Walter for the Consideration of One hundred & thirty Pounds at times to be paid.

Ordered that the Church wardens in Company with Maj'r Joseph Foster & Maj'r John Dandridge do meet at some convenient time to Execute mutual Bonds between the Church wardens, w'ch said matter together with his Security the Rev'd * * for the performance of the Contract.

That all the male Tithables belonging to Wm. Grey, Gent., & the like belonging to Capt. John Derritour & at his own house, John Ross * Martin & * * Largison be added to the Gang belonging to Wm. Easley.

D. Mossom, Min'r; Jos. Foster, Jno. Dandridge, Daniel Parke Custis, Jos. Marston; Rich'd Littlepage, Ambrose Dudley, Church Wardens.

---

At a Vestry held for St. Peter's Parish, September the 29th, 1740.

PRESENT:

The Rev'd Mr. Mossom, Min'r; Coll. Wm. Macon, Coll. Daniel Parke Custis, Maj'r John Dandridge, Maj'r Jos. Foster, Mr. Walter Clopton, Mr. David Patteson, Mr. Chas. Massie, Mr. Jos. Marston, Vestrymen; Capt. Richard Littlepage, Mr. Ambrose Dudley, Church Wardens.

St. Peter's Parish,                Dr.

| | |
|---|---:|
| To the Rev. Mr. Mossom his Salary to September the 29th, Cask to Do., a L, 640 p Ct. | 16640 |
| To James Holmes his Salary to September 29th | 1800 |
| To Richard Brokas, Sexton, his Salary | 630 |
| To the Rev'd Mr. Mossom for Deficiency in Glebe Land, 1600 lbs. Tobo. | 1600 |
| To Cask to Do. a 4 p Ct., 64, Hugh Grindley for keeping Chas. Goodwin | 514 |
| To Alice Moor for keeping Mary Major | 450 |
| To David Patteson for keeping Mary Hazard | 700 |
| To John Weaver for keeping Margaret Grumbal | 700 |
| To Maj'r Dandridge for 2 List of Tithables & Copy of the new Oaths | 95 |
| To Mr. Ben. Waller for a Copy of List of Tithables | 18 |
| To Richard Brokas for his wife washing the Surplice | 50 |
| To Capt. Richard Littlepage Allowed for Delinquents, 21 | 620 |
| To £5 to Capt. Doran for Salivating Eliz'th Taylor a 14 P. | 715 |
| To Coll. Wm. Macon his Acco't being £13. 13. 7½ in Tobo. a Do. p. D. | 524 |
| To Antho. Colt his Acct. being £3, 19s, 4D., a Do. | 566 |
| To David Patteson his Acco't being 6s at Do. | 39 |
| To Coll. Macon for Cloathing Andrew Farney, £1, 10S. in Tobo. at Do. | 215 |
| To Hannah Pearson for Curing Andrew Farney's Leg. | 300 |
| To Doct'r Arnotto Acco't being £7 at Do. | 1000 |
| To John Amos for his wife's being discharged out Levy in 1738 | 26 |
| To 5 lb. Tobo. p Poll. on 1027 Tithables Leveyed as P Order | 5135 |
| To the Collection a 6 p. ct., 1950, A. Rem't out from the Collector, 471 | 2421 |
| | 34918 |

    Per Contra        Cr.,

By 1027 Tithables a 34 lb. Tobo. p Poll. ............... 34918

St. Peter's Parish, in Cash      £ S D
To Mr. Powers for Prosecuting the Presentin..1.. 1..6
To 12 Bottles of Wine to Capt. Littlepage a S4|..2.. 8..0
To 2 Bottles of Wine to Maj'r Dandridge a S5|..0..10..0

              3..19..6

Ordered that Hugh Grindley be allowed 450 lb. Tobo. for keeping Charles Goodwin the ensuing year.

That Alice Moor be allowed 450 lbs. Tobo. for keeping Mary Major the ensuing year.

That David Patteson be allowed 700 lbs. Tobo. for keeping Mary Hazard the ensuing year.

That John Weaver be allowed 600 lbs. Tobo. for keeping Margaret Grumbal the ensuing year.

That the Church Wardens be impowered to give Thomas Ashcraft credit in a Store for forty Shillings towards finding him in Cloathes for the ensuing year.

That Barnett Taylor be allowed 400 lb. Tobo for keeping Eliz'th Harris the ensuing year.

That 5 lb. Tobo. be Leveyed on Every Tithable Person in this Parish for Carrying on the Building a Vestry Room & Steeple & other Repairs of the Church, & that it be sold for ready money to the highest Bidder by the Collector & by him to be paid to the Churchwardens.

That Coll. Daniel Parke Custis & Mr. Walter Clopton be Chosen Churchwardens for the ensuing year, & were accordingly Sworn.

That the money arising by the fines & other money due to the Parish be paid to the Churchwardens towards Defraying the money Debt & other uses of the Parish.

That the Sume of Twenty Pounds be paid to Mr. William M *, Builder for Erecting * Porch According to Agreem't, & white washing & other Repairs of the inside of the Church, & that the money be p'd to him in 1742.

This Day the Parish Levy being Proportioned we find it amounts to the Sume of 34 lb. Tobo. P Poll. on 1027 Tithables w'ch S'd Sume of 34 lbs. Tobo. Mr. Wm. Clopton is impowered to Collect from Every Tithable Person in this Parish Provided

## VESTRY BOOK OF ST. PETER'S PARISH. 185

the S'd Clopton enter into Bond with Security to the Vestry for Performance of the same. Mr. Wm. Clopton has offered to give bond with his Securities, Mr. Walter Clopton & Mr. David Patteson, who are approved by the Vestry for his Performance of the Collection, & is to give Bond accordingly.

D. Mossom, Min'r; R. Littlepage, Jos. Marston, Jno. Dandridge, Jos. Foster, David Patteson, Ambrose Dudley; Daniel Parke Custis, Walt. Clopton, Church Wardens.

Recorded by JAMES HOLMES, Clk of the Vestry.

At a Vestry held for St. Peter's Parish September the 29th, 1741.

PRESENT:

The Rec'd Mr. Mossom, Min'r; Coll. Wm. Macon, Capt. Rich'd Littlepage, Capt. Mich'll Sherman, Mr. Ambrose Dudley, Maj'r Jon. Dandridge, Mr. Joseph Marston, Mr. David Patteson, Mr. Chas. Massie, Vestrycen; Coll. Parke Custis, Mr. Walter Clopton, Church Wardens.

St. Peter's Parish,     Dr.

| | |
|---|---:|
| To the Rev'd Mr. Mossom, his Salary to September the 29th, Cask to Do. at 4 p ct., 640 | 16640 |
| To James Holmes his Salary to Sept'r the 29th, Richard Brokas his Salary, 630 | 2430 |
| To Hugh Grindley for keeping Charles Goodwin | 450 |
| To Alice Moor for keeping Mary Major | 450 |
| To David Patteson for keeping Mary Hazard | 700 |
| To John Weaver for keeping Marg't Grumbal | 600 |
| To Burnet Taylor for keeping Eliz'th Davis | 400 |
| To Mr. Ben. Waller for Copy of List of Tithables | 18 |
| To Richard Brokas his wife washing the Surplice | 50 |
| To Coll. Macon his Acco't £11, 8S., 9½d. in Tobo. a 2d. | 1373 |
| To Mr. Wm. Massie his Acco't £1, 2S., 6d., in Tobo. at Do. | 135 |
| To Coll. Custis his Acco't £1, 4S., 0d. in Tobo. a Do. | 144 |
| To Mr. Wm. Clopton Acct. for Delinquents | 578 |
| To Mr. Powers his Acco't for Prosecuting the Present-in'ts | 600 |
| To Maj'r John Dandridge his Acco't | 311 |

To Mr. Walter Clopton for keeping a bastard child of
  Mary Ashberry ................................. 50c
To Thos. Addison for being overcharged on Levy in 1740   34
To Edward Birch his Acco't, 45, Barnet Taylor, his Acco't
  400 ............................................ 445
To Amey Burke for Cleaning the Church ............ 100
To 7 lb. Tobo. on 1048 Tithables Leveyed as p Order .. 4336
To the Collection a 6 p Ct., Remnant due from the Col-
  lector ......................................... 2338

      Per Contra,      Cr.      35632

By 1048 Tithables a 34 lb. Tobo. P Poll., ............. 35632

Ordered that James Ashcraft be allowed forty Shillings * * for keeping his father, Thos. Ashcraft, the ensuing year.

That Phillis Moon be allowed 700 lb. Tobo. for keeping her son, John Moon, for the ensuing year.

That Thomas Davis be allowed his Acco't for burying Peter Davison, being 326 lb. of Tobo.

That Hugh Grindley be allowed 450 lbs. Tobo. for keeping Charles Goodwin the ensuing year.

That Alice Moor be allowed 450 lb. Tobo. for keeping Mary Major the ensuing year.

That David Patteson be allowed 700 lbs. Tobo. for keeping Mary Hazard the ensuing year.

That John Weaver be allowed 700 lbs. Tobo. for keeping Margaret Grumbal the ensuing year.

That Alice Ross be allowed 400 lb. Tobo. for keeping John Downe the ensuing year.

That Israel Austin be allowed 250 L. Tobo. for keeping his brother, Leonard Austin, the ensuing year; and likewise the S'd Leonard to be discharged Paying his Parish Levy.

That Mrs. Coopers Male Tithables be added to Mr. Hartwell's Levy.

That Mr. Derricourts' male Tithables be added to Martin Hewlett's Levy.

That Maj'r Footes' & the Rev'd Mr. Mossom's male Tithables be added to Coll. Macon's.

That Stephen Broker be appointed sexton of this Parish in

the Room of his father, Rich'd Broker, Dec'd, w'ch the same allowance as usual.

That Chas. Barker be allowed 500 lb. of Tobo. towards his support & maintenance.

That 7 1 of Tobo. be Levyed on Every Tithable person of this Parish towards discharging the Parish debts and other disbursements.

That two Church Folio Comon Prayer Books be sent for, neatly bound in Turkey Leather & Letters on the back in gilt Letters, vizt., (St. Peter's Parish), by Coll. Wm. Macon, (2 Folios 50 P. Ct. on the First Cost.)

That the Church Wardens be impowered to Employ some Person to free the Church Yard and all about it from all Rubbish, Filth & Nastiness.

This Day the Parish Levy being proportioned we find it amounts to the Sume of £34 Tobo. p. poll. on 1048 Tithables, w'ch Sd Sume of Tobo. Mr. Walter Clopton is impowered to Collect from Every tithable Person in this Parish, provided the Sd Clopton enter into bond with Security to the Vestry for performance of the Same. Mr. Walter Clopton has offered to give bond with his Securityes, Capt. Mich'll Sherman & Mr. Joseph Marston, who are approved by the Vestry for his performance of the Collection & is to give bond accordingly.

Daniel Parke Custis, Walt. Clopton, Church Wardens; D. Mossom, Min.; Wm. Macon, Jo. Foster, Jno. Dandridge, Mich'll Sherman, Jo. Marston, David Patteson, Ambrose Dudley.

Recorded by JAMES HOLMES, Clerk of the Vestry.

At a vestry held for St. Peter's Parish June the 3rd, 1742.

PRESENT:

Coll. Daniel Parke Custis, Mr. Walter Clopton, Church Wardens.

The Rev'd Mr. Mossom, Min'r; Major Joseph Foster, Major John Dandridge, Capt. Mich'll Sherman, Mr. Joseph Marston, Mr. David Patteson.

Ordered that the Church Wardens agree with some person to mend the Church windows & to Provide a Rope and Chain for the Bell.

That Mr. Walter Clopton, Parish Collector, be impowered to sell all the Tobacco which was Levyed upon the Sev'll Tithables of this Parish at the Vestry held on Sept'r the 29th, 1741, for ready money at July Court Ensuing, as also the Tobacco arising by Fines.

That Maj'r Foster be Desired to speak to Sam'll Duvall and Edward Russell in Relation to erecting Dormant windows for the Roof of the Steeple & Return their opinion by the next Vestry.

That Coll. Daniel Parke Custis be Desired to agree with some workmen for erecting the Font.

That Coll. Wm. Macon be impowered to send for a handsome surplice & one Communion Table Cloth & two Napkins of the best Damask at 50 p. cent. upon the first cost.

That the Church Wardens, together with Maj'r Foster & Maj'r Dandridge, Settle the amo'ts with Capt. Richard Littlepage for all the Tobacco in his hands as Collector.

That Notice be given for a Vestry to be held on Saturday, the 24th Day of July next Ensuing.

D. Mossom, Min'r; Jos. Foster, Jno. Dandridge, Jos. Marston, Mich'll Sherman, David Patteson; Walt. Clopton, Church Warden.

---

Att a Vestry held for St. Peter's Parish, September the 29th, 1742.

PRESENT:

The Rev'd Mr. Mossom, Min; Mr. Chas. Massie, Coll. Wm. Macon, Mr. David Patteson, Maj'r John Dandridge, Maj'r Jos. Foster, Joseph Marston, Captain Rich'd Littlepage, Mr. Ambrose Dudley, Vestrymen; Coll. Daniel Parke Custis, Mr. Walter Clopton, Church Wardens.

St. Peter's Parish,           Dr.

To the Rev'd. Mr. Mossom, his Salary to September the
  29th .......................................... 16000
To Cask to do. at 4 p. cent. ...................... 640
To James Holmes his Salary to Sept. the 29th ........ 1800
To Stephen Broker, Sexton, his Salary ................ 630
To James Ashcraft for keeping his father, Chas. Ashcraft,
  40 m. Tobo. a 15 ................................ 267

| | |
|---|---|
| To Phillis Moon for keeping her son, John Moon ....... | 700 |
| To Thomas Davis for burying Peter Davison ........... | 326 |
| To Hugh Grindley for keeping Charles Goodwin ........ | 450 |
| To Alice Moor for keeping Mary Major .............. | 450 |
| To David Patteson for keeping Mary Hazard .......... | 700 |
| To John Weaver for Mary Turnbull ................. | 700 |
| To Alice Ross for keeping John Downs ............... | 400 |
| To Mr. Ben. Waller for a copy of the List of Tithables .. | 18 |
| To Sarah Broker for washing the Surplice ............ | 50 |
| To Coll. Wm. Macon his acco't being £4, 11s., 3½d. in Tobo. a 15 ....................................... | 609 |
| To Capt. Wm. Massie his acco't, 2, 8, 11 in Tobo. a Do... | 326½ |
| To Mr. Antho. Cole his acco't, 0, 11, 8, in Tobo. a Do. ... | 79 |
| To Dr. Arnott his acco't 1, 9, 4, in Tobo. a Do. ......... | 196 |
| To Mr. Walter Clopton his acco't ................... | 772 |
| To Mr. David Patteson his acco't a 0, 6, in Tobo. a Do... | 57 |
| To Maj'r John Dandridge his acco't .................. | 114 |
| To John Dollard his acco't, 1, 8, 6, in Tobo. a Do. ...... | 154½ |
| To Frances Morris, her acct., 3, 0, 2 ................. | 401 |
| To Stephen Broker for keeping 2 children of Ann Lewis.. | 80 |
| To Isral Austin for keeping his Brother .............. | 250 |
| To Coll. Custis for keeping the Church Yard & Swinging the Font ........................................ | 150 |
| To John Phillips for his Support .................... | 600 |
| To Cornelius Matthews for the Support of his mother .. | 500 |
| To Charles Barker for his Support ................... | 400 |
| To 7 lb. Tobo. on 1084 Tithables Leveyed as pr. order.... | 7588 |
| To a Ballance due from the Collector ................ | 420 |
| | 35288 |

Ordered that James Ashcraft be allowed forty Shillings for keeping his Father, Thos. Ashcraft, the ensuing year.

That Phillis Moon be allowed £700 of Tobo. for keeping her son, John Moon, for the ensuing year.

That Hugh Grindley be allowed £450 Tobo. for keeping Charles Goodwin the Ensuing year.

That Alice Moor be allowed £450 Tobo. for keeping Mary Major the Ensuing year.

That David Patteson be allowed £700 for keeping Mary Hazard the ensuing year.

That John Weaver be allowed £700 for keeping Margaret Grumuall the ensuing year.

That Israel Austin be allowed £250 for keeping his Brother the Ensuing year.

That John Phillips be allowed for his support 600 ll. for the Ensuing year.

That Cornelius Matthews be allowed for the Support of his mother 500 lb. for the Ensuing year.

That Charles Barker be allowed for his Support £400 for the Ensuing year.

That the Rev'd Mr. Mossom be paid the Sume of 10 lb. Curr't money by Coll. Wm. Macon of money being in his hands, w'ch Sd Sume is given as a Present by the Gent. of the Vestry.

That the Persons mentioned in the Prayer of George Poindexter's Petition be under the Overseer w'ch shall be appointed by the next Court.

That Coll. Wm. Macon & Mr. Joseph Marston be chosen Church Wardens for the Ensuing year & were accordingly Sworn.

That Coll. Wm. Macon, Maj'r Joseph Foster, Coll. Custis & Maj'r Dandridge or any two of them agree with Mr. Edward Russell towards Repairing the Spire & Erecting Dormant windows for the Steeple.

That the Collector sells what Tobo. he has in his hands for ready money to the highest Bidder when thereunto required by the Church Wardens.

This day the Parish Levy being proportioned we find it amounts to the Sume of 7 1 Tobo. p. poll. on 1084 Tithables, w'ch Sume of Tobo. Mr. Walter Clopton is impowered to collect from Every tithable person in this Parish, provided the sd Clopton Enter into Bond with Security to the Vestry for Performance of the Same. Mr. Walter Clopton has given Bond with his Securityes, Mr. Charles Massie & Mr. Ambrose Dudley, who are appointed by the Vestry for his Performance of the collection & is to give Bond accordingly.

D. Mossom, Min'r; Jno. Dandridge, Rich'd Littlepage, Chas.

Massie, Ambrose Dudley, Walter Clopton, Daniel Parke Custis, David Patteson; Wm. Macon, Jos. Marston, Church Wardens. Recorded by JAMES HOLMES, Clerk of the Vestry.

At a vestry held for St. Peter's Parish, September the 24th, 1743.

PRESENT:

The Rev'd Mr. Mossom, Min'r; Mr. Chas. Massie, Mr. Ambrose Dudley, Mr. Walter Clopton, Mr. Thos. Butts, Coll. Daniel Parke Custis, Maj. Jos. Foster, Maj. Jon. Dandridge, Capt. Rich'd Littlepage, Capt. Mich'll Sherman; Col. Wm. Macon, Mr. Jos. Marston.

St. Peter's Parish.

| | |
|---|---:|
| To the Rev'd Mr. Mossom his Salary to September the 29th | 16000 |
| To Cask to Do. a 4 p. ct. | 640 |
| To James Holmes his Salary to September the 29th | 1800 |
| To Stephen Broker, Sexton, his Salary | 630 |
| To James Ashcraft for keeping his Father, 40s. in Tobo. a 5 | 267 |
| To Phillis Moon for keeping & cloathing her son | 967 |
| To Hugh Grindley for keeping Chas. Goodwin | 450 |
| To Alice Moor for keeping Mary Major & a child | 1050 |
| To David Patteson for keeping Mary Hazard | 700 |
| To John Mason for keeping Mary Grumbal | 700 |
| To Israel Austin for keeping his Brother | 250 |
| To John Phillips for his Support | 600 |
| To Cornelius Matthews for the Support of his Mother | 500 |
| To Charles Barker for his Support | 400 |
| To Coll. Wm. Macon his acco't, £12, 10, 9, in Tobo. a 15.. | 1731 |
| To Coll. Wm. Massie his acco't £2, 5, 11, in Tobo. a Do... | 317 |
| To David Patteson his acco't £0, 9, 0, in Tobo. a Do. | 62 |
| To Stephen Brokar for Erecting a horse block | 50 |
| Brought Forward | 27114 |
| To Hannah Irby for her Attendance agt Willis Osling | 67½ |
| To Ann Irby for her Attendance agt., Do. | 45 |
| To Mr. Clopton for Delinquents | 665 |
| To Mr. Ben. Waller for a Copy of the List of Tithables.. | 18 |

| | |
|---|---:|
| To George Heath as a Further Addition to his wife's charge | 200 |
| To Maj'r John Dandridge his acco't | 601 |
| To Capt. Richard Littlepage his acco't | 41 |
| To Hannah Morgan her acco't | 101 |
| To John Ellmore his acco't | 900 |
| To Thomas Martin, his acco't | 200 |
| To the Rev'd Mr. Mossom for the Deficiency of Glebe | 1600 |
| To Cask to Do. a 4 P. ct. | 64 |
| | 31616½ |
| To 12 lb. of Tobo. on 1063 Tithables Leveyed as P. Order | 12750 |
| To the Coll'n a 6 pr. ct. | 2658 |
| | 47030 |
| To a Rem'r due From the Collector | 805 |
| | 47835 |

Per Contra,              Cr.
By 1063 Tithables a 45 lb. Tobo. P. Poll. ........... 47835

Ordered the presenting of Mr. Davis Patteson's Resignation of the office of a Vestryman by the Rev'd Mr. David Mossom to the Vestry. & Mr. Mossom informing the Vestry that when Mr. Patteson Resign'd he desired him to acquaint the Vestry that it was his Request Capt. William Massie might Succeed him, it is the unanimous vote of the Vestry that Capt. Massie be a Vestryman, & he is accordingly chosen. The Clerk is ordered to give him Notice that he is chosen into that office.

That Coll. Wm. Macon Pay Mr. James Power what Fees shall appear to be due to him for prosecuting the presentents of the grandjury.

That the Rev'd Mr. David Mossom be allowed the Sume of Sixteen hundred pounds of Tobo. & cask for the Deficiency of a Glebe & the Same Sume to be continued yearly till a Loyall Glebe is provided for him.

That James Ashcraft be allowed Forty Shillings for keeping his Father, Thos. Ashcraft, the Ensuing year.

That Phillis Moon be allowed 967 of Tobo. for keeping & cloathing her son, John Moon, for the Ensuing year.

## VESTRY BOOK OF ST. PETER'S PARISH. 193

That Hugh Grindley be allowed £450 of Tobo. for keeping Charles Goodwin the Ensuing year.

That David Patteson be allowed £300 of Tobo. for keeping Mary Hazard the Ensuing year, & in case She proves worse to be allowed Further as the Levy shall think proper.

That Israel Austin be allowed £250 of Tobo. for keeping his Brother the Ensuing year.

That John Phillips be allowed for his Support 600 lb. of Tobo. for the Ensuing year.

That Cornelius Matthews be allowed for the Support of his mother 500 lb. of Tobo. for the Ensuing year.

That Samuel Bailey be allowed £450 of Tobo. for keeping Mary Major the Ensuing year.

That Henry Strange be allowed £700 of Tobo. for keeping Margaret Grumbal the Ensuing year.

That Coll. Wm. Macon & Mr. Jos. Marston be continued church wardens for the Ensuing year.

That the church Wardens Sell the Quantity of 13561 lb. of Tobo. to the highest Bidder for ready money for the Use of the Parish & be impowered to Demand the Same from the Coll'r.

This day the Parish Levy being proportioned we Find it amounts to the Sume of £45 of Tobo. P. Poll. on 1063 Tithables, w'ch Sd Sume of Tobo Mr. Julius Burbige is impowered to collect From Every Tithable Person in this Parish, Provided the Sd Burbidge Enters into Bond with Security to the Vestry for Performance of the Same. Mr. Julius Burbidge has offered to give Bond with his Securityes. Maj'r Jos. Foster & Maj'r Jn. Dandridge, who are approved by the Vestry for his Performance of the Collection & has given Bond Accordingly.

D. Mossom, Min'r; John Dandridge, Mich'll Sherman, Ambrose Dudley, Thos. Buttes. Jo. Foster, Rich'd Littlepage, Daniel Parke Custis. Chas. Massie, Walt. Clopton; Wm. Macon, Jo. Marston, Church Wardens.

Recorded by JAMES HOLMES, Clerk of the Vestry.

Att a Vestry held for St. Peter's Parish November the 17, 1743.

PRESENT:

The Rev'd Mr. Mossom, Min'r; Mr. Charles Massie, Maj.

John Dandridge, Mr. Ambrose Dudley, Capt. Michael Sherman, Coll. Daniel Parke Custis; Coll. Wm. Macon, Mr. Jos. Marston, Church Wardens.

Pursuant to an Order of Vestry made the 24th of September last, that the Clerk give Notice to Capt. William Massie that he is chosen Vestryman in the place of Mr. David Patteson, who has resigned, & that he Appear at the next Vestry to take the Oathes required by Law to Execute the Office of a Vestryman, & Capt. Massie appearing Accordingly was this Day Sworn before Coll. Wm. Macon & Coll. Daniel Parke Custis, two of his Ma'ties' Justices of the Peace for the County of New Kent, & after Capt. Massie was Sworn the Vestry Proceeded to appoint the Severall Persons to Procession the Lands as the Law Requires, & Ordered them to be Recorded in the Processioning Book.

Ordered that Major Foster's hands be added to Wm Moor's Levy.

That George Walton's hands, Judith Waddell's hands, Wm. Moor's hands & Stephen Broker, be added to Noel Waddill's Levy.

That the Vestry of St. Peter's Parish or any Seven of them meet at the Glebe at ten of the clock in the Forenoon the 5th Day of December next, (if Fair), if not, the next Fair Day, & treat with any Persons For a Sufficient Quantity of Land to make the said Glebe Legall.

That the Fines now in the hands of the Church Wardens be Distributed among the Poor of the Parish at this time instead of Easter Tuesday at the Discretion of the Church Wardens, & that when Distributed, att the next Vestry they Account to whom the Same so Disposed.

D. Mossom; Chas. Massie, Daniel Parke Custis, Ambrose Dudley, Rich'd Littlepage, Wm. Massie, Jno. Dandridge, Mich'll Sherman; Wm. Macon, Jo. Marston, Church Wardens.

Recorded by JAMES HOLMES, Clk. of the Vestry.

At a Vestry held for St. Peter's Parish September the 29th, 1744.

PRESENT:

The Rev'd David Mossom, Min'r; Maj'r John Dandridgge, Capt. Rich'd Littlepage, Capt. Wm. Massie, Mr. Walter Clopton,

VESTRY BOOK OF ST. PETER'S PARISH. 195

Mr. Thomas Butts, Mr. Chas. Massie, Coll. Dan'll Parke Custis, Maj'r Jos. Foster, Mr. Ambrose Dudley, Vestrymen; Coll. Wm. Macon, Mr. Jos. Marston, Church Wardens.

St. Peter's Parish, Dr.

| | |
|---|---:|
| To the Rev'd Mr. Mossom his Salary to September the 29th | 16000 |
| To Cask to Do. a 4 P. ct. | 640 |
| To the Rev'd Mr. Mossom for the Deficiency of Glebe | 1600 |
| To Cask to Do. a 4 P. ct. | 64 |
| To James Holmes his Salary to September the 29th | 1800 |
| To Stephen Broker, Sexton, his Salary | 630 |
| To Sarah Broker for washing the Surplice these 2 years | 100 |
| To James Ashcroft for keeping his Father | 600 |
| To Hugh Grindley for keeping Charles Goodwin | 450 |
| To David Patteson for keeping Mary Hazard | 800 |
| To Israel Austin for keeping his Brother | 250 |
| To John Phillips for his Support | 600 |
| To Cornelius Matthews for the Support of his Mother | 500 |
| To Samuel Bailey for keeping Mary Major | 450 |
| To Henry Strange for keeping Marg't Grumbal | 700 |
| To Phillis Moon for keeping her Son | 967 |
| To George Heath for keeping John Vincent, an orphan child | 600 |
| To Sarah Broker for keeping Christ'r Bendall in his Sickness | 300 |
| To Maj. John Dandridge his acco't | 380 |
| To Mr. Ben. Waller for a copy of the List of Tithables | 18 |
| To Capt. Wm. Massie his £3, 3, 10, in Tobo. at 10 P. ct. | 638 |
| To Rich'd Crump, Sen'r, his Acco't, £4, 2s., 0, in Tobo. at Do. | 419 |
| To Coll. Macon his acco't, £8, 17, 4, in Tobo. at Do. | 1744 |
| | 30280 |
| To George Taylor for keeping Catherine Taylor in Child bed | 400 |
| To Hannah Morgan for keeping Marg't Foster 4 weeks | 400 |
| To Sarah Broker as part of her Fee for Bringing Cath. Taylor to Bed | 30 |
| | 31110 |

Ord'd that the Sume of 12750 lb. of Tobo be Levyed for
the use of the Parish .......................... 12756
                                                 ─────
                                                 43866
To the Coll'n at 6 P. Ct. .......................... 2632
                                                 ─────
                                                 46498
To a Rem'r due from the Coll'r ....................   54
                                                 ─────
                                                 46552
    Per Contra,              Cr.
By 1058 Tithables at 44 lb. Tobo. Pr. Poll............ 46552

Ordered that James Ashcraft be allowed 600 lb. of Tobo. for the Support of his Father in Lieu of the 40 Ordered him last year.

That Phillis Moon be allowed 967 lb. of Tobo. for keeping her son, John Moon, the Ensuing year.

That Ann Patteson be allowed 800 lb. of Tobo. for keeping Mary Hazard the Ensuing year, & in case she proves worse to be allowed Further as the Vestry shall think proper.

That Israel Austin be Allowed 250 lb. Tobo. for keeping his brother the Ensuing year.

That John Phillips be allowed for his Support 600 Lb. Tobo. for the Ensuing year.

That Cornelius Matthews be allowed for the support of his mother 500 lb. Tobo. for the Ensuing year.

That Samuel Bailey be allowed 450 lb. Tobo. for keeping Mary Major the Ensuing year.

That Henry Strange be allowed 700 Tobo. for keeping Marg't Grumbal the Ensuing year.

That Charles Hughes & Edward Morris be Discharged From Paying their Parish Levyies.

That Ship. Richardson be likewise Discharged From Paying his Parish Levy until such time as he Recovers his health.

That Maj'r John Dandridge & Capt. Wm. Massie be appointed Church Wardens for the Ensuing year.

That Coll. Macon be Paid his Cask acco't out of the Tobo. now to be sold by the Church Wardens, w'ch amounts to the Sume of £14 l, 3.10.

That the Church Wardens Pay Julius Burbidge the Quantity

of 365 lb. Tobo. out of the Tobo. now to be Leveyed for Delinquents.

That the Church Wardens Sell the Tobo. now in hand to the highest Bidder for ready money.

That the Church Wardens Sell the Quantity of £12756 of Tobo. to the highest Bidder for ready money for the use of the Parish & be impowered to Demand the Sume from the Collector.

That the Church Wardens be impowered to take up Money on interest if any Sho'd be wanting after the Tobo. in hand is Sold in Order to Discharge Phil. Poindexter.

That James Ashcraft be allowed 600 lb. of Tobo. for keeping his Father the Ensuing year.

That Wm. Moor's hands be added to Martin Hewlett's Levy.

This Day the Parish Levy being proportioned we find it amounts to the Sume of 44 lb. of Tobo. P. Poll. on 1058 Tithables w'ch S'd Sume of Tobo. Capt. Wm. Hoctaday is impowered to collect from every tithable Person in this Parish, Provided the S'd Hockaday Enter into Bond with Security to the Vestry for Performance of the Same, Capt. Wm. Hockaday has offered to give Bond with his Securityes, Maj'r Joseph Foster & Maj'r John Dandridge, who are approved by the Vestry for his Performance of the Collection, & has given bond Accordingly.

D. Mossom, Min'r; Jos. Foster, Thos. Buttes, Chas. Massie, Wm. Macon, Daniel Parke Custis, Jos. Marston, Rich'd Littlepage, Walt. Clopton, Ambrose Dudley; John Dandridge, Wm. Massie, churchwardens.

Recorded by JAMES HOLMES, clk. of the Vestry.

---

At a Vestry held for St. Peter's Parish November the 13th, 1744.

PRESENT:

The Rev. Mr. Mossom, Min'r; Maj. Jos. Foster, Capt. Rich'd Littlepage, Coll. Daniel Park Custis, Mr. Walter Clopton; Maj. John Dandridge, Capt. Wm. Massie, Church Wardens.

Whereas, it Appears to the Vestry after having Examined the seveall credits and debts that there is due the Sume of Eighty Pounds From the Parish to the Creditors, it is Ordered that the Church Wardens take up the said Sume of Eighty Pounds upon Interest upon the Credit of the Parish for the Discharging the aforesaid Debt.

D. Mossom, Min'r; Rich'd Littlepage, Jos. Foster, Walt. Clopton, Daniel Parke Custis; Jno. Dandridge, Wm. Massie, Church Wardens.

Recorded by JAMES HOLMES, Clk. of the Vestry.

Whereas, it has this 16th Day of December, 1744 in Regard of the incapacity of Stephen Brokar in officiating his office of Sexton of this Parish, it is agreed upon by the consent of the Rev'd Mr. David Mossom, Min'r, Capt. Wm. Massie, Church Warden; Coll. Daniel Parke Custis, Mr. Walter Clopton & Mr. Chas. Massie, Vestrymen, that William Furbish be Appointed to officiate as Sexton of this Parish untill Such time as the Sd Stephen Broker Shall be Capable of Attending in Person & that the Sd Furbish be allowed for so attending out of the Salary of the Said Brokar.

At a Vestry held for St. Peter's Parish September the 28th, 1745.

The Rev'd Mr. Mossom, Min'r; Col. Wm. Macon, Mr. Jos. Marston, Coll. Daniel Parke Custis, Mr. Chas. Massie, Coll. Jos. Foster, Capt. Rich'd Littlepage, Capt. Mich'll Sherman, Mr. Walter Clopton, Vestrymen; John Dandridge, Wm. Massie, Church Wardens.

| St. Peter's Parish, | Dr. |
|---|---|
| To the Rev'd Mr. Mossom his Salary to September the 29th | 16000 |
| To Cask to Do. at 4 P. ct. | 640 |
| To the Rev'd Mr. Mossom for the Deficiency of Glebe | 1600 |
| To Cask to Do. a 4 P. ct. | 64 |
| To James Holmes his Salary to Sept. the 29th | 1800 |
| To Stephen Brokar for the time he attended as Sexton | 157 |
| To Wm. Forbess's Salary From the 16th of Dec'r to the 29th Inst. | 473 |
| To James Ashcraft for the Support of his Father | 600 |
| To Phillis Moon for the Keeping her son, John Moon | 967 |
| To Ann Patteson for keeping Mary Hazard | 800 |
| To Israel Austin for Keeping his Brother | 250 |
| To Cornelius Matthews for keeping his Mother | 500 |

VESTRY BOOK OF ST. PETER'S PARISH. 199

| | |
|---|---|
| To Samuel Bailey for keeping Mary Major | 450 |
| To Henry Strange for keeping Marg't Grumbal | 700 |
| To Sarah Brokar for washing the Surplice | 50 |
| To Mr. Ben. Waller for a copy of the List of Tithables.. | 18 |
| To Maj. John Dandridge his account | 385 |
| To Capt. Massie his acco't £15, 6, 10, in Tobo. a 12\|6 pe. ct. | 2455 |
| To Anne Patteson her account ,£0, 11, 6, in Tobo. a Do... | 92 |
| To James Holmes his account £0, 3, 0, in Do. a Do. | 24 |
| To Rich'd Crump, Sen'r, his account, £0, 17, 16, in Do. a Do. | 140 |
| To Wm. Forbes for Erecting 2 horse Blocks | 100 |
| To Jane Richison her account for keeping Eliz'th Lewis.. | 400 |
| To Hannah Crump for keeping Ben. Crump, an orphan child, 8 months | 600 |
| To John Green his account £1, 5, 0, in Tobo. a Do. | 200 |
| To Rich'd Jones his account | 100 |
| To James Gilliam for keeping an Orphan child 9 months.. | 700 |
| | 30265 |
| To the Sume Leveyed upon the Sev'll Tithables | 13439 |
| | 43704 |
| To Collection upon the Same | 2622 |
| Per Contra, Cr., | 46326 |
| To 1102 Tithables at 42 Pr. Poll. | 46284 |
| By a Rem'r due to the Collector | 42 |
| | 46326 |

Ordered That Mary * * be paid 800 lb. of Tobo. for keeping her mother, Marg't Grumbal, the Ensuing year.

That Wm. Forbes be Paid 600 lb. Tobo. for keeping John Jeffers's child the Ensuing year.

That Hannah Crump be Paid 600 lb. of Tobo. for keeping an Orphan Child the Ensuing year.

That Mr. Clopton be impowered to agree for a woman to attend to Eliz'th Lewis.

That Cornelius Mattheys be paid 500 lb. of Tobo. for keeping his Mother the Ensuing year.

That Samuel Bailey be Paid 500 lb. of Tobo. for keeping Mary Major the Ensuing year.

That Israel Austin be Paid 250 lb. of Tobo. for keeping his Brother the Ensuing year.

That Phillis Moon be Paid 967 lb. of Tobo. for keeping her Son the Ensuing year.

That Ann Patteson be Paid 900 lb. of Tobo. for keeping Mary Hazard the Ensuing year.

That James Ashcraft be Paid 700 lb. of Tobo. for keeping his Father the Ensuing year.

That Maj'r John Dandridge & Capt. Massie be Continued Church Wardens for the Ensuing year.

That Maj'r Wm. Gray be appointed a Vestryman in the Room of Mr. Thomas Buttes, Dec'd, & that the clerk give him Notice to attend accordingly.

This Day the Parish Levy being proportioned we Find it amounts to the Sume of 42 lbs. of Tobo. P. Poll. on 1102 Tithables, w'ch Sd Sume of Tobo. Capt. Wm. Hockaday is impowered to collect From Every Tithable Person in this Parish, Provided the Sd Hockaday Enter into Bond with Security to the Vestry for Performance of the Same, Capt. Wm. Hockaday has offered to give Bond with his Securityes, Coll. Jos. Foster & Maj'r John Dandridge, who are approved by the Vestry for his Performance of the Collection & has given bond accordingly.

That the Church Wardens Sell the Quantity of 13439 lb. of Tobo. to the highest Bidder for ready money for the use of the Parish & be impowered to Demand the Same From the Collector.

D. Mossom, Min'r; Wm. Macon, Jos. Foster, Rich'd Littlepage, Dan. Parke Custis, Jos. Marston, Chas. Massie, Walter Clopton; John Dandridge, Wm. Massie, Church Wardens.

---

At a Vestry held for St. Peter's Parish October the 11th, 1742.

PRESENT:

The Rev. Mr. Mossom, Min'r; Coll. Jos. Foster, Capt. Richard Littlepage, Mr. Charles Massie, Mr. Walter Clopton, Mr. Joseph Marston, Vestrymen; Major John Dandridge, Capt. Wm. Massie, Church Wardens.

VESTRY BOOK OF ST. PETER'S PARISH.    201

| | |
|---|---|
| St. Peter's Parish, Dr. | |
| To the Rev'd Mr. Mossom his Salary to September the 29th | 16000 |
| To Cask to Do. a 4 P. Ct. | 640 |
| To the Rev'd Mr. Mossom for the Deficiency of Glebe... | 1600 |
| To Cask to Do. a 4 P. Ct. | 64 |
| To James Holmes his Salary to Sept. the 29th | 1800 |
| To Wm. Forbess, Sexton, his Salary | 630 |
| To Marq Croix for keeping her Mother, Marg't Trumbal | 800 |
| To Hannah Crump for keeping an Orphan Child | 600 |
| To Cornelius Mattheus for Keeping his Mother | 500 |
| To Samuel Bailey for keeping Mary Major | 500 |
| To Israel Austin for keeping his Brother | 250 |
| To Stephen Moon for keeping his Brother | 967 |
| To Ann Patteson for keeping Mary Hazard | 900 |
| To Wm. Forbess for keeping John Jeffer's child 4 months | 200 |
| To James Ashcraft for keeping his Father | 700 |
| To Mr. Ben. Waller for a Copy of the List of Tithables... | 18 |
| To Maj'r John Dandridge his account | 91 |
| To Coll. Macon his account | 365 |
| To James Holmes his account, £0, 3s., 0d., in Tobo. a 12s.\|6d. P. C. | 24 |
| To Capt. Massie his account, £18, 14, 7, in Tobo. a Do... | 2947 |
| To Mary Forgeson for keeping Charles Goodwin | 500 |
| To Dominick Touger his account | 146 |
| To Sarah Brokar for curing Jo'n Moon's Leg & Washing the Surplce | 459 |
| To Hannah Pearson for curing Amey Binns | 300 |
| To Charles * his acount | 86 |
| To Ann Patteson her acco't £0, 5s., 0d., for burying Mary Hazard in Tobacco | 122 |
| To Daniel Carroll his acco't for keeping Christ. Venable.. | 100 |
| To George Wilkinson his acco't | 42 |
| To David Binns his acco't for keeping his Sister 3 months | 150 |
| To Wm. Forbess for burying John Forbes's child | 100 |
| | 31592 |
| To Collection a 6 P. Ct. | 1890 |
| | 33482 |

To a Ballance due from the Collector ................. 448

33930

Pr. Contra,            Cr.

By 1131 Tithables a * * * * Pr. Poll................. 33930

Ordered that David Patteson be allowed 800 lb. of Tobo. for keeping Margaret Trumbal the Ensuing year.

That Hannah Crump be allowed 600 lb. of Tobo. for keeping an Orphan child the Ensuing year.

That Cornelius Matthews be allowed 500 lb. of Tobo. for keeping his mother the Ensuing year.

That Samuel Bailey be allowed 500 lb. of Tobo. for keeping Mary Major the Ensuing year.

That Israel Austin be allowed 250 lb. of Tobo. for keeping his Brother the Ensuing year.

That Stephen Moon be allowed 967 lb. of Tobo. for keeping his Brother the Ensuing year.

That James Ashcraft be allowed 700 lb. of Tobo. for keeping his Father the Ensuing year.

That Mary Forgeson be allowed 500 lb. of Tobo. for keeping Charles Goodwin the Ensuing year.

That Capt. Michael Sherman, Vestryman of this Parish, having Resign'd his office, by a note under his hand Dated this Day, & Directed to the Minister & Vestry, Capt. Richard Meux is chosen a Vestryman in the Sd Sherman's Stead.

That Capt. Richard Meux being Present at this Vestry, was Sworn into his office of a Vestryman before Coll Joseph Foster, one of his Ma'ties' Justices.

That Capt. Wm. Massie & Capt. Rich'd Meux be appointed Church Wardens for the Ensuing year.

That Thomas Cooc, James Pollard, Francis Barnes & Christ'r No * * * be added to the Levy whereof John Appurson is overseer.

That John Morris be Discharged from Laying his Parish Levy.

This Day the Parish Levy being proportioned we find it amounts to the Sume of 30 lb. of Tobo. P. Poll. on 1131 Tithables, w'ch Sd Sume of Tobo. Capt. Rich'd Meux is impowered to collect From Every Tithable Person in this Parish, Provided the Sd

Meux Enter into Bond with Security to the Vestry for Porformance of the Same. Capt. Rich'd Meux has offered to give Bond with his Securityes, Coll. Foster & Capt. Wm. Massie, who are approved by the Vestry for his Performance of the Collection, and has given bond accordingly.

D. Mossom, Min'r; Jos. Foster, Rich'd Littlepage, John Dandridge, Chas. Massie, Walt. Clopton, Jos. Marston; Wm. Massie, Rich'd Meux, Church Wardens.

Recorded by JAMES HOLMES, Clk of the Vestry.

At a Vestry held for St. Peter's Parish by adjournment Oct'r 3rd to 16th, 1747.

The Rev'd Mr. Mossom, Min'r; Mr. Ambrose Dudley, Coll. Jos. Foster, Mr. John Parke, Coll. Dan'l Parke Custis, Mr. Joseph Marston, Coll. William Macon, Capt. Rich'd Littlepage, Mr. Walter Clopton, Vestrymen; Capt. Rich'd Meux, Capt. William Massie, Church Wardens.

| St. Peter's Parish, | Debt'r. |
|---|---|
| To the Reverend Mr. Mossom his Salary to Septem'r the 29th | 16000 |
| to Cask to do. at 4 p. Cent. | 640 |
| to the Reverend Mr. Mossom for the Deficiency of the Glebe | 1600 |
| to Cask to do. at 4 p. cent. | 64 |
| To James Holmes his Salary to Sept'r 29th | 1800 |
| to William Forbess his Salary as Sexton | 1000 |
| to David Patterson for keeping Margaret Grumbal | 800 |
| to Hannah Crump for keeping an Orphan Child | 600 |
| to Cornelius Matthews for keeping his mother | 500 |
| to Sam'l Bailey for keeping Mary Major | 500 |
| to Israel Austin for keeping his Brother | 250 |
| to Stephen Moon for keeping his Brother | 976 |
| to James Ashcraft do. his Father | 700 |
| to Mary Taliaferro, do. Charles Gooding | 500 |
| to Mr. Waller for a Copie of the List of Tithables | 18 |
| to Maj'r John Dandridge for 2 Copies do. | 36 |
| To Sarah Broker for washing the Surplice | 150 |
| to the Collector for Delinquents including the Ballance due | 329 |

to Margery Clart for keeping Christopher Bendall ..... 400
to Dan'l Carroll for do ........ do. ................. 300
to Capt. William Massie's Acco't, £17, 10, 2½, in Tobo.
at 11 p. ct. ........................................ 3180
to Robert Clopton for making a Coffin for Geo. Mason 10| 90
to James Ashcraft for Burying Thomas Ashcraft, £1, 8s.,
7½, ............................................... 251
to the Reverend Mr. Mossom for 6 Bottles of Wine, 1.
4, 0 .............................................. 220
                                                    ─────
                                                    30901
to 6 lb Tobo. p. Poll. ............................ 6690
                                                    ─────
                                                    37591
to Collection at 6 p. Cent. ....................... 2256
                                                    ─────
       Per Contra                                   39847
By 1118 Tithables at 36 lb. Tobo p. Poll.............. 40248

Remains due to the Parish from the Collector, 401 lb. Tobo.

The office of a Parish Clk. and Clk. of the Vestry becoming void by the Death of James Holmes, William Baker is chosen in the said Offices by the Minister and Majority of the Vestry, and took the Oaths as required by Law.

Capt. Richard Meux is Continued Church Warden for the Ensuing year, and Mr. Ambrose Dudley is Chosen Church Warden in the Room of Capt. William Massie.

Being the Opinions of the Vestry that Maj. William Gray is Legally removed Out of the Parish & his office of a Vestryman becoming Void, Mr. Geo. Webb is Chosen in his Room; the Clk. is to give him Notice to attend the next Vestry.

Ordered that the Church Wardens Demand Alice Warren's Child from Gideon Beltes if he is removing out of the Colony, and Binds the s'd Child to Jos. Crump.

Ordered That Israel Austin for keeping his Brother the Ensuing year have 500 lb. Tobacco.

Ordered That Daniel Patterson have 800 lb. Tobo. for keeping Margaret Grumbal the Ensuing year.

Ordered that Cornelius Matthews have 600 lb. Tobo. for keeping his mother the Ensuing year.

Ordered That the Church Wardens remove Mary Major to another place, &c.

Ordered Mary Fargesson be allowed 500 lb. Tobo. for keeping Chas. Gooding the Ensuing year.

Ordered Edward Lewis be allowed 1200 lb. Tobo. for keeping his mother the Ensuing year.

This Vestry is adjourned to Oct'er the 24th, 1747.

David Mossom, Min'r; William Macon, Joseph Foster, Daniel Parke Custis, John Parke, Walter Clopton, William Massie, Vestrymen; Richard Meux, Ambrose Dudley, Church Wardens.

Recorded by WILLIAM BAKER, Clk. of the Vestry.

---

At a Vestry held for St. Peter's Parish which was continued by adjournment from the 24th of this Instant, Octob'r, to the 31st.

PRESENT:

The Reverend Mr. Mossom, Min'r; Capt. Rich'd Littlepage, Mr. Matt'w Anderson, Mr. John Parke; Capt. Richard Meux, Mr. Ambrose Dudley, Church Wardens.

Ordered That 6 lb Tobacco p. Poll. be levy'd on every Tithable in this Parish and that the Collector deliver the Said Tobo. to the Church Wardens who are impowered & required to Sell the same for ready Money at the best Market that shall Offer.

Mr. Ambrose Dudley being Chosen Church Warden in the Room of Capt. William Massie at the Vestry held Oct'r the 16th, 1747, was accordingly Sworn this Day before Capt. Richard Littlepage.

Ordered that Agness, the Bastard Child of Alice Warren, who had been formerly Bound to Gideon Beltes, be Bound by the Church Wardens to Francis Harris, the said Gideon Beltes having resigned the Indenture.

This day the Parish levy being Proportioned we find it amounts to the Sum of 36 lb. Tobo. p. Poll. on 1118 Tithables, which said Sum of Tobacco Capt. Rich'd Meux is impowered to Collect from Every Tithable Person in this Parish. the said Meux having already Entered into Bond with his Security, Mr. Ambrose Dudley and Mr. Matt'w Anderson, who are approved by the Vestry for his Performance of the Collection.

David Mossom; Richard Littlepage, David Mossom, Min'r;

Richard Littlepage, Walter Clopton, Will'm Massie, Matt'w Anderson, John Parke, Vestrymen; Richard Meux, Ambrose Dudley, Church Wardens.

Recorded by WILLIAM BAKER, Clk. Vestry.

At a Vestry held for St. Peter's Parish Sep'r 29th, 1748.

PRESENT:

The Rev'd Mr. Mossom, Min'r; Capt. Rich'd Meux, Col. Jos. Foster, Capt. Wm. Massie, Mr. Geo. Webb, Mr. Walter Clopton, Mr. Ambrose Dudley, Capt. Rich'd Littlepage and Colo. Will'm Macon; Capt. Rich'd Meux, Mr. Ambrose Dudley, Ch. Wardens.

Mr. Geo. Webb was this day Sworn into the office of a Vestryman before Colo. Jos. Foster & Capt. Wm. Massie, having been Chosen into the said Office the last Vestry in the Room of Maj'r Will'm Gray, who has Remov'd himself out of the Parish.

| St. Peter's Parish, | Dr. | lb. Tobo. |
|---|---|---|
| To the Rev'd Mr. D. Mossom his Salary to ye 29th Sep'r | | 16000 |
| To Cask. 4 p. ct. | | 640 |
| To Do. for Deficiency of a Glebe | | 1600 |
| To Do. 4 P. Ct. for cask | | 64 |
| To Wm. Baker's Salary to be pd. to Jos. Crump | | 1800 |
| To Wm. Forbush, Sexton, his Salary | | 1000 |
| To David Patteson for Margaret Grumball | | 800 |
| To Hannah Crump for an Orphan Child | | 600 |
| To Cornelius Matthews for his Mother | | 600 |
| To Geo. Waddell for Mary Major, Rec'd of Sam'l Bailey | | 535 |
| To Israel Austin for his Brother | | 500 |
| To Mary Fergeson for Char's Gooding | | 500 |
| To Mr. Waller for Copia List. | | 18 |
| Mr. Dandridge 2 Do. | | 36 |
| To Sarah Broker for Washing | | 150 |
| To the Collector for Delinquents | | 1712 |
| To Margery Clark for Christ'er Bendal | | 600 |
| To Edward Lewis for his mother | | 1200 |
| To Capt. Massie's Acct., £10, 0, 6½ a 12\|6 | | 1204 |
| To Alex. Fargisson for Sarah Turner | | 600 |
| To Jas. Clarkson—his Levy | | 30 |

VESTRY BOOK OF ST. PETER'S PARISH. 207

To Henry Scrugs .................................. 36
To Wm. Forbush for Andrea Fernea ................ 100
To do. for clearing the Church yard ................ 50

Carried Forward ........................... 30375
To 6 lb. Tobo. P. Poll. for the Parish Use .......... 6660
To Collecting at 6 P. ct. ........................... 2222

                                                  39257
Contra,                    Cr.

By Ballance due from the Collector last year .......... 401
By 1110 Tithes a 35 lb. P. Poll. ................... 38850

                                                  39251
Ballance due to the Collector ....................... 6

                                                  39257

Ordered that the Ch. Wardens do Provide for the Orphan Child of Agnes Crump, Deceased.

That David Patterson have 800 lb. Tobo. for keeping Mary Grumbal.

That Cornelius Matthews have 600 lb. for keeping his mother.
That Sam'l Bailey have 500 lb. for keeping Mary Major.
That Mary Fargison have 500 lb. for Chas. Gooding.
That Edward Lewis have 1200 lb. for his mother.
That Will'm Forbush have 400 lb. for Andrew Fernea.
That Mr. Ambrose Dudley be continued ch. Warden, and that Mr. George Webb be ch. Warden in the Room of Capt. Rich'd Meux.

That the high Sheriff be collector for this Parish the ensuing yeare.

Collo. Foster and Mr. Webb Securityes.

This day the Parish Levy being Processioned we find it amounts to the Sum of 35 lb. Tobo. p. poll. on 1110 Tithables, which said Sum of Tobo. Capt. John Richardson is Impowered to Collect from Every Tithable in the Parish.

Ordered that the Clerk of the Vestry Deliver to the Present Collector the List of Delinquents Return'd to the Vestry by the late Collector in 1746 & 1747, to be Levy'd as the Law Directs, and to be accounted for to the Ch. Wardens for the use of the Parish.

D. Mossom, Min'r; Walter Clopton, Rich'd Littlepage, Will'm Massie, Will'm Macon, Rich'd Meux, John Parke; Geo. Webb, Ambrose Dudley, Ch. Wardens.

Recorded by JOHN RYAN, Clk. Vestry.

At a Vestry held for St. Peter's Parish by Adjournment from Sept. 29th to October the 11th, 1749.

PRESENT:

The Rev'd Mr. Mossom, Min'r; Colo. Will'm Macon, Colo. Jos. Foster, Col. D. P. Custis, Mr. Jos. Marston, Capt. Rich'd Meux, Mr. John Parke, Vestrymen; Mr. Geo. Webb, Mr. Amb. Dudley, Church Wardens.

| St. Peter's Parish, | Debter, | lbs. Tobo. |
|---|---|---|
| To the Rev'd Mr. D. Mossom's Salary to the 29th Sept. | | 16000 |
| to Cask to do. at 4 P. Cent. | | 640 |
| to the Rev'd Mr. Mossom for deficiency of a Glebe & Cask | | 1664 |
| to John Ryan's Salary as Clerk of the Church & Vestry | | 1800 |
| to Will'm Forbes, Sexton, his Salary | | 100 |
| to Cornelius Matthews for Maintaining his Mother | | 600 |
| to Samuel Bailey for Mary Major | | 500 |
| to James Turner for Charles Goodwin | | 500 |
| to Maj'r Dandridge for 2 Lists Tithables | | 36 |
| to Mr. Benja. Waller for 1 Do. | | 18 |
| to Sarah Brooker for washing the Ch. Linnen | | 150 |
| to Will'm Meanly for the Support of his Daughter | | 700 |
| to Margery Clark for keeping two Bastard Children | | 1000 |
| to Capt. Littlepage for Chex Linnen for the Children | | 66 |
| to Hannah Crump for keeping a Bastard Child | | 700 |
| to Will'm Forbes for keeping Andrew Fornea | | 400 |
| to Edward Lewis for maintaining his mother | | 1200 |
| to Allow'd Will'm Hewlet on acct. of a Bastard Child | | 200 |
| to Allow'd the Collector for Delinquents as P. Acct. | | 451 |
| to Mr. Webb. acct. £9, 2, 5, in Tobo. at 14 P. ct. | | 1303 |
| to Colo. Macon's Do., £1, 6, 3, at Do. | | 187 |
| to the Collector for Ballance due to him the Last Levy | | 6 |

29121

Collector's Salary at 6 P. ct. .......................... 1747

Debt carried forward and to the Parish Debt brought over 30868
The Parish Cr't.—By the Collector for Delinquents of last
year by him received ............................ 792
By 1151 Tithables at 26 P. Poll. .................... 29926
Ballance due to the Coll'r to be allowed next year ........ 150

30868

Ordered that Eliza. Morris be allowed 400 lbs. Tobo. for the keeping of Andrew Fornea.

That the two Bastard Children of Mary Dunsten be Bound out by the Church Wardens.

That the Bastard Daughter of Mary Dixon, Dec'ed, be bound to Will'm Hewlet by the Ch. Wardens, The Vestry allowing the said Hewlet 200 lb. Tobo.

That the Church Wardens pay the Rev'd Mr. Mossom's acct, viz., 24, which he deliver'd at the last Vestry, which at present is mislaid.

That the Church Wardens pay to Alex'r Fargisson his acct, viz., 3, 9|1, which he Delivered to the last Vestry.

That the Church Wardens pay the Rev'd Mr. Mossom 24| for the Preceeding year.

That the Church Wardens pay Doc'r Newyear Smith's acct, 1|6,

That Mr. Geo. Webb be continued Church Warden and that Mr. John Parke be chosen Church Warden in the Room of Mr. Ambrose Dudley.

That all the Tithables belonging to Mr. Rich'd Farrell's Quarter, Augustine Pasley, David Ross, John Ross, & John Ross, the son of Rich'd Ross, & John Downs be added to the Gang under Michael Harfield, Surveyor.

That the Bastard Children of Mary Dunston be Committed to the care of Jane Davis till they can be bound out. She being allowed after the Rate of 500 lb. Tobo. P. Ann. for Each child.

Mr. John Parke took the Oath of Church Warden & John Ryan Clerk of the Parish & Vestry.

This Day the Parish Levy being Laid we find it amounts to the sum of 30076 Pounds of Tobo., which being Divided by 1151 the Number of Tithables this present year, makes 26 lb Tobo. P.

Poll., which sum of 26lb. Tobo. Mr. John Richardson, High Sheriff, is impowered to Collect, he Entering into Bond with Security for the Performance of his office, D. P. Custis & Jos. Foster, Gent., Securities. Bond to be given to the Church Wardens by New Kent Nov'r Court.

D. Mossom, min'r; D. P. Custis, Jos. Foster, Jos. Marston, Rich'd Meux, Amb. Dudley; Geo. Webb, John Parke, Church Wardens.

Recorded by JOHN RYAN, clk. Vestry.

At a Vestry held for St. Peter's Parish by Adjournment from ye 29th Sept. past to ye 26th of Novem'r, 1750.

PRESENT:

The Rev'd Mr. Mossom, Min'r; Colo. Wm. Macon, Mr. Walt. Clopton, Colo. Jos'h Foster, Mr. Amb. Dudley, Colo. D. P. Custis, Mr. Jos'h Marston, Mr. Rich'd Meux, Mr. Matt'w Anderson, Vestrymen; Mr. Geo. Webb, Mr. John Parke, Church Wardens.

| St. Peter's Parish Debt'r. | lbs. Tobo. |
|---|---|
| To the Rev'd Mr. David Mossom's Sallary to ye 29th Sept'r Past | 16000 |
| To Cask to Do. at 4 P. Cent. | 640 |
| To the Rev'd Mr. Mossom's Deficiency of a Glebe & Cask to Do. | 1664 |
| To Jno. Ryan his Sallary as Clerk of the Parish & Vestry, deducting 103 lb. Tobo. | 1800 |
| Paid by Jno. Armistead to George Walton | * * |
| To Wm Forbes, Sexton, his Sallary | 1000 |
| To Mr. Geo. Webb's acct for Goods Deliver'd for ye Poor, £6, 12, 6, Tob. a 2 P. ct. | 795 |
| To Colo. Wm. Macon's Acct. for Do., delivered Do., £3, 19, 4, in Tobo. a 2 P. C. | 476 |
| To Mr. Nath'l Noah's Acct. for Goods delivered by, Order, £6, 14, 8, a do. | 808 |
| To Capt. Wm. Massie's Acct. for goods deliver'd, £7, 19, 2, in Tobo. a do. | 955 |
| To Eliza Morris for a P. stockings for Andrew Furnea, o o l. 1. 6 in Tobo. a do.. | 9 |
| To Mr. Geo. Heath for keeping Christ. Bendall 2 mo. Burying him & Digging his grave, &c. | 300 |

VESTRY BOOK OF ST. PETER'S PARISH. 211

| | |
|---|---|
| To John Hutchinson's Acct. for keeping Mary Mahone, £2-17-6, Tobo. a do. | 345 |
| To Cornelius Mattheys for keeping his mother | 600 |
| To Samuel Bailey for keeping Mary Major | 500 |
| To Maj'r Dandridge for Copy two Lists Tithables | 36 |
| To Mr. Benja. Waller for one Do. | 18 |
| To Sarah Brooker for washing the Church Linnen | 150 |
| To Wm. Meanly for the Support of his Daughter | 700 |
| To Jane Davis for keeping Mary Dunstan's Bastard Children | 1000 |
| To Hannah Crump for keeping a Bastard child | 700 |
| To Eliza. Morris for keeping Andrew Furnea | 400 |
| To Edw. Lewis for keeping his Mother 8 mo. & Burying her | 950 |
| To Mary Clopton for keeping Mary Jozard | 300 |
| To Jane Brothers for Charles Askew, 17s., 6d. | 105 |
| To Sarah Brooker towards her maintenance | 200 |
| To Martha Hight toward her maintenance | 300 |
| To James Turner for keeping Charles Goodwin | 500 |
| To Mary Anderson towards her maintenance | 300 |
| To Mary Spencer for the Support of her Daughter | 300 |
| To Rich'd Crump Jurs., Acct. Allow'd, £0, 17, 9¾, In Tobo. at 2d. p. lb. | 107 |
| To the Collector for Delinquents Return'd | 1040 |
| | 32998 |
| To Ballance due to ye Collector last year P. | 150 |
| To the Collector's Sallary a 6 P. Cent. | 1984 |
| | 35137 |
| Contra, Cr. | |
| By 1156 Tithables at 30 lb. Tobo. P. Poll. | 34680 |
| Ball. due to ye Collector to be allowed Next year | 457 |
| | 35137 |

Ordered That Eliza. Morris be alloyed 400 lb. Tobo. for keeping Andrey Furnea.

That Cornelius Mattheys be alloy'd for keeping his mother 600 lb. Tobo.

That Samuel Bailey be alloy'd for keeping Mary Major 500 lb. Tobo.

That James Turner be allow'd for keeping Charles Goodwin 500 lb. Tobo..

That Mary Clopton be allow'd for keeping Mary Gogan 500 lb. Tobo. the Ensuing year.

That Hannah Crump be allow'd for keeping a Bastard Child 600 lb. Tobo.

That Samuel Plumley be appointed Sexton in the Room of Wm. Forbes, Dec'ed, with the like Sallary that Forbes served for.

That Mr. Matthew Anderson be Appointed Church Warden in the Room of Mr. George Webb.

The Vestrymen now Present have agreed to meet upon Easter Tuesday next in Order to Settle the Accts. Relating to the Parish.

This Day the Parish Levy being laid we find it amounts to the Sum of 35137 Pounds of Tobo., which being Divided by 1156, the Number of Tithables this Present Year, makes 30 lb. Tobo. P. Poll., which sum of 30 lb. Tobo. Mr. John Armistead is impowered to Collect, he Entering into Bond with his Securities, Colo. Joseph Foster & Mr. John Parke for the Performance of this office.

This Day Mr. Matthew Anderson took the oaths to the Government & of a church Warden before Colo. William Macon & Colo. Joseph Foster.

D. Mossom, Min'r; William Macon, D. P. Custis, Jos'h Foster, Walter Clopton, Rich'd Meux, Ambrose Dudley; John Parke, Matth'w Anderson, Church Wardens.

At a Vestry met in the Vestry Room of St. Peter's Parish and held August ye 24th, 1751.

### Present:

The Rev'd. Mr. D. Mossom, Min'r; William Macon, Walter Clopton, Ambrose Dudley, George Webb, Vestrymen; John Parke, Ch. Warden.

The members Present Subscribed to be conformable to the Doctrine and Discipline of the Church of England as by Law Established.

Upon the Motion made by the Rev'd Mr. Mossom that there are now Several Vacancies in this Vestry by the Death of Mr. William Massie, the Removal of Mr. Matthew Anderson into an-

VESTRY BOOK OF ST. PETER'S PARISH. 213

other Parish and County, And the Resignation of Mr. Meux, Signified by a Letter under his hand dated August 12, 1751, Directed to this Vestry, and delivered by Mr. Parke, Church Warden.

Resolved, That Mr. John Lewis and Mr. William Hopkins be appointed Two of the Vestry Men of this Parish, and that the Clerk do give them Notice thereof.

Mr. Jesse Scott and Mr. William Gray were also nominated, and upon taking the votes of the Minister and Vestry here present, the same were equally divided, and ye Election of One of them Refer'd to ye Next Vestry.

PRESENT: Richard Littlepage, Gent.

Elizabeth Forbes, Widow of Wm. Forbes, late Sexton, is appointed to Execute that Office in the Room of Samuel Plumley, lately Deceased.

William Macon, Gent., is appointed Church Warden in the Room of Mr. Matthew Anderson, Lately Removed.

Upon Consideration of an Order of the Court of James City County bearing date July 8th, 1751, and also an Order of the Court or New Kent County dated July 11, 1751, directing the Vestry of this Parish to divide the Lands into Precincts and to appoint Persons to Procession the same according to Law.

Ordered That all Lands in this Parish be Continued and divided into Twenty Precincts, the same that have been hitherto Accustomed to be Processioned, and that the Persons whose Names are Under Specified in Each Precinct Respectively, do Procession the Same, and Return to the Vestry an Account of their Proceedings; That is to say, in Precinct

No. 1. John Roper and Henry Atkinson.
No. 2. George Poindexter & William Poindexter.
No. 3. William Perkins & Jonathan Patteson.
No. 4. Walter Clopton & Robert Jarratt.
No. 5. Jesse Scott & George Waddill.
No. 6. Anthony Cole & John Waddill.
No. 7. William Macon & Martin Hewlet.
No. 8. Richard Crump & William Clopton.
No. 9. John Parke & Edward Bacon.
No. 10. Charles Mannin & Joseph Ellyson.
No. 11. Thomas Martin & Devereux Clopton.
No. 12. Robert Ellyson & William Johnson.

No. 13. James Roberts & Walter Daniel.
No. 14. Charles Crump & Henry Scrugs.
No. 15. George Wilkinson & Ambrose Dudley.
No. 16. Thomas Moss & Richard Meanley.
No. 17. Francis Barnes & Joseph Weaver. .
No. 18. William Vaughan & William Gregory.
No. 19. William Vaiden & Thomas Hilliard.
No. 20. Thomas Pinchback & Jacob Ragland.

And that Such Processioning shall be by them Respectively made between the Last day of September and the Last day of March next coming, as to them shall seem most convenient.

Ordered That a Vestry be summoned and held on Monday, the 30th day of September next, for laying the Parish Levy and for dispatch of other parochial affairs. And the Church wardens do give Notice to all persons who they shall be informed have in their hands any money or Tobacco due to this Parish, That they do Appear at the said Vestry to give account thereof.

D. Mossom, Min'r; Walter Clopton, Rich'd Littlepage, Ambrose Dudley, Geo. Webb; William Macon, John Parke, Church Wardens.

At a Vestry held at the Vestry Room of St. Peter's Parish the 30th day of September, 1751.

The Rev'd Mr. D. Mossom, Min'r; Capt. Rich'd Littlepage, Mr. George Webb, Mr. Joseph Marston, Vestrymen; Colo. Wm. Macon, Colo. D. P. Custis, Mr. Walter Clopton, Mr. Ambrose Dudley; John Parke, William Macon, Church Wardens. Colo. William Macon (by order of the last Vestry being appointed Churchwarden in the Room of Mr. Matthew Anderson, lately Removed) This day took the Oath of a Church Warden.

Mr. John Lewis & Mr. William Hopkins being Elected Vestrymen at the last Vestry held for this Parish, This day took the Oaths Required by Law, and Subscribed to be Conformable to the Doctrine and Discipline of the Church of England, and were thereupon Admitted members of the Vestry.

PRESENT:

John Lewis, William Hopkins.

Mr. William Hopkins Elected Church Warden in the Room of Mr. John Parke, and this day took Oath of Church Warden.

Pursuant to a Reference of the last Vestry, the Election of Mr. William Gray & Mr. Jesse Scott to be a Vestry-Man in the Room of Mr. Rich'd Meux, who then Resign'd. Mr. William Gray being this day duly Elected, took the Oaths Required by Law, and Subscribed to be Conformable to the Doctrine and Discipline of the Church of England, and was thereupon admitted a member of this Vestry.

| | |
|---|---:|
| To the Rev'd Mr. Mossom's Salary to the 29th Instant | 16000 |
| To Cask & Shrinkage—8 P. cent. | 1280 |
| To the Rev'd Mr. Mossom for Deficiency of a Glebe—cask & shrinkage | 1728 |
| To John Ryan's Salary, Clerk of the Parish & Vestry | 1800 |
| To Eliza. Forbes, Sexton, including 3. 4. o. lb. Tobo. to be paid by the Collector to El'za, the Widdow of Sam'l Plumley, late Sexton, dec'ed | 1000 |
| To Eliza. Morris for keeping Andrew Furnea | 400 |
| To Cornelius Mattis for keeping his mother | 600 |
| To Sam'l Bailey for keeping Mary Major | 500 |
| To James Turner for keeping Charles Goodin | 500 |
| To Mary Clopton for keeping Mary Gozard | 600 |
| To Hannah Crump for keeping a Bastard Child | 600 |
| To William Meanley for the Support of his Daughter | 700 |
| To Major Dandridge for 2 Lists of Tithables | 36 |
| To Mr. Benja. Waller for 1 Do. | 18 |
| To Sarah Brooker towards her maintainance | 300 |
| To Martha Hithe the Same | 300 |
| To Mary Anderson towards his support | 300 |
| To Mary Spencer for the Support of her Daughter | 300 |
| To Sarah Brooker for washing the Church Linnen | 150 |
| To Jane Davis for keeping two Bastard Children | 1000 |
| To Richard Tomson towards his Support | 400 |
| To George Barker towards his Support | 500 |
| To Millinton Dixon for Burying Charles Asque | 450 |
| To Noel Waddill for Burying two Persons | 300 |
| To Edward Patteson for Lidia Philips | 200 |
| | 29962 |
| To the Collector's Salary at 6 P. Cent. | 1798 |
| To Do. for the Ballance of Last Levy's due to him | 457 |
| To Do. for Insolvents, in 1750 | 964 |

Contra, Cr.
By 1136 Tithables at 30 lb. Tob. P. Poll. .............. 34080
Ballance in the Collector's hands to be Accounted for to the
  Vestry ........................................... 899
                                                     ─────
                                                     33181

Pursuant to an Order made last Vestry Mr. Lewis Webb having Registered the Processioning Orders and Returns of 1747 in the Vestry Book, this day Returned the same, which being Examined by the Church Wardens, were found to be truly Registered.

Ordered That the Several Sums Under Specified by the Church Wardens in money, vizt:

                                                £ S. D.
To Parke Bailey his account allow'd ................ 1. 2. 2
To Colo. William Macon ......................... 3.10. 9
To Matthew Anderson's Estate .................... 2.18. 6
To George Heath ............................... 8.
To Farqr. Matheson ............................ 1.16. 0
To Rich'd Crump, Jr., to repairs to the Church ..... 10.00 0
                                                ─────────
                                                £ 19.15. 5

Ordered That Charles Pearson be Allow'd 400 lbs. Tobo. for keeping Andrew Furnea.

That Cornelius Matthews be allowed 600 lbs. Tobo. for keeping his mother.

That Sam'l Bailey be allowed 500 lbs. Tobo. for keeping Mary Major.

That James Turner be allowed 500 lbs. Tobo. for keeping Charles Goodwin.

That Mary Clopton be allow'd 600 lbs. Tobo. for keeping Mary Gozard.

That Hannah Crump be allow'd 600 lbs. Tobo. for keeping Agathe Crump's Child.

That James Morris be allow'd 900 lbs. Tobo. for keeping Mary Dunstan's Bastard children during their Continuance with him.

Ordered That all persons indebted to the Parish do account with the Church Wardens and Pay their Hands the Several Sums due from them, and in failure of Payment, the Church Wardens are required to bring suit for the Recovery of the Same.

VESTRY BOOK OF ST. PETER'S PARISH. 217

Ordered That the Church Wardens bring suit against John Hoy, of Albemarle County, upon the Acco't of two Bastard Children born of the body of Mary Dunstan, which Bastards were sworn to the said Hoy by the said Dunstan, and at present are and have been for some years Past, very chargeable to this Parish.

This day the Parish Levy being laid we find it amounts to the Sum of 33181 Pounds of Tobacco, which being Divided by 1136, the Number of Tithables this Present Year, Amounts to 30 lb. P. Poll., which Sum of 30 lb. Tobo. P. Poll., Maj'r William Gray is impowered to Collect, he giving Bond with his Securities, Mr. Walter Clopton, & for the Performance of his office.

D. Mossom, Min'r; Dan'l Parke Custis, John Lewis, Rich'd Littlepage, Joseph Marston, George Webb, Ambrose Dudley, Walter Clopton, William Gray, John Parke, Wm. Macon, Wm. Clopton, Church Wardens.

At a Vestry Met in the Vestry Room of St. Peter's Parish, and held the 20th day of Nov'r, 1752.

PRESENT:

The Rev'd Mr. D. Mossom, Min'r; Mr. John Parke, Mr. Walter Clopton, Mr. Ambrose Dudley, Vestrymen; Colo. William Macon, Mr. William Hopkins, Church Wardens.

Ordered That Col. William Macon and Mr. William Hopkins be continued Church Wardens for the Ensuing year.

| St. Peter's Parish, | Dr. | lbs. Tobo. |
|---|---|---|
| To the Rev. Mr. Mossom's Salary to the 29th Septem'r.. | | 16000 |
| To Cask & Shrinkage 8 P. ct. | | 1280 |
| To the Rev'd Mr. D. Mossom for Deficiency of a Glebe, cask & Shrinkage | | 1728 |
| To John Ryan's Salary as Clerk of the Church & Vestry to ye 29th Sep'r | | 1800 |
| To Eliza. Forbes, Sextones till the 25th March | | 500 |
| To Edward Beltes, Sexton, from the 25th March till ye 29th Sep'r | | 500 |
| To Cornelius Mattis for keeping his Mother | | 600 |
| To Samuel Bailey for keeping his Mother-in-Law | | 500 |
| To James Turner for keeping Charles Goodin | | 500 |

| | |
|---|---|
| To Mary Clopton for keeping Mary Gozard ........... | 600 |
| To William Meanley for the Support of his Daughter.... | 500 |
| To Mr. Benja. Waler for a Copy List Tithables ......... | 18 |
| To Sarah Broker towards her Maintainance ........... | 300 |
| To Mary Hithe toward her Maintainance .............. | 300 |
| To Mary Anderson towards her Support ............. | 300 |
| To Mary Spencer towards the Support of her Daughter .. | 600 |
| To Sarah Broker for washing the Church Linnen ...... | 150 |
| To Charles Pearson's Acc't allow'd for keeping Andrew Fornea 6 mo. ...................................... | 200 |
| To William Terrell's Acc't Allow'd for keeping Do. 6 mo. | 200 |
| To Mr. Jonathan Patteson's Acc't allow'd 16\|1 in Tobo a 12\|6 P. Ct. ..................................... | 135 |
| To Edward Richardson's Acc't 13\|4 In Tobo. a Do. ..... | 107 |
| To Francis Harris's Acc't 13\|9 In Tobo a Do. .......... | 110 |
| To Maj'r John Dandridge's Acc't allow'd .............. | 212 |
| To William Perkins for 5 Horse Blocks ............... | 132 |
| To Gideon Massie for keeping Geo. Barker 8 Mo. ....... | 300 |
| To Capt. Jesse Scott his Acc't allow'd ................. | 1200 |
| To Unity Raymond towards her Support .............. | 500 |
| To the Collector for Delinquents Return'd ............ | 540 |
| To Richard Crump, Jun'r's Acc't Allow'd, £3. 6. 9., In Tobo a 12\|6 P. Ct. ................................. | 534 |
| To Alex'r Fargison for Burying John Turner ......... | 150 |
| To Sarah Crump for keeping Mary Bailey 4 mo. ........ | 350 |
| | 30846 |
| To the Collector's Salary at 6 P. ct. ................... | 1850 |
| | 32696 |

JOHN L. POINDEXTER.

Contra.,          Cr..

| | |
|---|---|
| By Tobo. due from the Collector last year ............. | 899 |
| By 1025 Tithables at 31 lb. Tobo. P. Poll. ............. | 31775 |
| By a Remainder due to the Collector to be allow'd him next year ........................................ | 22 |
| | 32696 |

Ordered That Mr. Edmund Bacon, Capt. Jesse Scott, and Mr.

## VESTRY BOOK OF ST. PETER'S PARISH. 219

Jonathan Patteson be appointed Vestry Men in the Room of Colo. Joseph Foster & Mr. Joseph Marston, Dec'ed, and Maj'r William Gray, who is Removed out of this Colony, And that the Clerk do give them Notice to attend at the Next Vestry to be held for this Parish.

That Colo. William Macon do Pay Mr. John Street 10|10 for his Trouble in Surveying and Laying off an acre of Land given by Capt. William Taylor for the Use of St. Peter's Church, and that he Pay Mr. Bartlot Anderson 10|10 for writing a Deed for the said Land.

That Colo. William Macon do Pay Richard Thomson £2, S10; John Reynolds, £3; Charles Hughes, £2; Mr. William Hopkins, £1; And Mr. Parkes Bailey, 12|6.

That the Rev'd Mr. D. Mossom Deliver to the Clerk of the Vestry Maj'r John Dandridge's Receipt for the Bonds due to Mr. David McGill, Exec'r, in the year 1735.

That Edward Bettes be Appointed Sexton in the Room of Eliza. Furbes, whose Salary being the 29th of Sept. Last.

This Day the Parish Levy being laid we find it Amounts to the Sum of 32696 Pounds of Tobo., which being Divided by 1025, the Number of Tithables this Present year Amounts to 31 lb. Tobo. P. Poll., which Sum of 31 lb. Tobo. P. Poll., Mr. John Armistead is impowered to Collect, he giving Bond with his Securities, Mr. Ambrose Dudley and Mr. John Parke, for the Performance of his Office as Collector.

Signed by D. Mossom. Min'r; Walter Clopton, Ambrose Dudley, John Parke, Vestrymen; William Macon, William Hopkins, Church Wardens.

Recorded by JOHN RYAN, Clerk of the Vestry.

---

At a Vestry held at the Vestry Room of St. Peter's Parish the 29th Day of Sept., 1753.

PRESENT:

The Rev'd Mr. D. Mossom, Min'r; Colo. D.P. Custis, Mr. John Parke, Mr. John Lewis, Vestrymen; Colo. William Macon, Mr. William Hopkins, Ch. Wardens.

Mr. Edmund Bacon, Mr. Jesse Scott & Mr. Jonathan Patteson being Chosen Vestrymen at the last Vestry, and the Clerk being Ordered to give them Notice of the Same, They Accordingly appeared at this Vestry, and Quallify'd themselves as the Law Directs by taking the Oaths Appointed & Subscribing to be Conformable to the Doctrine & Discipline of the Church of England, & Subscribing the Test, and are admitted to their places in the Vestry.

PRESENT:

Mr. Edmund Bacon, Mr. Jesse Scott, Mr. Jonathan Patteson.

| St. Peter's Parish, | Dr. |
|---|---|
| To the Rev'd Mr. David Mossom's Salary till 29 Sept'r.. | 16000 |
| To Cask & Shrinkage 8 P. Ct. | 1280 |
| To the Rev'd Mr. Mossom for Deficiency of a Glebe, Cask & Shrinkage | 1728 |
| To John Ryan's Salary as Clerk of the Parish & Vestry.. | 1800 |
| To Edward Bettis, Do., as Sexton, till Sep'r 29 | 1000 |
| To Cornelius Mattis for keeping his Mother | 600 |
| To Sam'l Bailey for keeping Mary Major | 500 |
| To James Turner for keeping Charles Goodwin | 500 |
| To Mary Clopton for keeping Mary Gozard | 600 |
| To William Meanley for keeping his Daughter | 500 |
| To Mr. Benja. Waller for One list Tithables | 18 |
| To Sarah Broker towards her maintenance | 300 |
| To Do. for washing the Church Linnen | 300 |
| To Mary Anderson towards her support | 300 |
| To William Terrell for keeping Andrew Furneau | 400 |
| To Colo. Jno. Dandridge for Two Lists Tithables | 36 |
| To Mary Spencer towards the Support of her Daughter.. | 600 |
| To Sarah Green towards her support | 300 |
| To Unity Raymond towards her support | 500 |
| | 27112 |
| To Tobo. Ordered to be Levyed for the use of the Parish | 12611 |
| | 39723 |
| To the Collector's Salary at 6 P. ct. | 2383 |
| To Ballance due to the Collector last year | 22 |
| P. Contra, Cr. | 42128 |
| By 1137 Tithables at 37 lb. Tob. P. Poll. | 42069 |
| Ballance due to the Collector to be allow'd him next year.. | 59 |
| | 42128 |

VESTRY BOOK OF ST. PETER'S PARISH. 221

Ordered That Colo. William Macon & Mr. William Hopkins be continued Church Wardens for the Ensuing year.

That the Church Wardens do pay to John Reynolds Three Pounds, and unto Rich'd Thomson Forty Shillings.

That the Church Wardens do Settle with Mr. John Armistead for the Money in his hands due to the Parish, and Receive the Same and account with the Vestry for it.

That the Sum of 12611 of Tobo. be Levy'd for the use of the Parish, and to be Sold by the Church Wardens as Soon as it can be collected.

This Day the Parish Levy being Laid we find it to amount to the Sum of 42128 Pounds of Tobo., which being Divided by 1137, the Number of Tithables this present year, Amounts to 37 Pounds of Tobo. P. Poll. and a Remainder of 59 lb. Tobo, Which Sum of 37 lbs. Tobo. P. Poll., Mr. John Armistead is Impowered by this Vestry to Collect, he giving Bond with his Securities, Mr. John Parke and Mr. Jonathan Patteson for the due Performance of his Office as Collector.

David Mossom, Min'r; Dan'l Parke Custis, John Parke, John Lewis, Edmund Bacon, Jesse Scott, Jonathan Patteson, Vestrymen; William Macon, William Hopkins, Church Wardens.

Recorded by JOHN RYAN, Clerk of the Vestry.

At a Vestry held for St. Peter's Parish the 28th Day of September, Anno Dom., 1754.

PRESENT:

The Rev'd Mr. D. Mossom, Min'r; Colo. Dan'l Parke Custis, Capt. Edmund Bacon, Mr. John Parke, Mr. John Lewis, Mr. Geo. Webb, Mr. Jesse Scott, Mr. Walter Clopton, Mr. Jonas Patteson, Vestrymen; Colo. William Macon, Mr. William Hopkins, Church Wardens.

| Saint Peter's Parish, | Dr. | lb. Tobo. |
|---|---|---|
| To the Rev'd Mr. D. Mossom's Salary to the 29th Sept'r | | 16000 |
| To Cask & Shrinkage 8 P. Ct. .................... | | 1280 |
| To the Rev'd Mr. D. Mossom for Deficiency of a Glebe, Cask & Shrinkage ............................ | | 1728 |
| To John Ryan's Salary as Clerk of the Parish & Vestry.. | | 1800 |
| To Do. for washing the Church Linnen ............. | | 150 |

To Edward Bettis, Sexton, his Salary .............. 1000
To Cornelius Mattis for keeping his mother........... 600
To Sam'l Bailey for keeping Mary Major ............ 500
To George Waddill for keeping Charles Goodwin ....... 500
To Mary Clopton for keeping Mary Gozard ........... 600
To William Meanley for keeping his Daughter ......... 700
To Mr. Benjamin Waller for a Copy of a list of Tithables   18
To Sarah Brooker to be Disposed of for her Use by the Ch.
    Wardens ........................................ 600
To Colo. John Dandridge for 2 Lists of Tithables...... 36
To Mr. Jona. Patteson for keeping Andrew Furneau .... 600
To Mary Spencer for keeping her Daughter .......... 600
To Sarah Green towards her Support ............... 300
To Unity Raymond towards her Support ............. 500
To 10 lb. Tobo. P. Poll. Levy'd P. Order of the Vestry .. 11596
To John Reynolds towards his Support .............. 500
To Mr. Jonas. Patteson's Acc't Allow'd in Tobo. at 12|6
    Pr. Ct. ........................................ 206
To Mr. William Terrell's Acc't, £1, 1, 0, allow'd in Tobo.
    at Do. ........................................ 161
To Richard Crump, Jun'r, for Repairs ............... 50
To the Collector for Delinquents & former Ballances .... 1299
To John Vaiden, Patroller's Parish Levy ............. 37
                                                    41355
To the Collector's Salary a 6 P. Ct. ................. 2481
                                                    43836
Contra—P. 1159 Tithables at 38 lb. Tobo. P. Poll. ....... 44042
Ballance to be Accounted for by the Collector in Laying
    the Next Levy ................................. 206

Ordered That Colo. William Macon & Mr. William Hopkins be Continued Church Wardens till the Next Vestry.

That Mr. John Armistead do pay the Sum of £13, 15, of which is the Sum he has Received for fines into the hands of Colo. William Macon, Church Warden.

That Mr. William Hopkins do also pay to the said Colo. Macon the Sum of £7, 5, which he has now in his hands and is due to the Parish.

VESTRY BOOK OF ST. PETER'S. PARISH. . 223

Whereas, it appears to the Vestry that Colo. William Macon's Acc't, which he has this Day Produced, is just, & there is a ballance in his hands due to the Psh. of £34, 1, 6½; he is to keep the Said Ballance till it is Ordered to be disposed of by the Vestry, together with the other sums to be paid to him.

This day the Parish levy is laid and we find it amounts to the Sum of 43836 lb. Tobo., which being Divided by 1159, the Number of Tithables in the Parish this Present year, Amounts to 38 lb. Tobo. P. Poll., Whereof John Hopkins is Appointed Collector, To the Performance of which he has given Bond with his Securities, Mr. John Parke and Mr. Edmund Bacon.

D. Mossom, Rect'r; Dan'l Parke Custis, George Webb, Walter Clopton, John Lewis, John Parke, Edmund Bacon, Jesse Scott, Jona. Patteson, Vestrymen; William Macon, William Hopkins, Ch. Wardens.

Recorded by JOHN RYAN, Clerk of the Vestry.

---

At a Vestry held for St. Peter's Parish, the 13th Day of 7br, 1755, for appointing Processioners, and doing other Parish Business.

PRESENT:

The Rev'd Mr. D. Mossom, Min'r; Colo. D. P. Custis, Mr. Geo. Webb, Mr. John Parke, Capt. Elm. Bacon, Mr. John Lewis, Mr. Walter Clopton, Mr. Jesse Scott, Mr. Jonathan Patteson, Vestrymen; Mr. William Hopkins, Churchwarden.

Pursuant to an order of the Court of James City County, Dated July the 14th, And also an order of the Court of New Kent County, Dated June the 12th, 1755, Directing the Vestry of the Parish to Divide the Lands therein into Precincts and appoint Persons to Procession the Same According to Law.

Ordered That all the Lands in this Parish be Divided into twenty Precincts, the same that have been hitherto Processioned, and that the Persons whose Names are Under Specified in each Precinct Respectively do Procession the Same. and Return to the Vestry an account of their Proceedings; That is to say,

No. 1. John Ryan & Henry Atkinson.
No. 2. Geo. Poindexter & Wm. Poindexter.
3. Jona. Patteson & Robt. Baily.
4. Walter Clopton & Robt. Jarrett.

5. Jesse Scott & George Waddill.
6. John Waddill & Noel Waddill.
7. William Macon & Martine Hewlett.
7. Rich'd Crump, Jr., & William Clopton.
9. John Parke & Edward Bacon.
10. Charles Manning & Joseph Ellyson.
11. Thomas Martin & Devereux Clopton.
12. Rob't Ellyson & Francis Harris.
13. Edw'd Morgan & John Dollard.
14. Charles Crump & Henry Scruggs.
15. Geo. Wilkinson & Ambrose Dudley.
16. Thomas Moss & James Christian.
17. Francis Barns & Joseph Weaver.
18. William Gregory & John Green.
19. William Vaiden & Thomas Hilliard.
20. John Wilkinson & Jacob Ragland.

And that Such Processioning Shall be by them Respectively made between the Last day of September, and the last day of March Next Ensuing, as to them Shall Seem most meet and Convenient.

Ordered That Colo. William Macon and Mr. William Hopkins be Continued Church Wardens till the next Vestry.

That a Vestry be held on Monday the 29th of this Instant for Laying the Parish Levy, and doing other Parochial Business.

Signed by the Rev'd Mr. David Mossom, Rector; Dan'l Parke Custis, Walter Clopton, George Webb, Edmund Bacon, John Parke, John Lewis, Jun'r, Jesse Scott, Jonathan Patteson, Vestrymen; Mr. William Hopkins, Church Warden.

Recorded by JOHN RYAN, Clk. of the Vestry.

At a Vestry held at the Vestry Room of St. Peter's Parish for Laying the Parish Levy & doing other Parochial Business the 29th day of Sept., 1755.

PRESENT:

The Rev'd Mr. D. Mossom, Rector; Colo. Daniel Parke Custis, Mr. Walter Clopton, Mr. Ambrose Dudley, Mr. John Parke, Mr. Edward Bacon, Mr. Jonathan Patteson, Mr. Jesse Scott, Vestrymen; Colo. William Macon, Mr. William Hopkins, Church Wardens.

| St. Peter's Parish, | Dr. | lb. Tobo. |
|---|---|---|
| To the Rev'd Mr. D. Mossom's Salary to this day | | 16000 |
| To Cask & Shrinkage 8 Per Centum | | 1280 |
| To the Rev'd Mr. D. Mossom for Deficiency of a Glebe, cask, &c | | 1728 |
| To John Ryan's Salary as Clerk of the Parish Vestry | | 1800 |
| To John Ryan for washing the Church Linnen | | 150 |
| To Cornelius Matthews for keeping his mother & Burying her | | 350 |
| To Sam'l Baily for keeping Mary Major, Levy'd for Geo. Waddill | | 500 |
| To George Waddill for keeping Charles Goodwin | | 500 |
| To Mary Clopton for keeping Mary Godard | | 600 |
| To William Meanley for keeping his Daughter | | 700 |
| To Mr. Benjamin Waller for a Copy of a List of Tithables | | 18 |
| To Colo. John Dandridge for a Copy of 2 Dos. | | 36 |
| To Eliza. Morris for keeping Andrew Furneau | | 600 |
| To Mary Spencer for keeping her Daughter | | 600 |
| To Sarah Green towards her Support | | 300 |
| To Unity Raymond towards her Support | | 500 |
| To John Reynolds towards his & his wife's Support | | 500 |
| To Thomas Waddill for keeping Mary Bailey & Burying her | | 360 |
| To Eliza. Carrol Relieving Mark Flange | | 250 |
| To John Waddill for Burying Alice Warren | | 75 |
| To the Collector for Delinquents Retain'd | | 364 |
| To Martha Williams for her Relief | | 250 |
| To Colo. William Macon's Acc't for Goods deliver'd for the use of the Poor; & Richard Crump's acc't for Repairs in the Church, £12, 19, 9, in Tobo. a 2d. P. lb. | | 1558 |
| | | 30019 |
| To the Collector's Salary at 6 P. Centum | | 1801 |
| P. Contra. | Cr. | 31820 |
| By 1178 Tithables at 27 Tobo. p. Poll. | | 31806 |
| By Tobo. due to the Collector to ballance | | 14 |
| | | 31820 |

Ordered That the Vestry with the Consent of the Minister proceed to the Choice of Church Wardens in the Place of Colo. William Macon and Mr. William Hopkins, whose office Expires at this Vestry; And accordingly Mr. Edmund Bacon and Mr. Jonathan Patteson are Chosen Church Wardens, and have Qualified themselves by taking the Oaths Requir'd by Law, before Colo. Daniel Parke Custis in the presence of the Minister and Vestry.

Order'd That George Forbes, Son of Eliza. Forbes, be Levy free for the future.

This Day the Parish Levy being laid, we find it amounts to the sum of £31820 Tobo., which being Divided by 1178 Tithables, as appears by the list, it amounts to the Sum of 27 lb. of Tobo. P. Poll.; and a Remainder of 14 lb. Tobo. due to the Collector. Whereof Colo. William Macon, High Sheriff, is appointed Collector to the true Performance of which he has given Bond together with Colo. Daniel Parke Custis, his Security.

D. Mossom, Rector; Daniel Parke Custis, Walter Clopton, Ambrose Dudley, Rich'd Littlepage, William Macon, William Hopkins, John Parke, Jesse Scott, John Lewis, Jun'r, Vestrymen; Edmund Bacon, Jonathan Patteson, Church Wardens.

JOHN RYAN, Clk. of the Vestry.

---

At a Vestry met and held upon the Glebe Land the 30th day of Sept'r, 1755.

PRESENT:

The Rev'd Mr. D. Mossom, Rector; Colo. William Macon, Colo. Dan'l Parke Custis, Mr. Ambrose Dudley, Mr. John Parke, Mr. John Lewis, Mr. William Hopkins, Mr. Jesse Scott, Vestryment; Capt. Edmund Bacon, Mr. Jonathan Patteson, Church Wardens.

The gentlemen of the Vestry having this day met upon the Glebe Lands to Consult about building a Glebe, have come to the following Resolutions:

1st. That an house be built upon the land which was bought of Philip Poindexter, as near as Conveniently may be to the house of the said Poindexter.

2ly. That all such houses as are Required by Law be forthwith built and advertisements Published in the Gazette to give Notice to Undertakers to that Purpose.

VESTRY BOOK OF ST. PETER'S PARISH. 227

3ly. That the 14th day of November Ensuing be the day fixed for the Meeting and Treating with Undertakers if it be a fair day; if not, next fair day upon the Said Land.

D. Mossom, Rector; Dan'l Parke Custis, William Macon, Ambrose Dudley, John Parke, John Lewis, Jun'r, William Hopkins, Jesse Scott, Vestrymen; Edmund Bacon, Jonathan Patteson, Church Wardens.

Recorded by JOHN RYAN, Clerk of the Vestry.

At a Vestry held at the Vestry Room of St. Peter's Parish ye 29th Day of Sept'r, Anno, 1756.

PRESENT:

The Rev'd Mr. D. Mossom, Min'r; Colo. William Macon, Colo. D. P. Custis, Mr. Amb. Dudley, Mr. John Parke, Mr. Jesse Scott, Mr. Walter Clopton, Mr. Rich'd Littlepage, Vestrymen; Capt. Edmund Bacon, Church Warden.

| St. Peter's Parish | Cr. lb. Tob. |
|---|---|
| To the Rev'd Mr. D. Mossom, Salary to the 29th Sept'r. | 16000 |
| To Cask & Shrinkage 8 P. ct. | 1280 |
| To the Rev' Mr. Mossom for Deficiency, Glebe, Cask, &c. | 1728 |
| To John Ryan's Salary as Clerk of the Parish and Vestry | 1800 |
| To Do. for washing the Church Linnen | 150 |
| To Edward Betti's Salary as Sexton | 1000 |
| To Sam'l Bailey for keeping Mary Major | 500 |
| To Thos. Moss for keeping Charles Goodwin | 600 |
| To Mary Clopton for keeping Mary Godard | 600 |
| To William Meanley for keeping his Daughter | 700 |
| To Mr. Benja. Waller for a Copy of a List of Tithables.. | 18 |
| To Colo. John Dandridge for 2 Copy's Do. | 36 |
| To Eliz. Morris for keeping Andrew Furneau | 700 |
| To Mary Spencer for keeping her Daughter | 600 |
| To Sarah Green towards her Support | 300 |
| To Unity Raymond towards her Support | 500 |
| To Martha Williams towards her Relief | 250 |
| To Eliz. Plumley to be paid the Ch. Wardens towards her Relief | 400 |
| To the Ch. Wardens for the Support of Agness Crump's Child | 500 |

| | |
|---|---:|
| To John Reynold & his wife towards their Support | 600 |
| To Mr. Jonathan Patteson's Acc't, £9, 2, 1½ In Tobo. at 14\|P. Cent. | 1300 |
| To Rich'd Thompson towards his Support | 500 |
| To Mr. Jesse Scott's Acc't, £4, 0, 0, In Tobo. at 14\|P. Cent. | 571 |
| To Tobacco Levy'd for the Use of the Parish | 9000 |
| | 39633 |
| To the Collector's Salary at 6 P. Cent. | 2378 |
| | 42011 |

P. Contra, Cr.

| | |
|---|---:|
| By 1233 Tithables at 34 lb. Tobo. P. Poll | 11922 |
| By a Ballance due to the Collector, to be Levy'd for him Next Year | 89 |
| | 42011 |

Ordered That Capt. Edmund Bacon and Mr. Jonathan Patteson be Continued Church Wardens for the Ensuing year.

That Mr. William Vaughan be Appointed a Vestry Man in the Room of Mr. William Hopkins, Dece'd; And that the Clerk do give him Notice to attend at the Next Vestry to be held for this Parish.

This Day the Parish Levy being Laid, We find it amounts to the Sum of 42011 Pounds of Tobacco, which being Divided by 1233, being the Number of Tithables, as appears by the Lists, for this Present year Amounts to the Sum of 34 lb. Tobo. P. Poll., tor, which Sum Mr. Gill. Armistead is Impowered to Collect of Every Tithable in the Parish this Present year; To the true Performance of which he has given Bond Together with Colo. Dan'l Parke Custis and Colo. Wm. Macon, his Securieies.

D. Mossom, Rector; Dan'l Parke Custis, William Macon, Amb. Dudley, John Parke, Jesse Scott, & Walter Clopton, Vestrymen; Edmund Bacon, ch. Warden.

Recorded by JOHN RYAN, Clk. Vestry.

---

At a Vestry held at the Vestry Room for St. Peter's Parish the 29th Day of September, 1757.

## VESTRY BOOK OF ST. PETER'S PARISH.    229

### PRESENT:

The Rev'd D. Mossam, Min'r; Colo. William Macon, Mr. John Parke, Capt. Rich'd Littlepage, Mr. Ambrose Dudley, Capt. Jesse Scott; Capt. Edmund Bacon, Church Warden.

| St. Peter's Parish, | Debtor. | lb. Tobo. |
|---|---|---|
| To the Rev'd Mr. David Mossom's Salary to Sept. 29th.. | | 16000 |
| To Cask & Shrinkage 8 P. Ct. on Do. | | 1280 |
| To the Rev'd Mr. Mossom for Deficiency of a Glebe, Cask, &c. | | 1728 |
| To John Ryan's Salary as Clerk of the Parish & Vestry.. | | 1800 |
| To Eleanor Ryan for Washing the Church Linnen | | 150 |
| To Edward Bettis's Salary as Sexton | | 1000 |
| To Sam'l Bailey for keeping Mary Major | | 500 |
| To Thos. Moss for keeping Charles Goodwin | | 600 |
| To Mary Clopton for keeping Mary Godard | | 600 |
| To William Meanley for keeping his Daughter | | 700 |
| To Mr. Benjamin Waller for a Copy of a List of Tithables | | 18 |
| To Mr. William Clayton for Two Copies Do. | | 36 |
| To Eliza. Morris for keeping Andrew Furneau | | 700 |
| To Mary Spencer for keeping her daughter | | 600 |
| To Sarah Green towards her Support | | 300 |
| To Mr. Jonathan Patteson's Acct., £8, 10, 3¾ Allow'd in Tobo. a 14 P. ct. | | 1216 |
| To Colo. William Macon's Acc't 13\|6\|2 Allow'd in Do. at Do. | | 97 |
| To Thos. Moss's Acc't for keeping Agness Crump's Child, £1, 5 6, a Do. | | 180 |
| To Wm. Meanley's Acc't for building a Shedd for his Daughter | | 100 |
| To Mary Reynolds towards her Support | | 300 |
| To Martha Williams towards her Support | | 250 |
| To the Church Wardens for the Use of Eliza. Plumley ... | | 400 |
| To Thos. Moss for keeping Agness Crump's Child | | 600 |
| To the Ch. Wardens for the Use of Rich'd Thomson | | 600 |
| To Do. for the Use of John Simco | | 1000 |
| To John Dollard for Burying Charles Morris | | 200 |
| To Rich'd Taylor for keeping Bolton's Child, £2, 10, a 14 P. ct. | | 356 |

| | |
|---|---:|
| To Do for keeping the Same Child the Ensuing year, £5 a 14 P. ct. | 714 |
| To Mr. Barns' Acc't for a Coffin for Agness Crump and keeping her child | 560 |
| To Do. for keeping the Said Child the Ensuing year | 714 |
| To Mr. John Armistead's acc't 18\| in Tob. at 14 P. Ct. | 128 |
| To 4 lb. Tobo. P. Poll., Levy'd for the Use of the Parish | 5008 |
| To the Collector for Ballance due to him Last Levy | 5098 |
| To Do for Delinquents last year | 198 |
| To John Hopkins acc't allow'd | 196 |
| | 38918 |
| To the Collector's Salary at 6 P. ct. | 2335 |
| Total Sum | 41253 |

| P. Contra, | Cr. | lb. Tobo. |
|---|---|---:|
| By 1252 Tithables at 33 lb. Tobo. P. Poll | | 41316 |
| Ballance due from the Collector to the Parish | | 63 |
| | | 41316 |

Ordered That Mr. Thos. Ivy & Mr. Stephen Furneau Holmes do pay the Vestry 1600lb. Tob. with Cask, Shrinkage, &c., for the use of the Parish, and for not finishing the Glebe Work according to Agreement.

Mr. William Vaughan having been Chosen by the last Vestry to serve as a Vestryman in the Room of Mr. William Hopkins, Dece'd, hath this Day duly Quallified himself by taking the Oaths Required by Law, and is, therefore, admitted a Member of this Vestry.

Capt. Edmund Bacon & Mr. Jonathan Patteson by Consent of the Minister and Vestry, are Continued Church Wardens for the Ensuing year.

Mr. Lewis Webb, & Mr. Izard Wilkinson are Chosen Vestrymen to Serve in the Room of Colo. Daniel Parke Custis, Dece'd, and Mr. John Lewis is Remov'd out of the Parish, and that the Clerk do give them notice to meet at the next Vestry to be held for this Parish.

John Taylor, John Bird, and William Meanley, upon their Petition are set Levy free.

This day the Parish Levy being Laid & we find it amounts to the Sum of 41253 Pounds of Tobo., which being Divided by 1253, the Number of Tithables for this Present year, amounts to 33 lb. Tobo. P. Poll., and a Ballance due as above, which Sum of 33 lb. Tobo. P. Poll., Mr. Lain. Jones is Appointed to Collect, having Enter'd into Bond with his Securities, Colo. William Macon & Mr. William Clayton, for the due Performance of his Office.

Signed by D. Mossom, Rector; Will'm Macon, Rich. Littlepage, Amb. Dudley, John Parke, Jesse Scott and William Vaughan, Vestry-men; Edmund Bacon, Church Warden.

Recorded by JOHN RYAN, Clk. Vestry.

At a Vestry held at the Vestry Room for St. Peter's Parish the 20th Day of February, 1758.

PRESENT:

The Rev'd Mr. D. Mossom, Min'r; Colo. William Macon, Mr. George Webb, Mr. Walter Clopton, Mr. John Parke, Mr. Jesse Scott, and Mr. William Vaughan, Vestrymen; Capt. Edmund Bacon, Mr. Jonathan Patteson, Ch. Wardens.

Mr. Lewis Webb and Mr. Izard Wilkinson having been Chosen Vestry-men at the last Vestry, have this day taken the Oaths as appointed by Law; and Subscribed the Test and Declaration, are thereupon admitted Members of this Vestry.

Capt. Edmund Bacon, Church Warden, having Render'd an Acc't to the Vestry, the Ballance now in his hands is £19, 1:. 5¼.

It appearing to the Vestry that the new Chimney at the East End of the Glebe House, is of great advantage and Conveniency to it; and it is agreed by the Vestry that another New Chimney be Erected at the West End of the Said House; and that the Church Wardens with Colo. William Macon, Capt. Jesse Scott, Mr. Lewis Webb, Mr. John Parke and Mr. Izard Wilkinson, do meet at the Glebe to agree with the workmen for the Performing of the said work, when they shall judge Proper, and as soon as Conveniently they can.

Ordered That Rich'd Crump have five of Madam Custis's male Tiths from the Brick House & Old Quarter to work upon his Road, and that those Tiths be Excused from working Upon any other Road.

Order'd That William Bailey's & Joseph Pargeson's male Tiths be added to Martin Hewlet's gange, and that they be Excused from working Upon any other Road.

Ordered That Mrs. Eliza. Vaughan's, Philip Austin's, and George Walton's Male Tiths be added to Noel Waddell's Gange; and that they also be Excused from working Upon any other Road.

Ordered That the fine by the Presentment of the Grand Jury against Martin Hewlet be Remitted.

Ordered That the fine by the Presentment of the Grand Jury against Rich'd Crump be Likewise Remitted.

William Macon, Sen'r; Walter Clopton, John Parke, Jesse Scott, William Vaughan, Lewis Webb, Izard Wilkinson, Vestryment; Edmund Bacon, Jonathan Patteson, Church Wardens.

At a Vestry held for St. Peter's Parish on Monday, the 26th June, 1758.

PRESENT:

The Rev'd D. Mossom, Min'r; Colo. William Macon, Mr. John Parkes, Mr. Lewis Webb, Mr. Walter Clopton, Mr. Jesse Scott, Mr. William Vaughan, Mr. Izard Wilkinson, Vestrymen; Capt. Edw'a Bacon, Church Warden.

Order'd That Mr. William Clayton be Appointed and Chosen a Vestryman to Serve in the Room of Mr. George Webb, Dece'd.

Richard Crump having Presented his account for work done to the Church, &c., it is ordered that the Church Wardens Pay him the Sum of Twenty Pounds Curr't Money in full Satisfaction for all the work done by him for the Parish to this day.

D. Mossom, Min'r; William Macon, John Parke, Jesse Scott, Walter Clopton, William Vaughan, Lewis Webb, Izard Wilkinson.

Recorded by JOHN RYAN, Clerk of the Vestry.

At a Vestry held at the Vestry Room of St. Peter's Parish on Wednesday, the 22nd of November, Anno. Dom., 1758.

PRESENT:

The Rev'd Mr. D. Mossom, Min'r; Mr. Lewis Webb, Mr. John Parke, Mr. Walter Clayton, Mr. Jesse Scott, Mr. William Clayton, Capt. William Vaughan, Capt. Rich'd Littlepage; Capt. Edward Bacon, Mr. Jonathan Patteson, Church Wardens.

VESTRY BOOK OF ST. PETER'S PARISH. 233

St. Peter's Parish, Dr. lb. Tobo.

| | |
|---|---|
| To the Rev'd Mr. D. Mossom's Salary to the 29 of Sept'r | 16000 |
| To Cask & Shrinkage on Do. 8 P. Ct. | 1280 |
| To John Ryan's Salary as Clerk of the Ch. & Vestry to 7 br. 29 | 1800 |
| To Edward Bettis, Sexton, to Sept. 29 | 1000 |
| To Elleanah Ryan for washing the Church Linnen | 150 |
| To Mary Clopton for keeping Mary Godard | 600 |
| To William Wilkinson for keeping Mary Major | 500 |
| To Will'm Meanly for keeping his Daughter | 700 |
| To Mr. Benja. Waller for a Copy of a list of Tithables | 18 |
| To Mr. William Clayton for Two Copy's Do. | 36 |
| To Mary Spencer for keeping her Daughter | 600 |
| To Eliza. Morris for keeping Andrew Furneau | 700 |
| To Sarah Green towards her Support | 300 |
| To Mary Reynolds towards her support | 300 |
| To Martha Williams towards her Support | 250 |
| To the Church Wardens for the Use of Eliza. Plumley | 400 |
| To Ditto for the Use of John Simcoe | 1000 |
| To Do. for the Use of Rich'd Tomson | 600 |
| To Mr. Lewis Webb's Acc't, £1, 18, 11, In Tobo. at 2d. | 233 |
| To Mr. Lain. Jones for Ballance of his Acc't | 66 |
| To the Rev'd Mr. Mossom's Acc't,£2, 7, 0, In Tobo. at 2d. | 252 |
| To the Ch. Wardens for the Use of Jane Pond | 800 |
| To Ditto for Will'm Meanley's Use | 200 |
| To Do. for John Tayloe's Use | 200 |
| To Do. for Mary Amos | 200 |
| To Rich'd Crump's Acc't, £5, 6, 10, in Tob. at 2 P. Cent.. | 641 |
| To Mr. Jesse Scott's Acct. £4, 15, 0, In Tobo. at Do | 570 |
| To Tobo. Levy'd for additional Work done to the Glebe.. | 5000 |
| | 34396 |
| To the Collector's Salary at 6 P. Centum | 2063¾ |
| Total Sum | 36459¾ |

Pr. Contra, Cr.

| | |
|---|---|
| By 1259 Tithables at 29 lb. Tob. P. Poll. | 36511 |
| Ballance Due from the Collector to the Parish | 51¼ |
| Prof. | 36511 |

Orders. Capt. William Vaughan and Mr. Lewis Webb are appointed and Chosen Church Wardens for the Ensuing year.

Mr. Jonathan Patteson * * * Rendered his Acc't. The Ballance Due from him to the Parish * * * Pounds, Ten Shillings and Two Pence, which Sum he is O * * * & Pay to Mr. Stephen Homes, and Mr. Thomas Joy.

This day the Parish Sum being * * * * * 59. The Nuumber of Tithables for this Present year amounts to 29 lb. Tobacco P. Poll., and a Ballance due to the Parish as above, whereof the Church Wardens are Appointed Collectors, and by Security for the due Performance of his office as Collector.

D. Mossom, Rector; Walter Clopton, Rich'd Littlepage, John Parke, Edmund Bacon, Jesse Scott, Jonathan Patteson, William Clayton, Vestrymen; William Vaughan, Lewis Webb, Church Wardens.

Dr.      St. Peter's Parish to Mr. Wm. Walker.

|  | £ | S | D |
|---|---|---|---|
| 1741 To Building a Steeple according to the first agreement | 130.. | 0.. | 0 |
| To making a New Door, & Door Case, Painting the great West Door, Mending the Plaistering, White Washing the Church, Mending the Floor & Sleepers in Sev'll of the Pews | 8.. | 0.. | 0 |
| To making a large Palisade Gate | 4.. | 0.. | 0 |
| To Painting the Stairs | 0.. | 15.. | 0 |
| To Making a Table for the Vestry Room | 1.. | 5.. | 0 |
| To Making 3 Benches for Do. | 0.. | 12.. | 0 |
|  | 146.. | 12.. | 0 |
| Taken from this account | 6.. | 5.. | 0 |
| Allowed | 140.. | 7.. | 0 |

Contra.           Cr.

| | £ | S | D |
|---|---|---|---|
| By cash Rec'd of Maj. John Dan * * | 40.. | 0.. | 0 |
| By Do. Rec'd of Capt. Rich'd Litt. * * | 30.. | 0.. | 0 |
| By Do. Paid Wm. Atkinson as P. | 48.. | 0.. | 0 |
| By Do. Pd. Mr. Farg'r' Mathes * * | 37.. | 2.. | 9 |
| By Do. Pd. the Rev'd Mr. David Mossom | 15.. | 4.. | 6 |
| | 140.. | 7.. | 0 |

[These last pages are much mutilated.]

# INDEX.

Addison, 186.
Adams, 19, 121, 122, 125, 130, 132, 133, 145, 176.
Alais, 69.
Alldridge, 18, 45, 109.
Alexandrian, 338.
Alford, 8, 11, 15, 17, 49, 63, 105, 114, 118, 119, 120, 131, 172.
Allen, 17, 77, 79, 80, 83, 84, 85, 86, 89, 90, 91, 92, 93, 94, 95, 96, 97, 98, 99, 100, 103, 105, 109, 135, 156.
Allin, 45, 80, 102, 104, 106, 107, 112, 113, 114.
Alloway, 168, 170.
Amess, 131.
Amoss, 45, 66, 137, 139, 140, 142, 176, 183.
Anderson, 10, 69, 81, 82, 83, 211, 212, 215.
Andrewson, 18.
Apperson, 138, 154.
Armistead, 210, 222, 230.
Arnott, 189.
Arnotto, 178, 183.
Ashburton, 92.
Ashbury, 173.
Ashcraft, 45, 138, 140, 186, 188, 189, 196, 208.
Askew, 85, 108, 161, 163, 164, 165, 167, 215.
Atkinson, 6, 8, 9, 11, 12, 18, 72, 81, 110, 124, 172, 213, 223.
Austin, 18, 52, 87, 90, 92, 107, 130, 132, 134, 140, 142, 162, 186, 189, 193, 208, 232.

Bacon, 19, 24, 92, 213, 224, 230.
Badford, 44.
Bailey, 174, 193, 196, 211, 215, 216, 223, 232.
Baisy, 124, 126, 128, 129, 131, 132.
Baizey, 133.
Baker, 18, 26, 27, 45, 162, 204.
Ball, 3, 6, 7, 8, 9, 10, 11, 15.
Barbridge, 167.
Barker, 5, 17, 18, 85, 163, 187, 215.
Barkwell, 152.

Barley, 161.
Barn, for Glebe, dimensions, &c., 157.
Barnes, 29, 202, 214, 224, 230.
Bassett, 5, 9, 7, 10, 11, 12, 13, 14, 16, 17, 18, 20, 21, 22, 24, 25, 28, 29, 31, 34, 38, 39, 42, 44, 45, 46, 47, 49, 50, 52, 55, 58, 59, 60, 62, 63, 64, 65, 68, 70, 71, 75, 76, 77, 79, 83, 84, 85, 86, 88, 89, 90, 91, 92, 93, 94, 95, 96, 97, 99, 100, 102, 103, 104, 106, 107.
Bathurst, 14, 29, 43, 44, 47, 48, 50, 51.
Batte, 18.
Baughn, 18, 81, 110.
Bayle, 51, 52.
Beateson, 18.
Becket, 64.
Bedford, 43, 123, 124, 126, 129, 131, 133, 137, 142, 147, 148.
Belfry, 132, 134.
Bell, 92, 187.
Bell, for church, 127.
Beltes, 204, 217.
Benches, for church, 172.
Benskin, 13.
Bettis, 162.
Beverdam Swamp, 69.
Bibles, 80.
Binns, 201.
Birch, 161, 163, 186.
Bird, 18, 19.
Bishop of the Plantation, 78.
Black Creek, 45, 151.
Black Creek Mill, 9.
Blackwell, 18, 51, 60.
Blair, 4, 144.
Blissland Parish, 3.
Bodford, 17.
Bodlay, 9.
Boe, 36.
Bogg, 30.
Bollosk, 18.
Bolskly, 20.
Bolton, 228.
Book, 17.

Booker, 148.
Booth, 32.
Boots, 18.
Borross, 18.
Bostick, 18.
Botler, 18.
Botte, 25.
Botts, 17.
Boughleys, 165.
Boughon, 120.
Bound, 45.
Bourn, 124, 137.
Bourne, 57.
Bouster, 35.
Bouston, 34.
Bowe, 40, 41.
Bowker, 3, 4, 45, 46, 47, 49, 50, 51, 52, 53, 55, 57, 59, 60, 61, 63, 64, 65, 67, 70, 71.
Bradbury, 45.
Bradby, 29, 97.
Bradshaw, 29.
Bray, 43, 44, 45, 46, 57, 72, 85.
Brick Chapel, 74.
Brick Church, 53, 58, 61, 62, 65, 71, 80, 91, 104, 109, 126.
Brick House, 117.
Bricklayers, 64, 71.
Brick Wall, dimensions, material, &c., 126.
Bricks, 57, 112.
Britt, 18.
Brigman, 85.
Brock, 21.
Brodie, 3, 104, 105, 106, 107, 110, 111, 112, 114, 115, 116, 117, 118, 119, 120, 122, 123, 124, 126, 127.
Brook, 119.
Brokar, 173, 175, 201.
Brokas, 172, 173, 177, 179, 192.
Brooke, 3, 18, 129, 130.
Brooker, 118, 152, 154, 155, 156, 186, 194, 208.
Brookes, 110, 120, 140, 148, 151, 156, 158, 161, 163, 165, 170, 172, 211.
Brothers, 109, 110, 114, 149, 152, 211.
Brown, 18, 60, 62, 141, 142, 145, 148, 156, 163.
Browne, 72, 142.
Browning, 66.
Brownscale, Bromscale, 3, 128, 130, 131.
Broxom, 18.
Bryan, 18, 60, 62, 66, 72.

Bugg, 97, 120, 121, 123, 124, 131, 137, 139, 142, 148.
Buggs, 41.
Bulkley, 18, 32.
Burbidge, 193.
Burke, 186.
Burley, 69.
Burnett, 36.
Burrass, 41.
Burrow, 85.
Burrows, 43, 49, 50, 52, 65, 72.
Burruss, 18.
Butts, 31, 63, 66, 72, 73, 76, 77, 79, 80, 81, 83, 85, 86, 89, 90, 91, 92, 93, 94, 95, 96, 97, 99, 102, 103, 111, 113, 124, 126, 130, 170, 172, 179, 192, 193, 208.
Carefoot, 82.
Carr, 3, 5, 6.
Carlton, 6, 7, 9, 11.
Carpenter, 50, 59, 158.
Carroll, 201, 204, 225.
Carter, 148, 173.
Casements, 75.
Cash, 16.
Casks, for Tobo., 6-234.
Cattle, 41.
Cawdry, 18.
Cedar Posts, 44.
Chain Carrier, 81.
Chamberlayne, 142, 145, 176, 178, 190.
Chamberlayne's Ferry, 171.
Chamberlayne's Ordinary, 172.
Chandler, 17.
Chappell, 45, 67, 161.
Chapel of Ease, 78.
Chapman, 40, 41.
Chex, linen, 208.
Christian, 224.
Chickahominy Swamp, 54, 62, 69, 75, 139, 151.
Childs, 64, 65, 67, 68, 71, 73, 75, 83.
Chilloe, 18.
Chimney to Glebe House, 231.
Church Benches, 234.
Church Wardens, 8, 30, 105, 125, 145, 176, 193, 208, 232.
Church Yard Cleaning, 187.
Church Bell, 84.
Church Cloth, 82.
Church Plate, 34, 82.
Clapboard, 88.
Clark, 28, 31, 82, 151, 208.
Clarke, 18, 45, 80.
Clarkson, 49, 72, 82, 206.

Clarkston, 17.
Claxton, 92.
Claybourne, 18.
Clayton, 17.
Clopton, 33, 36, 37, 38, 41, 49, 50, 59, 61, 68, 71, 79, 80, 89, 91, 96, 105, 121, 145, 176, 193, 208, 224.
Clough, 56, 60, 72, 82, 91, 97, 101, 107.
Colam, 107.
Cole, 213.
Collum, 118.
Collings, 3, 133, 142.
Colt, 177, 180, 183.
Comrie, 163, 165.
Conding, 17.
Cooc, 202.
Cooke, 120, 122.
Coopers, 180.
Commissary, 143.
Communion Cloth, 28, 158, 163.
Communion Wine, 34, 60.
Corley, 67.
Cox, 17, 19, 29.
Craford, 10, 16, 22, 28, 31, 39, 45, 49, 51, 59, 65, 68, 75, 81, 83.
Crawford, 14, 18, 44.
Croix, 201.
Crump, 15, 17, 29, 45, 57, 63, 85, 98, 129, 139, 140, 162, 164, 172, 177, 195, 208, 211, 232.
Cruse, 178, 179.
Curteen, 34.
Custis, 4, 172, 181, 191, 209, 210, 211, 230.
Cypress Shingles, 157.
Dabonei, 14.
Dabnee, 11, 13.
Dabney, 6, 7, 9.
Dabnie, 12, 16.
Dabboni, 5, 14, 15, 18, 20, 21, 22, 26, 28, 31, 34.
Dalton, 167.
Dandridge, 163, 169, 176, 177, 192, 193, 208, 211, 234.
Daniel, 32, 41, 45, 213.
Davis, 17, 19, 32, 50, 159, 162, 168, 172, 209, 211, 215.
Davison, 186.
Delahay, 45.
Dennet, 149.
Deprosse, 18.
Derritour, 182.
Derricourt, 186.
Diet, 61.
Dike, 142, 145.

Dikes, 155.
Dillon, 19.
Dixon, 209.
Dod, 72.
Dodd, 135.
Dollard, 45, 189, 224.
Dood, 149, 152.
Doran, 129, 135, 183.
Doritt, 18.
Dowie, 17.
Downe, 173, 175.
Downs, 173, 209.
Drummond, 124, 130, 133.
Drysdale, 4, 144.
Dudley, 174, 176, 177, 192, 193, 208, 209, 213, 224.
Dunston, 209, 211.
Duvall, 188.
Dwelling House, 118.
Easley, 182.
Eastor, 18.
Edloe, 69.
Edwards, 24, 29.
Effingham, 14.
Ellis, 64.
Ellison, 18, 20, 45.
Ellyson, 213, 224.
Elmore, 92, 192.
Engleebricht, 18.
Epecon, 17.
Epperson, 135.
Essex Co., 125.
Exchange, bills of, 7.
Fargisson, 206.
Farney, 183.
Farrell, 162, 175, 209.
Faulkner, 23, 32, 34, 36, 37, 40, 42, 60, 101.
Fergisson, 45.
Fernea, 207.
Ferrall, 173.
Field, 131.
Finch, 156.
Fisher, 29. 32, 33, 35.
Flange, 226.
Fleming, 10, 18, 92, 117, 138.
Flinch, 45.
Font, 173.
Fontaine, 132.
Footes, 186.
Forbes, 199, 210, 213, 215, 226.
Forbess, 3, 132, 201, 208, 226.
Forbush, 206.
Forgesson, 205.
Forgeson, 57, 85, 201.
Fornea, 209.
Forster, 8, 12, 17, 19, 22, 23, 29, 30,

39, 45, 49, 50, 59, 60, 68, 70, 79, 82, 89, 92, 99, 100, 112.
Foster, 102, 112, 170, 173, 177, 192, 193, 208, 209, 220.
Gardner, 45, 87, 91, 97, 101, 105, 107, 110, 116, 118.
Garrat, 18, 45.
Gates, 155.
Gates to Church, 127.
Gawlin, 173.
Gentry, 18, 60, 69.
Geofrige, 80.
Gibbs, 36.
Gibson, 36, 40, 45.
Giles, 32, 40.
Gilliam, 17, 46, 137, 139, 140, 199.
Glass, 10, 62, 75.
Glebe, 87, 154, 162, 194.
Glebe House, 95, 96, 112, 128, 134, 276.
Glebe House, plans and directions for, 96, 112, 113.
Glebe House, materials, &c., 112, 113.
Glebe Kitchen, 159.
Glebe Land, 54, 167.
Gogan, 212.
Gontin, 18, 25, 65, 72.
Gooch, 18.
Gooding, 205.
Goodwin, 103, 104, 110, 114, 139, 140, 142, 146, 148, 164, 168, 172, 175, 177, 179, 185, 191, 193, 208, 212, 216.
Gordon, 3, 19, 21.
Gore, 128, 129, 130, 132.
Gray, 3, 4, 95, 96, 97, 99, 100, 103, 105, 200, 208, 213.
Green, 17, 29, 30, 120, 221, 222.
Greene, 224.
Greenhill, 143.
Greens, 117.
Gregory, 214, 224.
Grey, 95, 178, 182.
Grimley, 149.
Grindley, 17, 179, 183, 191, 193, 208.
Gross, 18.
Grumbal, 178, 181, 191, 195, 208.
Guilam, 119.
Guillam, 131, 133, 142, 145.
Gulshell, 36.
Gunton, 40.
Hall, 69, 71, 73.
Hare, 87.
Harfield, 172, 209.
Harman, 17, 18.

Harper, 122.
Harris, 18, 45, 52, 97, 122, 224.
Hart, 6, 8, 11, 15, 19, 25, 27.
Harte, 17.
Hartwell, 186.
Harvey, 70, 84, 90, 118.
Hawle, 107.
Haggard, 142, 152, 156, 163, 165, 168, 170, 173, 177, 179, 182, 190, 193, 200.
Heath, 192, 195, 210, 216.
Helton, 100, 101, 108.
Henderson, 19, 92, 117, 135.
Hewlet, 171, 174, 208, 209, 213, 224, 232.
High Sheriff, 33, 50, 102, 210.
Hight, 18, 211.
Hilliard, 214, 224.
Hill, 17.
Hillon, 51.
Hilton, 34, 36, 39, 40, 43, 47, 51, 55, 56, 60, 65, 72, 77, 81, 85, 87, 90, 92, 97, 99, 101, 110, 114, 131.
Hinges, 88.
Hithe, 215.
Hockaday, 197, 200.
Hodges, 17.
Holmes, 172, 174, 177, 192, 195, 208, 230.
Holt, 123.
Hood, 69.
Hopkins, 213, 230.
Hopor, 20.
Horses, 40.
Horse Blocks, 158.
Horsley, 18.
Howard, 14, 45.
Howes, 36, 40, 43, 51.
Howle, 133.
Howles, 101.
Howsheus, 18.
Hughes, 18, 45, 62, 69, 73, 80, 87, 90, 149, 196.
Hulett, 162.
Hutchinson, 211.
Indian Corn, 40.
Indian Ross, 72.
Irby, 191.
Iron Work, 62.
Isard, 18.
Ivy, 230.
Jackson, 17, 30, 53, 58, 59, 60, 61, 65, 69, 72, 82, 84, 87, 88, 107, 116, 119, 120, 130, 162, 172.
James City, 19, 24, 54.
Jarrett, 17, 213, 223.

Jennings, 104.
Joanes, 7, 8, 9, 15, 17, 18, 20.
Johnson, 18, 19, 45, 67, 69, 119, 122, 126, 129, 133, 134, 137, 139, 142, 146, 213.
Jones, 5, 6, 45, 69, 231.
Jordan, 92.
Jonet, 142.
Joyners, 59.
Justice of Peace, 174.
Keeling, 101, 102.
Kemp, 163, 165, 173, 177, 179.
Kirby, 28.
Kimburrow, 69, 72, 73, 74, 81.
King, 18, 19, 25, 27, 51, 72, 87, 91.
Kitchen Dimensions and Materials, 134.
Knott, 68, 73.
Lang, 3, 4, 143, 145.
Landidge, 82.
Lansestor, 18.
Lathes, 69.
Lead, 75.
Leah, 41.
Leake, 47.
Lespleete, 90.
Levermore, 74, 84, 86, 88, 98, 102.
Lewes, 18.
Lewis, 38, 39, 42, 43, 45, 46, 47, 49, 50, 59, 64, 69, 117, 135, 141, 145, 176, 206, 211.
Lichfield, Bishop of, 3.
Lightfoot, 7, 17, 29, 40, 41, 43, 55, 63, 76, 77, 79, 83, 84, 89, 107, 135, 137, 172.
Littlepage, 6, 7, 13, 17, 27, 40, 64, 68, 69, 70, 71, 74, 75, 76, 80, 81, 82, 83, 84, 87, 88, 90, 98, 99, 103, 113, 114, 124, 129, 177, 180, 193, 208, 213, 234.
Littlepage, Madam, 162.
Lock and Key, 88.
London, 4.
London, Bishop of, 4.
Lyddall, 18, 25, 27, 71, 31, 39, 40, 49, 50, 57, 62, 69, 70, 74, 86.
Mackeney, 45, 51.
Macon, 5, 8, 10, 11, 17, 19, 20, 25, 29, 31, 35, 37, 38, 40, 49, 52, 53, 56, 59, 64, 133, 138, 142, 145, 176, 177, 192, 193, 208, 210, 213, 224.
Mackgeehe, 45.
Magrime, 55.
Maidlin, 69.
Major, 15, 17, 20, 33, 47, 63, 72, 107, 120, 170, 176, 177, 192.

Mallitt, 67.
Mannin, 213, 224.
Markgold, 17.
Marrohoe, 169, 171.
Marston, 141, 142, 143, 145, 157, 179, 192, 193, 208, 209, 210.
Martin, 18, 45, 69, 72, 81, 83, 101, 119, 138, 140, 165, 182, 192, 213, 224.
Mason, 17.
Mashay, 18.
Mask, 18, 83.
Massie, Massy, 69, 76, 77, 79, 80, 83, 85, 86, 89, 90, 99, 100, 112, 116, 132, 145, 176, 179, 193, 208, 210, 212.
Maryland Springs, 50.
Matheson, 216.
Mattheys, 211.
Mathews, 170, 193.
Mattis, 215.
Mattodequin Creek, 31, 69.
Meanley, 18, 208, 211, 214, 173.
Meas, 114.
Mecham's Creek, 66.
Medlook, 18.
Mems, 131.
Men's side of church, 159.
Meridie, 18.
Merriwether, 49, 50, 53, 55, 59, 63, 66, 68, 70, 76, 81, 83, 124.
Meux, 107, 131, 202, 209, 210, 215.
Middlesex, 4.
Milk House, 100.
Milk House, directions for, 100.
Miller, 32.
Millington, 17, 29, 30, 105, 107, 110.
Mills, 18, 81.
Mimb, 35.
Mims, 40, 48, 51, 56, 60, 66, 83, 84, 105.
Minns, 36, 37, 45, 72, 81, 87, 92, 97, 101.
Minge, 24.
Mitchell, 10, 15, 21, 45, 57, 85, 109, 125.
Mitshal, Mitshel, 6, 9.
Monrowe, 38, 39, 40.
Moorman, 18.
Moon, 17, 18, 65, 137, 157, 172, 186, 191, 195, 206.
Moore, 18, 45, 57, 62, 69, 72, 81, 83, 101, 120, 129, 130, 133, 135, 137, 139, 140, 173, 175, 177, 178, 179, 192, 194, 208.
Moreau, 3, 39, 42, 44.

Morgan, 18, 45, 80, 87, 139, 140, 142, 146, 148, 161, 163, 164, 172, 173, 175, 176, 192, 195, 207, 224.
Morris, 18, 26, 27, 29, 99, 130, 131, 142, 148, 152, 163, 196, 202, 209, 210, 211, 215, 216.
Moss, 14, 18, 20, 29, 30, 33, 35, 39, 42, 49, 51, 53, 58, 63, 66, 68, 70, 72, 75, 81, 82, 91, 107, 110, 161, 165, 214, 224.
Mossom, 3, 4, 147, 176, 177, 192, 193, 208, 209, 233.
Murrahoe, 172, 173, 175, 177, 178, 179, 181, 182.
Nails, 5, 22, 159.
Nance, 159.
Napier, 32, 34, 87, 91.
Nash, 130, 176.
Neenes, 45.
Nees, 40.
Netherland, 141, 145, 176.
New Kent Co., 3.
Nicholl, 57.
Nichols, 19.
Noah, 210.
Noden, 133.
Norkton, 18.
Norris, 85, 87, 89, 91, 92, 93.
Northe, 79.
Nuckols, 67.
Ornaments, 80.
Osling, 17, 119, 120, 123, 133, 137, 142, 146, 172.
Otey, 139, 141, 151, 153.
Oyster Shoals, 61.
Paddison, 17.
Page, 2, 4, 7, 10, 12, 15, 18, 19, 23, 27, 29, 31, 34, 39, 65.
Paine, 17.
Painters, 158.
Painting stairs, 234.
Paisley, 5, 172.
Palisade gate, 234.
Pamunkey river, 24.
Paper, 173.
Parish Debt, 209.
Parish Levy, 5, *et seq.*
Park, Parke, 5, 9, 11, 12, 15, 22, 36, 39, 42, 44, 45, 46, 49, 52, 53, 57, 59, 60, 63, 65, 68, 75, 76, 83, 86, 89, 91, 97, 100, 106, 113, 133, 209, 210, 224.
Parker, 28, 120, 156.
Parks, 6, 9, 13, 16, 18, 20, 24, 28, 31, 33, 36, 37, 38, 39, 63, 70, 71, 77, 109.

Pargeson, 232.
Pargestor, 18, 21, 26.
Pargetor, 30, 33.
Pasley, 17, 22, 65, 66, 209.
Pates, 18.
Patteson, 139, 141, 145, 176, 177, 183, 193, 206, 213, 215, 221, 230, 234.
Peard, 18.
Pearson, 142, 148, 152, 164, 165, 167, 168, 170, 172, 183.
Peasley, 6, 7, 10, 12.
Pedly, 36, 40, 43.
Peggs, 51.
Penix, 18.
Peraut, 72.
Perkins, 138, 213.
Perme, 5.
Perry, 3.
Pettison, 139.
Phillips, 19, 20, 189, 193, 215.
Physic, 108.
Pierce, 17.
Pine Plank, 159.
Pinchback, 151, 214.
Plank, &c., 157.
Plantine, 81.
Plasterers, 158.
Plate, 90.
Plumley, 212.
Pargistor, 25.
Poindexter, 5, 13, 15, 17, 22, 26, 27, 60, 65, 66, 72, 73, 76, 77, 79, 80, 82, 85, 86, 88, 90, 99, 101, 132, 145, 176, 213.
Polgreen, 13, 18.
Pollard, 202.
Pond, 162.
Pontin, 20, 21, 22, 25, 50.
Porch, 184.
Powers, 184, 185.
Prayer Books, 187.
Precincts, 213.
Price, 124.
Prior, 18.
Purde, 45.
Pyrant, 70, 81.
Quaker, 4.
Quit Rents, 152.
Ragglin, 18.
Ragland, 101, 214, 224.
Ray, 18.
Raymond, 123, 222.
Read, 152.
Realy, 18.
Red Oaks, 23.
Reese, 45.

Register Book, 51.
Rever, 5.
Reynolds, 222.
Rhodes, 35, 40.
Richardson, 157, 196, 210.
Richison, 199.
Rigoner, 6.
Roads, 65.
Roberts, 165, 213.
Robertson, 79.
Rock, 165.
Rodge, 29.
Rogor, 7. .
Ronalle, 18.
Rope and Chain, 187.
Roper, 8, 10, 12, 14, 17, 19, 20, 21, 22, 26, 28, 31, 33, 34, 36, 38, 42, 44, 47, 49, 81, 83, 137, 213.
Ross, 22, 36, 40, 41, 114, 162, 173, 182, 186, 209.
Russell, 188.
Ryan, 209, 223.
Sand, 69.
Sands, 18.
Sanders, 17, 18, 49. 51, 56, 60, 66, 72, 84, 101, 114, 116, 123.
Sanderson, 138, 148, 142.
Salaries of Ministers, 88, 101.
Sallivating, 178.
Sawyer, 61.
Schoolhouse, 53, 58, 104.
Scott, 71, 79, 80, 89, 90, 99, 100, 112. 120, 125, 126, 132, 133, 139, 156, 165, 213, 234.
Scruggs, 29, 32, 45, 62, 87, 90, 133, 137, 207, 213, 224.
Securities, 197.
Sellake, 3.
Sharp, 127.
Sheets, 173.
Sherman, 169, 174, 176, 177, 192, 193, 208.
Shoes, 37, 43.
Silver Chalice, 163.
Skelton, 127, 129.
Slater, 15.
Slattor, 8.
Smith, 5, 6, 7, 9, 17, 18, 19, 20, 22, 26, 27, 28, 31, 33, 36, 39, 41, 42, 44, 46, 47, 49, 50, 51, 52, 53, 59, 60, 63, 70, 87, 92, 107, 119, 120, 123, 124, 130, 174.
Snead, 18, 62, 82.
Sodder, 75.
Spear, 17, 121, 122.
Speares, 97.

Spencer, 18, 211, 221, 215.
Spurlock, 17, 29, 139.
Squire, 3, 70, 71, 74, 75, 77, 79, 80, 81, 83, 87, 90, 91.
Stafford Co., 182.
Stamp, 72.
Stanley, 45.
Steeple to Church, 181, 234.
Stocks, 80, 169.
Stone, 17.
Stone Swamp, 61.
Strange, 18, 107, 109, 193, 206.
Stringer, 83.
Shroasby, 85.
St. John's College, 4.
St. Paul's Parish, 79, 83, 84, 86.
St. Peter's Parish, 3, 234.
St. Stephen's Church, 4.
Surplice, 28, 43, 56, 81, 167.
Surveyor, 107.
Swanson, 31, 32.
Taliaferro, 203.
Talle, 18.
Tarr, 158, 160.
Tate, 18.
Taylor, 3, 4, 18, 9, 93, 96, 97, 99, 101, 103, 105, 107, 109, 111, 114, 124, 134, 135, 137, 142, 151, 152, 167, 179, 183, 195, 207, 228.
Teate, 56.
Terrell, 222.
Terroll, 19.
Thomas, 18, 130, 145, 151.
Thompson, 18, 101, 162.
Thornton, 110. 114, 119, 120, 130, 140, 145, 149, 153, 156.
Thorp, 137.
Timson, 56, 61, 110, 149, 161, 163, 164, 167.
Tinsley, 18.
Tinsley, 69.
Tithables, 6, 234.
Tobacco, 6, 234.
Tobacco, improvement of, 141.
Tobacco Plants, 139, 148.
Tobacco Stalks, 151.
Tobacco Strips, 151.
Tobacco Suckers, 151.
Tobacco Viewers, 153, 154.
Tomson, 171, 215.
Tony, 45.
Torker, 18.
Totopatomoys Creeke, 69.
Tonger, 201.
Tyler, 69.
Tudora, 151.

Turkey Leather, 187.
Turner, 7, 10, 11, 14, 16, 18, 19, 20, 21, 23, 25, 29, 30, 32, 34, 36, 38, 42, 43, 45, 50, 67, 72, 81, 117, 155, 171, 172, 208, 211, 212, 215, 216.
Turber, 35.
Undertakers, 227.
Uppehew, 73.
Upshear, 87, 90.
Vaiden, 214, 222, 224.
Vaughan, 17, 61, 73, 82, 118, 214, 228, 234.
Veere, 159.
Venable, 18.
Waddell, 17, 76, 77, 79, 80, 83, 86, 89, 90, 99, 100, 112, 119, 120, 124, 126, 133, 177, 192, 194, 208, 215, 224.
Waddy, 16, 18, 20, 33, 81.
Wady, 10.
Wainscot, 164.
Wakefield, 18.
Walker, 36, 43, 45, 105, 108, 118.
Wall, 18.
Waller, 183, 190, 211, 234.
Walton, 17, 18, 138, 145, 176, 210, 232.
Ware, 3, 22, 23, 24, 25, 26, 27, 28, 31, 32, 33, 38.
Warkman, 30.
Warren, 18, 204, 205.
Warsinan, 32.
Washington, 4.
Watkins, 110, 116, 122, 147, 149, 156.
Weaver, 124, 129, 134, 161, 162, 163, 164, 167, 186, 214, 224.

Webb, 17, 32, 34, 36, 39, 43, 48, 51, 56, 60, 65, 70, 72, 81, 209, 210, 212.
Well, 154.
Well Bucket, 101.
West, 18.
Wharton, 45.
White, 122.
Wiatt, 82.
Wicker, 123, 124, 126, 128, 129.
Wilde, 108, 110.
Wilkins, 17, 25, 50, 52, 72.
Wilkinson, 8, 11, 18, 25, 45, 51, 56, 60, 90, 138, 201, 213, 224, 230, 234.
Williams, 3, 17, 20, 21, 24, 90, 174, 226.
Williamsburg, 79, 127.
Wilmore, 139.
Wimsherfers, 43.
Winfield, 119, 120.
Winifree, 162.
Winfry, 107.
Wingfield, 36, 60.
Winkfield, 120.
Wine, 173, 184.
Winston, 10.
Willin, 34.
Witty, 18.
Wood, 7, 10, 11, 29, 30, 34, 36, 40, 43, 51, 56, 60.
Woody, 18.
Workmour, 5, 17.
Worthe, 182.
Wright, 5, 8.
Wyatt, 5, 7, 10, 12, 14, 16, 18, 20, 22, 23, 24, 25, 29, 31, 39, 44, 47, 49, 50, 52, 56, 59, 60, 62, 64, 69, 79, 83, 92.

www.ingramcontent.com/pod-product-compliance
Lightning Source LLC
Chambersburg PA
CBHW051056230426
43667CB00013B/2317